St. Louis Community College

Library

5801 Wilson Avenue
St. Louis, Missouri 63110

St. Louis Community College
at Meramec
Library

RED, WHITE,
AND BLUE PARADISE

HERBERT AND MARY KNAPP

Harcourt Brace Jovanovich, Publishers
San Diego   London   New York

RED, WHITE, AND BLUE
PARADISE

THE AMERICAN CANAL ZONE IN PANAMA

Library of Congress Cataloging in Publication Data
Knapp, Herbert, 1931–
    Red, white, and blue paradise.
    Bibliography: p.
    Includes index.
    1. Canal Zone.   I. Knapp, Mary, 1931–
II. Title.
F1569.C2K58   1985   972.87′5   84-4660
ISBN 0-15-176135-3

Designed by Jacqueline Schuman

Printed in the United States of America

First edition

A   B   C   D   E

For the Zonians—wherever you are.

It seems to me that I have never seen anything finer than this spirit at Panama. After years of hearing of the shame of corrupt politics and the inhumanity of industry in America, it is refreshing, indeed, to find here not only an exemplification of the ancient fiber of the race but a realization of its newest ideals.

Ray Stannard Baker

When the long account comes to be balanced, we may find that the United States will owe quite as much to the Panama enterprise on the moral as on the material side.

Willis J. Abbot

We live in Paradise and our handmaiden is Felicity.

*Unknown Zonian, living in
Paraiso, circa 1914*

It is a park-like civilization with practically no class distinctions.

Negley Farson

Acknowledgments

For their professional help and expertise, we would like to thank Joe Kane of the Panama Canal College Library; Beverly Williams of the Panama Canal Commission Library; Nan Chong, the Commission's Panama Collection Librarian; and her research assistants, Irene O. de González and Pat Booth.

We also want to thank all our students and friends on the Isthmus —Americans and Panamanians—for their interest in this project.

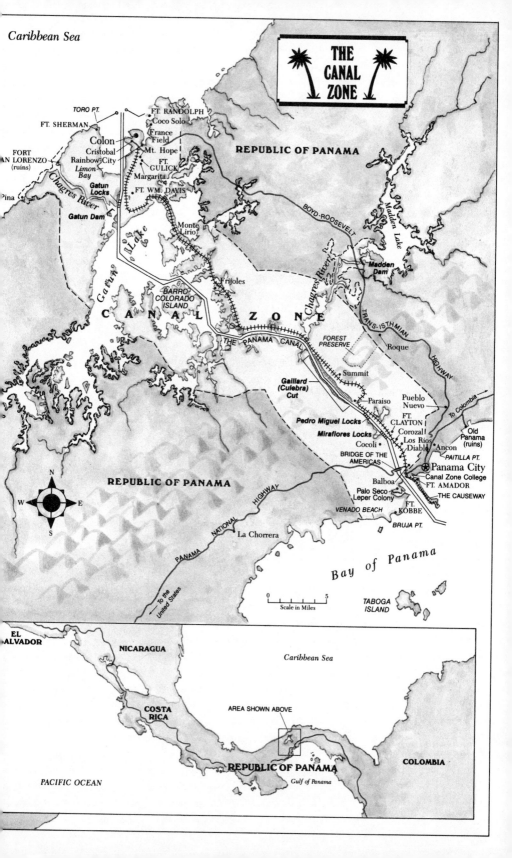

Contents

PART TWO

THE PANAMA CANAL ZONE—
CULTURAL VALUES AND CLASS CONFLICT

PART ONE
THE PANAMA CANAL ZONE– AN AMBIGUOUS UTOPIA

1
Learning from the Past

On October 1, 1979, the American Canal Zone in Panama disappeared, leaving behind only an abstract image of itself on old maps —a geographic ghost. Some Americans were glad to see it go and believe that the sooner it's forgotten, the better. But there are two good reasons to remember the Zone—to be haunted by it, even.

First, the Canal Zone showed what an American version of authoritarian socialism was like; second, it provoked illuminating comments from those who consider themselves superior to America's working class.

The Zone was the world's first workers' paradise—a star-spangled red, white, and blue postcapitalist society that was established while Russia was still groaning under the yoke of the Czar. And this American ministate in the tropics flourished for three-quarters of a century with relatively little change.

Only one of the men sent by President Theodore Roosevelt to run the Canal project in 1904 could possibly be called a social visionary: Charles Magoon, the Zone's second governor. His idea was to establish a model democratic government on the Zone for the edification of Latin America. When the chairman of the Isthmian Canal Commission, Theodore Shonts, heard about this, he bluntly told Magoon to forget it. The United States was in Panama to dig a canal—period.[1]

However, digging a canal across mountainous terrain in an inhospitable tropical environment during the early years of this century was no ordinary job. Its unusual problems required unusual solutions. In order to attract and keep competent workmen, the Canal Commission had to provide them with houses, schools, medical care, commissaries, and entertainment—in short, with a community. That community was not designed by intellectuals to illustrate a utopian social ideal, but it was designed to be a great deal more than a mere construction camp. Sponsored by the federal government, which expected it to last "in perpetuity," and located in the middle of a foreign country at "the crossroads of the world," the American Canal community was intended to be a credit to the United States. Indeed, George Washington Goethals, the chief engineer, expressly said so.[2] It should come as no surprise, then, that the Canal community reflected many of the ideas of America's most progressive political thinkers.

By 1911, the Zonians were aware and proud of the Zone's distinctive utopian character. In his Fourth of July speech that year, Goethals called the Canal workers the "advance guard in the new era of progress upon which our nation has now entered." Like the Puritans three centuries earlier, the Zonians believed they were living in a "Citty upon a Hill," and that the eyes of all the nations were upon them. Goethals said that they were "showing the world . . . that popular government, administered honestly and intelligently, is an agency for human welfare and happiness, as well as for national glory."[3] Another Zone official declared that the Zone was "a school of citizenship"—a place where individualistic Americans could learn community thinking.[4]

Visitors to the Zone were struck by its astonishing resemblance to the controversial utopia outlined by the radical American reformer Edward Bellamy in the late nineteenth century. "The dream of the late Edward Bellamy is given actuality on the Zone," trumpeted one visitor in 1913.[5] Another testified more soberly that it "strongly resembles what Bellamy dreamed years ago."[6] In 1928, a Zonian wrote that her community was "frequently" referred to as resembling Bellamy's utopia.[7] It was a similarity we often remarked on during our years as residents on the Zone.

Edward Bellamy is generally forgotten today, but he was the American equivalent of Marx—and just the sort of gentle, mystical, democratic reformer Marx despised. Both men wanted to change the world. To do this, the scholarly German wrote a great "scientific" answer book; the romantic American wrote a novel. He called it *Looking Backward*.

It appeared in 1887 and was the biggest publishing sensation since *Uncle Tom's Cabin*, appealing to "brains" and "roughnecks" alike, to both socialists and social belles. Clergymen, theosophists, and temperance advocates were agog over it. Union organizers, retired army officers, and anarchists all praised it. So did feminists. Frances Willard liked it so much she suggested its author must really be a woman—"a big-hearted, big-brained woman."[8]

In 1935, the philosopher John Dewey, the historian Charles Beard, and the editor of the *Atlantic Monthly*, Edward Weeks, working independently, prepared lists of the twenty-five most influential books of the previous fifty years. On each man's list, *Looking Backward* was second—right behind *Das Kapital*.[9]

But the immediate appeal of *Das Kapital* was not great. On the other hand, Bellamy's straightforward romance—after slow sales the first year—was an immense and explosive success throughout the world, but especially in the United States.

In 1932, Franklin D. Roosevelt was elected president, promising a New Deal for the American people. Two years later, Ida Tarbell, ex-muckraker and historian of Standard Oil, said that if there really was to be a "New Deal," Bellamy would deserve much of the credit. His famous book, she said, had gained a lasting hold on the popular imagination. His ideas were "woven into the thinking" of Americans.[10]

None of Roosevelt's New Deal reforms was as comprehensive as Bellamy would have wished, but while FDR was president, America made a start toward an approximation of Bellamy's dream, and it has continued to move in that direction ever since, though some reformers would say it has moved with unconscionable slowness.

It has moved slowly, however, because many Americans are of two minds about its direction. Few question Bellamy's goals of prosperity, equality, and brotherhood, but the giant bureaucracy that he proposed as the avant-garde of his utopia, and that FDR put into place, has not been an unqualified success. In many ways it has made America a more decent place to live; in others, it has proved unresponsive and oppressive. Moreover, Americans have seen in other nations how dreams similar to Bellamy's have skewed into totalitarian nightmares.

The trouble is that as of right now, Bellamy's is the only dream of a better world that we've got. As the twenty-first century approaches, we are still—most of us—dreaming variations of Bellamy's nineteenth-century dream of the future. (The late Mayor Daley of Chicago knew whereof he spoke when he delphically remarked that Americans have "a nostalgia for the future.")

Liberals think of that future as a welfare state; conservatives, as a managerial society. The differences don't amount to much. Both are orderly, rational societies governed by tenured bureaucratic elites. Recently, however, the sense of national purpose provided by Bellamy and other progressive reformers has begun to run out of steam. Unsure of what we want the future to be like, confused about what is possible, we must decide to rededicate ourselves to the general goals outlined by Bellamy and his followers, to modify them, or to strike out in a new direction. Before we decide, it seems wise to look closely at the Canal Zone.

The second reason to remember the Zone is that the fight to ratify the Carter-Torrijos treaties, which provided for the elimination of the Canal Zone and the transfer of the Canal to Panama, revealed a political division in our country that has yet to be seriously examined.

Opposition to the treaties was more widespread than the Carter administration had anticipated. No one could convincingly account for this. Liberals, of course, favored the treaties, which would divest the United States of its "colonial outpost" in Central America. But so did the brokers and bankers of Wall Street. So did the conservative heroes John Wayne and Bill Buckley. Even Senator Barry Goldwater spoke in favor of the treaties, though he ultimately voted against ratifying them in response to pressure from his constituents. Both the majority and minority leaders of the Senate favored ratification, as did ex-President Ford and all the most prestigious newspapers in the land.

So who was against them? The grass-roots character of the opposition puzzled analysts. Richard Hudson wrote in *The New York Times Magazine* that those opposing the treaties were functioning effectively "without an office in Washington or even one salaried lobbyist." He found this "amazing."[11]

Liberal journalists assured nervous senators that the Canal was not a bread-and-butter issue and thus would not play a significant role in the next election.

But class conflict is one of the things that can override bread and butter issues, and class conflict was what made the Canal debate so politically divisive.

The strongest supporters of the treaties were the status liberals, who used the debate to advance their own view of American history and of their rightful position in American society. According to them, America had nothing to be proud of in its relationship to Panama. Panama was the victim of a "colonialist situation," and America had to ratify the treaties in order to rectify years of wrongdoing.

This did not, as they say, play well in Peoria, where few people share the status liberals' guilt-ridden view of American history or their estimate of their own superiority. The status liberals see themselves as the compassionate, rational, disinterested, and cultured portion of society. They define themselves in contrast to America's "Babbitts" and "rednecks." (They think of the former as uncultured, moneymaking materialists; the latter, as uneducated, flag-waving, blue-collar types.) But many "Babbitts" and "rednecks" are Democrats, just like the status liberals. Indeed, the so-called "rednecks" should more properly be called union liberals. The Canal Zone was full of union liberals. Thus, the treaty debate did not divide the nation according to party but according to class—not "class" in the European sense of the word but in its looser American sense.

Class wasn't the whole story, of course. Many Americans simply thought that in their original form the treaties ignored important security interests of the United States. It was the strength of that objection that motivated Senators Howard Baker and Robert Byrd to revise the original State Department document. And it was their revisions that made ratification narrowly possible.

But ratification needn't have been such a near thing. Americans could have been rallied to support the treaties as the logical next step in a long and mutually beneficial relationship—a relationship that reflects considerable credit on the United States, no matter how stridently the government of Panama insists that it was oppressed. That was not, however, the way the treaties were presented to the American public.

Two years after the treaties were ratified, their most outspoken opponent was in the White House, and twenty senators who had voted for ratification were no longer in the Senate. The importance of the Canal as an issue varied from contest to contest but was a factor in all of them,[12] partly because it brought America's "class war" out of the shadows, if not into the open, and partly because it aroused widespread concern about how we mean to interpret our nation's past. What we finally decide in regard to that question will largely determine how our nation will respond to the future.

2

From Capitalism to Collectivism

THE FRENCH CONNECTION

The history and character of the American Canal Zone is inextricably bound up with the French attempt to dig a canal across the Isthmus of Panama in the 1880s. The French attempt was made by a private company. It attracted brilliant and heroic engineers, who performed "almost unbelievable feats of endurance," but they were never able to "knit their efforts into a homogenous whole."[1] Their work was undercut by stock swindlers, crooked suppliers, and competing subcontractors. Nothing illustrates better all that was wrong with late-nineteenth-century capitalism than the *Compagnie Universelle du Canal Interocéanique*. It failed to build a canal, left thousands of workmen dead, thousands of investors impoverished, and a very few men very rich. There was abundant evidence of bribery and corruption in the company's affairs.

The Americans who arrived in Panama fifteen years later, in 1904, were determined not to make the same mistakes. Their Canal project —sponsored by the federal government—was completely centralized, scrupulously honest, and displayed what was for the times an astonishing concern for the health and welfare of the least of its laborers.

Politically, however, the American Canal Zone was a uniquely ambiguous place. Curiously, the man responsible for this was a Frenchman who had been acting director general of the French canal company—Philippe Bunau-Varilla.

9

After the French project failed, Theodore Roosevelt tried to negotiate a treaty with Colombia to permit the United States to build a
canal across Panama, a province of Colombia at the time. When those
negotiations collapsed, Panama panicked, fearing it had lost its chance
for the canal forever. It had long been a rebellious province and
decided now, once again, to declare its independence. This time its
revolution succeeded. There were a number of reasons for this, but
one of the most important was the aid and counsel given to the leaders
of the revolution by Philippe Bunau-Varilla.

His goal was simple. He wanted to see the French canal in Panama
completed. But his motives were complex. His professional pride was
involved; he wanted the world to know the French engineers had been
right about the Panama route. National pride was involved, too: If
America finished the French canal, France would at least share the
glory. Finally, Bunau-Varilla had a financial stake in the bankrupt
French canal company. If its assets could be turned into cash, he
would profit. That last is what sticks American liberals. They assume
that profit was his main motive, but Bunau-Varilla was no one-
dimensional economic man. Profit, pride, and patriotism all played a
part in what he did.

When the Panamanian revolutionaries were discouraged, he encouraged them; when they were confused, he directed them; when
they were broke, he gave them money. Not as much as they wanted,
but enough. They asked for $6 million. He gave them $100,000.

"Our people will keep eternally engraved in their memory your
fruitful services," wrote Panama's President Domingo Obaldía in
1909,[2] and that was the last nice thing any Panamanian ever had to
say about Bunau-Varilla. He is the man they blame for taking advantage of their innocence and signing away their national dignity.
He is the author of the infamous "treaty no Panamanian signed."

It is true that the treaty Bunau-Varilla wrote and signed while he
was Panama's special representative was very favorable to the United
States, but a stiff ratification fight must have seemed like a real possibility. Many senators were still committed to the old American plan
for building a canal in Nicaragua. The anti-imperialists were furious

with Roosevelt for his shadowy complicity in Panama's convenient revolution. So were leading publishers.[3]

But Bunau-Varilla had made the United States an offer it could not refuse. Once the terms of the treaty were known and the treaty had been ratified by Panama, there was little doubt that it would be ratified by the Senate.

The most important thing in Bunau-Varilla's treaty was its offer to the United States of all the rights, power, and authority within the Zone—an area five miles wide on either side of the Canal—"which the United States would possess if it were sovereign of the territory." Furthermore, it offered "the use, occupation, and control" of the Zone "in perpetuity." The treaty did not offer the United States actual sovereignty over the Zone, only the right to *seem* to own the Zone forever.

After the treaty was ratified, the United States purchased all the private property within its new Zone. The Zone then belonged to the United States, but only in the sense that property belongs to its owner, not in the sense that land belongs to a nation. True, the Zone looked *as if* it belonged to the United States. Nevertheless, Panama sold only the appearance of sovereignty, not the real thing.

Americans acknowledged the difference with a shrug. Had not our philosopher William James taught us, "A difference that makes no difference is no difference"? But the fact that the United States could only act as if it were sovereign on the Zone only appeared to make no difference. It really prevented the Zone from ever becoming part of the United States and left the way open for its eventual return to Panama.

In retrospect, the terms of the treaty that Bunau-Varilla wrote seem less generous and more necessary for the success of the American project than anyone suspected—except perhaps Bunau-Varilla. Not long after the American ditchdiggers went to work, the merchants of Panama raised the price of food, just as they had when the French had tried to dig a canal there. Soon many Canal workers could not buy enough to eat.[4] The Americans raised everybody's wages. The Panamanians raised their prices. The Americans raised everybody's wages. Again, the Panamanians raised their prices. This time, Theodore Shonts, chairman of the Second Canal Commission, announced that the commission would establish commissaries to feed its own men. The local merchants were outraged, but thanks to Bunau-Varilla, the Americans were not at their mercy as the French had been; they could do as they pleased on their Zone.

Bunau-Varilla knew that the Americans could expect little or no cooperation from the local officials. The Panamanians looked back on the years of the French as the *"temps de luxe,"*[5] but no matter how much money the French spent in Panama, the city of Colón remained "a foul hole." After comparing it unfavorably to the slums of Naples and old Stamboul, a visitor remarked, "Need I say that the [French] canal company has no authority at Colón? Sanitation of the town is in the hands of the municipal council, which . . . prefers to concern itself with other matters."[6]

But because of Bunau-Varilla's treaty, the council's agenda was of no concern to the Americans. His treaty put the sanitation of the cities adjacent to the Canal Zone in American hands.

Bunau-Varilla was a patriot who risked his life in the Panama graveyard for the glory of France but made a fortune on the side in shady deals with the French canal company. He was an idealist who defied the French establishment by publishing the first evidence that his old classmate, Alfred Dreyfus, had been framed as a German spy by the generals of France.[7] But his idealism also involved him in the plot to detach Panama from Colombia, partly to serve his own financial interests. He was a very good man to have on your side—but he was a little crazy.

Bunau-Varilla saw his life as a long struggle against the international Prussian conspiracy.[8] To the Prussians, he attributed occult powers. They had been plotting, he said, to take over Europe since 1619! It was they, you see, who persuaded the French to put an Austrian archduke on the throne of Mexico in 1863. An Austrian! Is that not an "uncanny and striking fact"? He believed that the Prussians had persuaded France to violate the Monroe Doctrine in 1863, hoping that the ensuing quarrel between France and the United

States would prevent America from coming to the aid of France in 1916. According to Bunau-Varilla, the *apparently* innocent German dye industry was also part of Prussia's plot. Dye factories could be converted to munitions factories. You see it! Worst of all, Prussian agents had caused the failure of the French canal project in order to destroy French self-confidence. Prussian agents were everywhere, but thwarting them at every turn in Central America was one man— Philippe Bunau-Varilla!

It's easy to see why Senator Carmichael called him "the comic-opera representative of a comic-opera republic."[9] But Bunau-Varilla was comic only at a distance. Roosevelt said the man had the look of a duelist.[10] Certainly, Bunau-Varilla never lost sight of what was best for Bunau-Varilla, but he was right about the Panama route; he was right about the advice he gave to the revolutionaries; and he may have been right about the need for Panama to ratify the treaty without delay.

THE LAST WAHOO

None of the American engineers and roughnecks who went to Panama to build the Canal gave two cents for the political ambiguities of their nation's title to the Zone. They went looking for work and adventure.

In 1890, the superintendent of the Census had announced that the American frontier was no more. But between 1904 and 1914, when the Canal opened for business, there was a last American wahoo in Panama. Nature was still wild there; moreover, it was tropical, lending it some of the same horror for North Americans that the dark forests of Massachusetts had held for the Puritans. There were wild Indians in Panama, tropical bo's (hobos), and a few old-fashioned badmen. The Zone's first chief of police was George Shanton, the original Laramie Kid in Buffalo Bill's Wild West Show.[11]

An American in Panama could find the unexpectedness that was so much a part of the fascination of the frontier. A short trip upriver in a *cayuco* (log canoe), and he might come upon an Indian maiden "clad in all her innocence." In the city, he might wake up to the sound of gunfire. On election day in 1906, an American mechanic living on Santa Ana Plaza looked outside and decided to take the day off. From his window, he watched an all-day on-again, off-again battle in the park below. Men fought with canes and revolvers. Finally, policemen charged across the park with rifles blazing. "Many men fell, some lay still, and others got up and staggered off. Most of the shots were high and the falling twigs came down in a regular shower in the park. It was much like a Wild West show; the police yelling like Indians, waving their rifles in the air and firing as they ran."[12]

Like the mountain men who had walked into Taos some sixty years earlier, the diggers on the Panama frontier confronted a Latin American society. The locals lived by different rules, especially with regard to sex, work, and politics. An American man could feel liberated in Panama, accepting the Latin customs that gave him greater freedom, and rejecting as foreign those that would restrict him.

When he got tired of answering the call of the wild in the casinos, cantinas, and *casas de citas* of Panama City or Colón, he could refresh himself on a hunt in the jungle. There were plenty of strange animals to stir his imagination—jaguars, peccaries, tapirs, coatimundis, and especially alligators, Panama's equivalent of the North American buffalo.

Tourists, who were the equivalent on the Isthmus of Eastern dudes in the Old West, were often taken on alligator hunts. During excursion boat trips down Crocodile Creek, shots from repeating rifles would ring out from "every part of the deck, from the roof of the cabin, and from the pilot house." One local trapper was said to have taken 60,000 alligators in a single year[13] (164 a day?). Even if that report is exaggerated, it reflects the abandon with which the alligator was hunted and suggests the quantity of alligators in Panama's rivers and swamps.

HORSE SENSE AND HORSE PLAY

"Bo" Calloway, President Gerald Ford's campaign manager, called the Panama Canal America's turn-of-the-century moon shot. It's a good analogy, but the differences between the two projects are as important as their similarities. Both were engineering projects. Both were initiated by presidents who wanted to improve the nation's morale and prestige. However, there was a lot of skepticism about the value of the moon shot. Exactly what did we get for the billions it cost? The value of the Canal shortcut, on the other hand, was plain to everyone.

The Americans who backed Roosevelt on the Canal had mixed motives, of course. They wanted to show the world what America could do, and they wanted the military advantage that the Canal would produce. (The battleship *Oregon's* race around the Horn in 1898 to join the fleet at Santiago was still vividly remembered.) But Americans were proudest of the Canal's potential as an instrument for international peace and harmony. A journalist proclaimed that the Canal diggers were performing "a service to the cause of universal progress and civilization the worth of which the passage of time will never dim."[14]

Progress was no joke in those days. Faith in progress was what sustained people through the turmoil of the late nineteenth century. That faith was considerably eroded by the time the *Apollo* space vehicle landed on the moon. By then the general attitude toward technological progress was wary. People thought it might be out of control.

The space program was an enigma run by an acronym—NASA. The space engineers were anonymous. The nature they wrestled with was coded and stored in a computer. Sometimes the whole thing seemed more like a performance than an actual event.

That was never the case with the Canal project. The Canal diggers wrestled with a nature that could be seen and smelled and felt. The Canal engineers were identifiable people, and the job's technical problems were widely understood. Chief engineer John Stevens once declared wearily that he must be the only man in the country with no new ideas about how the Canal should be built.[15]

That is not to say the job was an easy one. In 1915, a historian wrote, "No single work ever undertaken by man called into play so many machines of different kinds . . . as the building of the Panama

Canal."[16] And a second-generation Zonian, in 1980, urged us not to forget, "This place was a world's fair of invention."

And so it was. But they were inventions that men who were intelligent and clever with tools could understand, repair, duplicate, and sometimes improve. The Panama Canal was the last triumph of "horse sense."

It may also have been the last triumph of "horse play." In spite of the Canal workers' gruff insistence on their absolute practicality, they kept acting like children—spiking the punch, getting into fights, playing tricks. A girl was married between dances at the Tivoli Hotel, while her parents, who disapproved of the match, were kept busy in the ballroom. The girl's friends saw to it that several extra "flashlights" were taken after the dance to allow time for the ceremony.[17]

One afternoon, chief engineer John Stevens, "as full of fight as a lumberjack," lunged at the State Department's chief representative on the Isthmus. And that worthy was boyishly proud of knocking Jackson Smith, the chief of Labor and Quarters, all the way down a flight of stairs.[18]

The physician responsible for wiping out yellow fever on the Isthmus, William Gorgas, and his two chief aides declared themselves a holiday and set out to navigate the unfinished Canal in a *cayuco*. But the truants had told no one of their plans and consequently nearly got themselves killed, since men were still blasting to widen the channel.[19] No one of comparable stature could behave like that today. Think of the reporters, the cameras, the fatuous smirks, and condescending comments on the six o'clock news.

THE AMERICAN ROUGHNECKS

Joseph Pennell went to Panama in 1912 to sketch the construction of the Canal—that "Wonder of Work," as he called it. In the notes that accompany his pictures, he wrote, "These engineers and workmen are the sort of Americans worth knowing."[20] They came from all over and from all kinds of backgrounds: John Baxter was there, with his degree from Harvard, as was Vesper Dillon, with his certificate from a sod schoolhouse. But they were all romantics. They called themselves "a Knight of the Throttle" or "a Knight of the Jackplane." Life was "the Battle for Bread." There were soldiers of fortune among them: Rufus Booth, who fought with the Cuban *insurrectos* against Spain before the United States intervened on the side of the rebels; Alexander Lundisheff, who began his life as the son of a man named Peacock, became a circus acrobat in Russia, and in the course of his career served in both the Mexican and American armies and in both the Colombian and American navies. There were adventurous women, too: Julia Frost, who had lived in Guatemala and Venezuela before coming to the Zone; Adelaide Mackereth, an army nurse in Cuba and a Red Cross nurse in Hiroshima during the Russo-Japanese War; and Miss Ruth Omealia of Kansas City, who, being at loose ends, tagged along when her brother-in-law, a locomotive engineer, went to Panama. She "caught on" as a telephone operator.[21]

Rose van Hardeveld and her husband were living in the wilds of Wyoming when he announced that he wanted to help America build the Canal. She was dismayed, but he was a newly naturalized Dutch immigrant, eager to testify through action to his new allegiance.

Arriving at Colón, Rose saw houses built on timbers above green water that was scabbed with filth and garbage. Her own house was full of bats and had an almost unbearable stench to it. The woman next door had taut yellow skin. Her little boy had pale lips, bad teeth, and a painfully distended abdomen. Rose wondered how long it would be before she and her rosy-cheeked children looked like that. She used oil-soaked swabs to fight back an invasion of ants, learned to keep the sugar bowl in a saucer of water, and gave way to "old-fashioned screaming hysterics" when her youngest daughter grew feverish.

Rose was one of the miscellaneous Protestants who formed the Christian League of Empire (*Emperador*, actually; it was an old Panamanian town). The league organized a Sunday school, much to Rose's relief: "And so in the midst of an alien people and in a strange country, it was given to us to keep our own ideals and teach our children in large measure the standards and culture of the United States."[22]

But she realized "with amazement and some amusement" that it was not until her children could buy ice cream cones and soda pop that "the last vestige of fear and uncertainty" left her.

Many times Rose neglected her housework to walk to the edge of the Cut and watch the work going on far below. And she quotes her husband as saying, "My answer to my own doubts every time, was faith in my country. I have always believed that America could accomplish anything she set out to do."[23] Which is, of course, a self-fulfilling prophecy.

THE FRONTIERSMAN AND THE BUREAUCRAT: STEVENS AND GOETHALS

The first chief engineer of the American Canal project never really took hold of the job. It was the next two, John Stevens and George Washington Goethals, who created the Zone and successfully carried forward the work. Stevens and Goethals were representative men— representative of different eras—and to an extent that would embarrass a novelist had he invented them.[24]

John Stevens was a self-reliant frontiersman, a man of the nineteenth century. Goethals, though only five years younger, was an organization man, a twentieth-century type. Appropriately, Stevens "burned up cigars like Grant in the Wilderness," while Goethals was "invariably smoking a cigarette."

Neither of them was a member of the First Canal Commission, also known as the Army-Navy Commission, that made such a mess of things on the Isthmus in 1904. Remembering vividly the financial scandal that had accompanied the collapse of the French canal project, the American commissioners were determined that no hint of waste or peculation would compromise the purity of the American project. Their job, as they saw it, was to make sure nobody made a mistake. So they debated endlessly about routine appropriations, hoping, apparently, that the earth and stone along the proposed path between the seas would, like some bureaucratic problem, "dissolve itself shortly" without anyone having to actually *do* anything.

It wasn't only their indecisiveness and timidity that paralyzed the project. Unwieldy army-navy procurement and accounting methods required bizarre quantities of paperwork. One hapless engineer found himself with 1,200 vouchers to fill out for the hire of 200 native carts —six vouchers per cart. Each sheet of the payroll had to be signed by the chief engineer, the division engineer, and the employee. A typical week's payroll weighed 103 pounds—and not nearly enough men had been hired yet to dig the Canal. Officials from four departments had to sign each requisition for a gallon of oil, and a carpenter had to have a written order before he could saw a ten-foot board in half.

Realizing things were "in a devil of a mess," Roosevelt appointed a new civilian commission and offered the job of chief engineer to John Stevens.[25]

Stevens hesitated. His wife urged him to accept. His whole life, she said, had been a preparation for just this job. He told Roosevelt he wanted "a free hand in all matters." Roosevelt promised, and "Big Smoke" Stevens packed for Panama.

He was a quiet man who did a lot of listening, but when he spoke, people stopped talking and remembered what he said. Recalling his first days on the Isthmus, he said, "Nobody was working but the ants and the typists." A yellow-fever epidemic was in progress. More workers were leaving than were arriving. Stevens told them, "There are three diseases on the Isthmus, yellow fever, malaria, and cold feet. The worst is cold feet. That's what's ailing you."

To a man who bragged that the railroad had had no collisions all year, Stevens said, "A collision has its good points as well as its bad ones. At least it indicates something is moving on the railroad." And he promised a division chief, "You won't get fired if you do something, you will if you don't do anything. Do something if it is wrong, for you can correct that, but there is no way to correct nothing."

Stevens referred to men as "high grade" or "degenerate," a judgment that had to do with their competence and versatility, but above all with their willingness to take risks and responsibility. He spent his long life (1853–1943) in an almost religious quest for responsibility. He admonished a group of young engineers never "even tacitly" to approve or carry out plans they knew to be wrong: "An engineer is morally responsible for any work that he undertakes to execute."

A man who believes that isn't going to get along with everyone. Indeed, a contemporary described Stevens as a man "looking for trouble." But not just any kind of trouble. He sidestepped a suggestion that he accept the presidency of the Great Northern Railway, a job that would have made him one of the most powerful men in the country. He said the job would require the practice of a diplomacy that he was temperamentally unfit to exercise.

What Stevens wanted was not power but responsibility, and the risk of failure that goes with it. For Stevens, the risk of failure was what gave meaning to life. That was why he wanted complete control of a job. It was also why he so often disobeyed his superior's instructions.

A man like Stevens needed a particular kind of employer, not a boss but a patron who could appreciate his work. He found his man in the railroad baron James J. Hill. Stevens came to Hill's attention by disobeying orders. As an assistant engineer, he was in charge of building a switchback line over the Cascade range for Hill's Great Northern Railway Company. When Stevens sent his plans to the main field office for approval, the chief engineer replied that the president of the company didn't like the look of a particular thirteen-degree curve. No work was to be done on that part of the roadbed until Mr. Hill himself had looked at it. "I decided differently," said Stevens, and when Hill saw what Stevens had done, he gave him a raise—much to the surprise of Stevens' immediate superior.

In 1882, Stevens went to work for the Canadian Pacific. He depreciated his technical knowledge at the time, remarking that only a little was needed, plus some "comprehension of the vagaries of human nature." He improved his knowledge of both while in Canada.

A few years later, back in the United States, Stevens found the Lost Marias Pass in the Rockies, whose existence had been rumored since the days of Lewis and Clark. He found another pass in the

Cascades that was later named after him. And he designed the railway tunnel under Seattle's business district. When he and his wife, Harriet, came to Panama, in 1905, he was fifty-two and knowledge-able about both the technical side of engineering and the vagaries of human nature.

Stevens did four important things in Panama. First, he organized a system for moving the dirt. That was the most important problem in Panama and something Stevens, as an old railroad hand, was particu-larly suited to deal with. Second, he began building a community for his workers so that they could bring their families and settle down to a long job. He expanded the commissary, built an ice plant, renovated the houses left by the French, and began work on schools, churches, police stations, jails, hotels, hospitals, post offices, and clubhouses. He even organized a brass band.

Third, he saw to it that the right people were put in charge or stayed in charge, among them William Crawford Gorgas, the doctor who claimed he could rid the Isthmus of yellow fever. In spite of his success in wiping out yellow fever in Havana after the Spanish-American War, few people believed Gorgas when he insisted that the disease was carried by mosquitoes. The age of the expert had not quite dawned, and when Gorgas made a nuisance of himself by demanding hundreds of thousands of dollars over his budget for screens and kerosene, the men of sound common sense on the Second Canal Commission decided he was a "theorist"—a crank. The chair-man nominated an osteopath he knew to take Gorgas' place.

Stevens didn't know anything about medicine. But he knew about men, and he believed Gorgas was the right man for the job. So in words "more forcible than elegant," which "perhaps would not bear repeating and paraphrased would lose much of their picturesque punch," he told the chairman what he could do with his osteopath.

Stevens backed Gorgas to the hilt—the only man on the commission to do so—and Gorgas repaid him with "a miracle." His men inspected every house on the Zone and in Panama's principal cities, overturning flower vases and ant guards (bowls of water placed under the legs of tables and beds)—everything containing standing water where a mosquito could breed. They sprayed and fumigated house by house, doing some houses several times. Men with cans strapped to their backs walked the streets and fields, squirting every ditch and puddle with kerosene. "The whole isthmus reeks of the stuff," wrote a reporter from the *London Times*.[26]

Almost all adult Panamanians were immune to yellow fever, or the black vomit as it was sometimes called. They found Gorgas' measures so irritating that some of them soured on the whole idea of a partnership with the Americans. The editor of *El Diario* grumbled that building the Canal and eradicating yellow fever were both delusions—merely examples of American boasting—and as the Panamanians danced the *tamborito*, their *cantadores* sang:

> *The Gringos invade our houses*
> *And tell us just what we must do.*
> *The Gringos are the bosses;*
> *Panameños, you are on the spot.*
> *They make us learn to walk the chalk,*
> *Like fence posts in a row,*
> *They dig and pave and scrub the streets;*
> *They're even cleaning up the jail.*
> *You might suppose that they are mad,*
> *But all Americanos act like that.*[27]

Gorgas pressed on, cleaning up the jails, the swamps, the streets, the markets—transforming Panama from an infamous pesthole to one of the most salubrious spots in the Americas.

The swift triumph of compulsory sanitation on the Isthmus astonished the world. It was one of the "miracles" that helped forge a new belief system based on the infallibility of the scientific expert and on the beneficial effects of social compulsion under his direction.

The fourth thing Stevens did was to persuade President Roosevelt and Congress to authorize a lock canal. It wasn't easy. Stevens was a witness before committees; he served on committees; he lobbied behind the scenes; and he wrote speeches for politicians who supported his plan. Roosevelt was only "luke-warm" about a lock canal. "I talked to Teddy like a Dutch uncle," Stevens recalled. The vote was thirty-six to thirty-one in favor of a lock-type canal.

He was a good lobbyist, but that wasn't work he was cut out for. And instead of easing off, the political demands of his job increased. Contractors began asking for a piece of the action. They invoked the names of Vice-President William Howard Taft and free enterprise. Finally Stevens wrote a letter to Roosevelt, complaining of the discomforts of being "continually subject to attack by a lot of people, and they are not all in private life, that I would not wipe my boots on in the United States." There were, he said, men "as competent and far more willing to pick up and carry the burden than I am," and went on to ask, "if in the next two or three months, you can see your way clear to let me follow other lines much more agreeable to me, I shall ever be your debtor."

Stevens was a quitter—no doubt about it. He never stayed with one company long. However, he had warned Roosevelt that he wouldn't necessarily stay in Panama until the job was done—only until its success or failure was assured. By 1907, its success was assured. Stevens predicted that the job would take eight more years. He overestimated by four and a half months.

The word *job* meant something different to him than it does to most of us. He once compared laying railroad track to "an absorbing drama" played by "actors who knew their parts and carried them through without a break." A journalist reported that when Stevens was working in the Southwest in the seventies, his boss offered $500 to the man who would walk across "a hundred or two miles of Apache country with a message." Stevens volunteered. When he returned, he is said to have refused the money. "The thing had been there to do, and it was the sort of thing he liked to do; he preferred to do it for its own sake—art for art."

That story may be apocryphal—at least in part—but the journalist who wrote it was on to something essential. Stevens was an artist—a maker—and when he had solved a job's "artistic" problems, he lost interest in it. He went on to other adventures in China and Russia during the Bolshevik Revolution, but the job he did in Panama was the high point of his career. And it brought an era to a close.

By the beginning of the twentieth century, men were using steamboats, steam locomotives, and steam shovels; they had telephones, the telegraph, dynamite, electric lights, and the trolley car. But these marvels had not displaced men and animals from their age-old central position in the accomplishment of work.

For all the Canal Commission's up-to-date equipment, it took an army of 53,679 men, most of them ordinary laborers, to dig a path between the seas.[28] And throughout the construction period, mules and horses hauled wagons, carriages, ambulances, and fire trucks. The Panama Canal was the last great project of men, mules, and steam; and Stevens was the last of the great self-educated, self-made engineers.

The kind of man Stevens was still haunts millions of Americans, like the ghost of someone they were supposed to be. There is no place in the modern corporate state for that kind of man, so people stay awake when they should be asleep, watching reruns of John Wayne movies, paying tribute to values they still honor but act upon only in dreams.

Stevens was the son of a Yankee farmer; George Washington Goethals, his successor in Panama, was the son of an immigrant Belgian woodworker.[29] Stevens went West to make himself into an engineer. Goethals went to school—City College, in New York City, then West Point—where he was made into an engineer—and into an officer and a gentleman. Stevens was perfectly aware of his own worth. He knew men who weren't good enough to wipe his boots on, but he searched throughout his life for adventure and challenging work, never for illustrious ancestors. He was a "politic roughneck." Goethals, as an officer and a gentleman, developed an interest in genealogy. "Goethals" was a name with aristocratic antecedents in Belgium.

After graduating, Goethals helped transform the laissez-faire volunteer army that fought the Spanish-American War as if it were an opportunity for individual self-expression into a relatively coherent, impersonal, bureaucratic fighting force. Then, in 1907, President Roosevelt sent him to Panama to replace Stevens.

Much to Goethals' surprise, everything about the Canal project was running smoothly. He couldn't understand why Stevens had quit. But Goethals quickly understood what he was up against as Stevens' replacement. The men loved Stevens. He was their kind of man— a roughneck who had raised himself by his own bootstraps to the place where he could talk like a Dutch uncle to the president of the United States. "I have never seen so much affection displayed for any man," Goethals wrote.

Petitions were circulated begging Stevens not to go. Work stopped as men poured into the port of Cristóbal on special trains to see him off. They sang his favorite songs. They wept. Ship whistles tooted. The band switched from "Hail the Conquering Hero" to "Auld Lang Syne." Finally, he was gone, and the workers turned to size up their new boss. They were expecting a military regime and weren't prepared to like it.

Goethals wrote to his son that he tried to disabuse the men of the idea of militarism. He never, for instance, appeared in uniform on the Zone, but in his first speech at a smoker in Corozal, he struck an ambiguous note: "Every man who does his duty will never have any cause to complain on account of militarism."

Marie Gorgas, wife of William Gorgas, resented what she believed was Goethals' "passion for dominating everything and everybody." She has passed on a secondhand story that makes him sound like a madman. Responding to a casual remark about the beauty of the Zone, he is supposed to have said, "Yes, it's a beautiful spot . . . and I love it! But I love it for other reasons than its beauty or the things I get from it. Above all, I love it for the power. . . . Wealth—salaries—these are nothing. It's power, power, power!"

She was a very Southern Lady; he, a somewhat introverted immigrant's son from Brooklyn. His virtues were not the kind she could appreciate, but her judgment of him is only modified and not contradicted by what his admirers said of him. Power really was "the relish and sweetness of his life."

He called himself a dictator. An admirer said he was "the most absolute despot in the world." But "dictator" and "despot" had different meanings in those days. Goethals was no Hitler or Stalin.

True, he had no patience with "kickers." He gave his men no "say" in how the Canal Zone was governed. But they were neither soldiers nor prisoners. They could vote with their feet, and they did. Every year of the construction period more than half of the American workers went home. Goethals said that gaining control of the work force in order to mold and direct it was "the big attractive thing of the job." He did this in two ways, by modifying the workers' environment and by personal counseling.

Joseph Bishop, Goethals' friend and biographer, explained that "Uncle Sam had no intention of becoming a benevolent landlord and caterer when he went to Panama. . . . But in order to get the best class of American workingmen, and keep them fit . . . he had to keep adding one thing after another until now there are government laundries, bakeries with automatic pie, cake, and breadmaking machines, electric-light factories, plants for roasting coffee and freezing ice-cream, a harness shop, livery stables, printing press, and an official newspaper, The Canal Record."

But comfort and convenience weren't enough. Goethals also provided what he termed "rational amusements." He subsidized each worker's membership in the YMCA and saw to it that the "Y" adopted a liberal policy about the participation of women. He encouraged theatricals and a baseball league. He knew the men wouldn't "stick" if their wives were unhappy, so he brought Helen Varick Boswell to the Isthmus to organize women's clubs. A civil engineer by trade, he was a social engineer by inclination: "My chief interest at Panama is not in engineering," he remarked, "but in the men. The Canal will build itself if we can handle the men."

Employees "on the line" had "more of a show" with Goethals than with Stevens, who gave his foremen a job and told them to do it. They could handle their men as they pleased within certain broad limits. What counted with Stevens was "horse sense and the nerve to try doubtful experiments" in order to "grapple with and solve unusual problems that arise."[30]

Goethals established a formal appeals system. He forbade the use of abusive language by those in authority. (Newspaper headlines blared: "Sunday-School Methods on the Canal.") And he expected his foremen to do exactly as they were told. In a speech at West Point, he told an anecdote about an officer who explained to his general why he had disobeyed orders. The general replied, "Your reasons for not doing it are the best I ever heard; now go do it."

Stevens' method left men free to discover better ways—and worse ones. To prevent the latter, he relied on his judgment of character. Goethals' method made it unnecessary for him to pick superior supervisors—although as a matter of fact, he generally did. But his system did not require them, and over the years did not always get them. However, Goethals could afford to abridge his subordinates' freedom only because he did not expect them to have to grapple with and solve unusual problems. That stage of the work was over when he got there.

But there were plenty of everyday, ordinary problems that could hamper the work of the Canal army. Goethals dealt with some of them at paternalistic Sunday-morning counseling sessions.

> *Don't hesitate to state your case, the boss will hear you through;*
> *It's true he's sometimes busy and has other things to do.*
> *But come on Sunday morning, and line up with the rest,*
> *You'll maybe feel some better with that grievance off your chest.*[31]

One Sunday a Jamaican demanded his wife's salary because he was the man of the house. He was refused. A housewife complained about poor meat. Men were there looking for recommendations for work in the States. Some men just wanted to say they had talked to "the Colonel." The scene has been likened to various exotic parallels —Saint Louis judging his people beneath the oak at Vincennes, for example. But closer to home, it is a lot like the sort of thing another George Washington was doing around the turn of the century—

George Washington Plunkitt, a Tammany Hall ward boss, who busied himself helping folks with the small problems of their lives in return for votes, and who, unlike most ward bosses, left a record of his activities: "very plain talks on very practical politics."[32] Goethals did not need votes; he did, however, need the support of a motivated work force, and he got it, partly by showing his interest in the small problems of his workers' lives.

During the Goethals regime, the organization of work on the Zone was transformed to the twentieth-century method, which is essentially the army method. It focuses men's attention upon rank and degree, upon prerequisites and specialization. To a large extent, men stopped looking for their chances and began defending their rights.

The United States was moving in the same direction, though less systematically. In 1900, the *Saturday Evening Post* had reported a marked increase in college enrollments in "the special departments in which young men are taught to be experts."[33] Charles R. Flint, president of U.S. Rubber, explained that in the formation period it was possible for men to go into different things and carry them through successfully: "Now the formation period is practically over. We have settled down to doing business under the new plan. . . . The business of the world is going to be divided up more and more into departments. Success is to be won in getting at the head of one of these departments. It is the twentieth century method."[34]

3

The United States:
A Society in Search of an Ideal

The Canal Zone needs to be understood in relation to "the twentieth-century method." The Zone's organization and atmosphere—indeed, its very existence—reflect the shift in national goals and personal values that took place in the United States between roughly 1890 and 1920.

The historian William G. McLoughlin has proposed that we think of American history as divided into four eras, each era introduced by a turbulent transitional period lasting about thirty years. During those transitional periods, Americans argue passionately with each other about who is responsible for what, about where the country is headed, and about what a good person should do. In the process, they establish a new consensus about goals and values, without, however, totally repudiating the past.

> with one hand we cling
> To the familiar things we call our own,
> And with the other, resolute of will,
> Grope in the dark for what the day will bring.[1]

Or, as McLoughlin says, "the old light never quite dies, and the process is never finished."

America's first shift in goals and values took place between roughly 1730 and 1760. Americans changed their minds about religion, making it more emotional and democratic, less authoritarian and intellectual.

Between 1800 and 1830, there was a shift from a conformist to an individualistic ethic. "New Light" preachers such as the evangelist Charles Grandison Finney rejected the old Calvinist doctrine of Predestination. They rejected the idea that an American citizen had to wait passively and nervously to see whether or not God would save him. Finney preached, "Don't wait for feeling, DO IT."² A few years later, Emerson was urging Americans to be self-reliant. An American was not *predestined!* Americans were in charge of their own destinies—they could Save themselves. And if they could do *that*, why surely they could save the Republic—indeed, the whole world. It was the American destiny, brothers and sisters, to *do it!*

So they did it. They no longer saw America as a refuge, but as a revolutionary instrument that could save the world by actively intervening in its affairs—by Americanizing it. However, no authority was supposed to tell them how to do this. The government, like God, was expected to keep hands off—to allow people to make their own decisions and to act individually or through voluntary associations, including voluntary military associations.

Missionaries went all over the world to Americanize the heathen by converting them to Christianity, progress, and democracy. Settlers, followed by the army, Americanized Texas and California. During the Civil War, Union idealists saved the Republic ("His truth is marching on") by Americanizing the feudal, foreign, slaveholding South. Sodbusters and cowboys Americanized the West.

But as the frontier began to disappear, Americans began feeling less and less like self-reliant individuals who were responsible for their own fates and more and more like helpless cogs in an impersonal economic machine. That was bad enough, but then the Darwinists began telling them that they were helpless cogs in an impersonal biological machine, too. In response to this challenge to their traditional faith in individual freedom and responsibility, Americans began a third period of debate about their basic goals and values. That period lasted from roughly 1890 to 1920.

During those years, dozens of reformers—secular and religious—proposed new social goals and better ways of doing things. One of the most influential of those reformers was Edward Bellamy, and the new consensus he did so much to shape marked a shift from individualistic to collectivist values. Nowhere did this shift happen more quickly or thoroughly than in the American outpost on the banks of the Panama Canal. "This is the lesson of Panama," asserted Albert Edwards, after a visit to the Zone: " 'Collective activity'— this new force which we are developing with such amazing success in the tropics, which we, Americans, have carried farther than any other nation—is worth considering as a means of solving our problems at home."[3]

Willis Abbot called the Zone "an education in collectivism" and quoted an unidentified banker who was touring the Zone: "The big thing is the spirit of paternalism, of modern socialism, of governmental parenthood, if you will, which is being engendered and nursed to full strength by Federal control of the Canal. This is no idle dream, and within five years, yes, within three years, it will begin to be felt in the United States."[4]

However, the Canal Zone itself was shaped by a larger movement that was already making itself felt in the United States, where a leader of the religious wing of the progressive reform movement, Walter Rauschenbusch, was telling his congregation that the "individualistic concept of personal salvation" had pushed out of sight "the collective idea of the Kingdom of God on Earth." Conversion, Rauschenbusch revealed, "is the transition from an unsocial to a social mind."[5]

Conversion was difficult, however, because men were as predestined by "the system," that is, by their environment, as the Puritans had been by their Calvinist God. "We must work on the environment, not merely on the heart of men," declared John Dewey, a leader of the secular wing of the reform movement.[6]

The "we" he referred to were members of the new class of experts who had been trained in colleges to rise above their environment and to look beyond their own self-interest. They would take responsibility for the common man and do for him what he could not do for himself—save him. They would do this by reorganizing society, by creating a new and better system.

To this end, they preached cooperation and social planning through federal regulatory and welfare agencies, union confederations, professional organizations, and interdenominational religious organizations. The reformers even "rationalized" children's play. In 1906, they founded the Playground Association of America to promote publicly funded playgrounds supervised by experts who would teach children socially beneficial *team* sports.[7]

The turn-of-the-century reformers were determined to bring Americans together in social harmony. At first they thought they could do this by wresting control of the country from the "special interests," through democratic reforms. But many of the college-educated reformers soon lost faith in the efficiency of democratic procedures. It seemed inappropriate to them that they should have to cater to the irrational, uninformed electorate, who often preferred a lout to an educated man. The reformers ended up, in McLoughlin's words, "suggesting a partnership of government and business under the wise regulation of social scientists—social planners and policy makers."[8] A stewardship not of the Elect, nor of the elected, but of the accredited, college-educated experts.

The reformers' primary values were collectivism (cooperation and systematization), professionalism, and most of all, efficiency. The American flag flying over the Panama Canal was hailed as "a symbol to the passing world of the efficiency of the United States."[9]

Engineers, it was thought, possessed these values more commonly and to a greater degree than other men. Hence, many reformers believed it was the engineers rather than the politicians who should be in charge of society. The minds of the engineers had been cleared of cant by the discipline of the machine process, and their achievements—transatlantic cables, transcontinental railroads, transoceanic canals—were bringing the world together in rational harmony. In Panama their achievement included not just the Canal but the American community on its banks—the only society in the world designed, constructed, and presided over from beginning to end by engineers.

4
Two Idealists in Search of a Society

THE WAY WE WERE

We spent nineteen years as teachers on the Zone and in the Canal Area, as it was called after the 1978 treaties went into effect. Early on we realized that the Zone was generally misunderstood by the journalists and visitors who came there for a few days and then went off to instruct others about what it was really like. But that wasn't surprising. Even those of us who lived there had a hard time understanding it. The Canal workers were very proud of the Zone's distinctly American character, but sometimes they complained that living there was like living in the Soviet Union.

It was years before we came to terms with that paradox. It simply wasn't enough to explain glibly that the Zone was a colony, or a military reservation, or a company town. Only when we learned that during the first third of this century the Zone had reminded people of Bellamy's utopia did we begin to understand how it could be so very American and yet cause people in moments of exasperation to compare it to the Soviet Union.

It was disturbing, however, to realize that the character of the Zone had been so strongly influenced by the goals and values of the progressive reformers, for that meant that when we arrived on the Zone in the fall of 1963, we should have loved it. As liberals, we were the ideological heirs of those reformers. What Bellamy and the other progressives had wanted, we still wanted—a safer, fairer, more efficient, equalitarian, and collectivist society—in a word, a more

33

"rational" society. Certainly, there was no more "rational" society on earth than the Canal Zone. But we didn't love it. By Christmas, we had decided to go home after our two-year commitment was up.

We changed our minds—but never felt really at home on the Zone. And our long sojourn in "utopia" left us with very mixed feelings about its advantages. While we were there, we modified or abandoned many of the socialist ideas we had hitherto cherished.

Back in the 1950s, we were fairly typical of a certain group of idealistic, semi-alienated, college-educated, antibusiness, would-be elitists. We had a vague feeling that there were too many poor people in the world, including us, too much respect for wealth instead of education, and too much money wasted on pointless product innovation and advertising. We wanted a more rational society, which would, incidentally, be more socialist, less wasteful—more efficient, less unjust.

We were atypical in that, as chance would have it, we found ourselves living in a community where our socialist ideals were largely realized. However, we were not unique; there were others on the Zone with backgrounds similar to ours, and some of them maintained their faith in the ideals of their youth by arguing that the Zone was not "really" socialistic. When pressed, however, they would admit that "real" socialism didn't exist anywhere—yet.

It is true that the Zone was not a perfect society, but it was an instructive approximation of Bellamy's American-style authoritarian socialism, and we think anyone dreaming of "real" socialism in America could profitably compare his dream to the Zone's reality.

In some ways, we were predisposed to modify our socialist sympathies even before we left the States. While we approved of the changes the progressives and their liberal heirs had made toward reorganizing society along more "rational" lines, we were fed up with organization men and team players. (On the Zone, of course, there was nothing but!) In the 1950s we made no connection between the idealistic collectivism that we advocated and the conformity that we deplored. It simply didn't register that there was a relationship between the suburban syndrome and the spirit of "Togetherness" on the one hand and the increasingly systematized and regulated character of American society on the other. We did not see that the safety and sterility of suburbia represented a triumphant reaction to the unsafe, unregulated, nonsterile (fertile but infectious) free-for-all of the late nineteenth century. We didn't think in terms of trade-offs but of perfection.

Also, in those days, we imagined that, as teachers, we had "risen above" our society. We identified with the social engineers, the managers of society—not of businesses. We shared their perspective and admired engineered solutions to society's problems, except when we felt we were the ones being engineered. That, we resented.

For instance, we were in favor of compulsory public education. We thought it was important for experts, like us, to have the right to infringe upon the freedom of students and parents to believe whatever silly thing tradition or local prejudice dictated. However, we resented the way school administrators compelled us to teach prescribed material in a prescribed way at a prescribed time. Those bureaucrats were infringing on our freedom—our right as professionals to make our own professional decisions about those things.

The progressives called public education "The Great Panacea."[1] By taking control of public education, they intended to undermine authority and tradition and teach Americans to think critically about "the system." And critical thinking was the part of our ideological inheritance from the progressives that we accepted most enthusiastically—and uncritically.

Naturally, we disapproved of indoctrination. Indoctrination was the antithesis of our rational, progressive ideal. So we preached secularism, relativism, and social engineering to our students, while assuring each other that we weren't really indoctrinating them. It was those old-fashioned teachers who were doing the indoctrinating—by teaching ethnocentrism, patriotism, and an uncritical respect for authority and tradition.[2]

It seems odd, now, how dear that fiction was to us, but we needed to believe in critical thinking. It enlarged our lives. Ill-paid and apparently insignificant, we were really secret agents working to Save

Civilization from Christianity, Capitalism, and the Dead Weight of the Past. As far as we were concerned, all traditional institutions and beliefs, from patriotism to the Rainbow Girls, represented the shackles of yesteryear, which we were for casting off. They were all threats or affronts to critical thinking.

Patriotism in particular aroused our scorn. It was so ethnocentric, so parochial. And if there was anything we didn't want to be out there in Kansas, it was ethnocentric or parochial. Patriotism was also a prejudice, and we were against prejudice.

Of course, we didn't consider ourselves unpatriotic. Not at all! We saw through more than we thought through, and could thus have it both ways—could be both patriotic Americans and detached, dispassionate, reasonable citizens of the world.

We loved our country. We were, after all, seeking to purify it, to recall it from its crass commercialism, racial bigotry, incessant breeding, and empty ritualism—its lack of logical rigor and moral passion. More than mere schoolteachers, we were self-ordained, self-elected preachers who, before our captive congregations, were carrying on the oldest and most characteristic American tradition: We were affirming our Americanness by denouncing America. We were delivering jeremiads.

IN THE AMERICAN GRAIN: DELIVERING JEREMIADS

The jeremiad is a kind of sermon. The Puritans, as Sacvan Bercovitch has shown, gave it its American form, and Americans have been using it ever since to focus and refocus their idea of themselves as Americans.

The European jeremiad is a lament: Man is depraved; there is no remedy; many are called but few are chosen; on your knees, brother. The American jeremiad has a different ending. The Puritan preachers lamented more energetically than their European counterparts but then announced the good news—that God's punishments were meant as correctives, as a means of recalling America to its mission, which was to be God's "peculiar garden of pleasure," "a City of Righteousness," a "Valley of Vision."

The Europeans accepted man's depravity as a fact of life and despaired, in a composed, equable way. Americans refused to accept it. They dreamed of a society where, as Perry Miller said, ". . . the fact could be made one with the ideal."³

Well, we were Americans, and that was our dream. So we castigated our nation for falling away from its ideals, for, as a Puritan put it long ago, looking to choose "a captain back for Egypt."⁴ That was how we felt when Eisenhower was elected instead of Stevenson in 1956. We were sure America had sold its soul for giant-finned cars and tract houses in the suburbs.

We weren't the only ones. The liberal magazines we read were full of articles criticizing America. But those articles were shrill, puny things. Who would step forth to preach the great jeremiad that would awaken the nation and recall it to its old progressive-liberal virtues?

In 1960 we thought it might be Kennedy with his "Ask not what your country can do for you, but what you can do for your country," but as it turned out, the master of the jeremiad in our time was not a liberal politician. He was a traditional ordained Christian preacher, Martin Luther King.

But King's crusade for racial equality—his great revival—did not arouse the nation until the 1960s. Back in the fifties, we had to make do with lesser men, among them, curiously, the British writer Graham Greene, a man who dislikes Americans intensely. (Twenty-two years later, he would play a minor role in the campaign to ratify the Panama Canal treaties by peddling the virtues of left-wing dictatorship to American intellectuals.) In his popular 1956 book *The Quiet American*, he contrasted a cynical, sad European character with an innocent, idealistic American. Greene's message was that it was better to be like the European (Mr. Worldly-Wise-Man), never expecting much in this vale of tears, than to be like the American, bounding about full of confidence and energy—and breaking things.

The Quiet American was a European jeremiad directed at Americans. But those Americans who liked it read it as an American jeremiad—a sermon joining "social criticism to spiritual renewal."⁵

True, Greene left off the word of hope at the end, but the citizens of a nation of immigrants are adept at finding hope where stay-at-homes see cause only for lamentation. Greene's American readers took *The Quiet American* as a self-help book. The message they got was, "Don't be naive and innocent. Be subtle. Be sophisticated. Improve yourself."

Just how to do that was spelled out two years later by William Lederer and Eugene Burdick in *The Ugly American*. Their book was also set in Southeast Asia and was about bumbling American diplomats and AID officials. But it was a true American jeremiad: You are wicked, brother, but you can be better!

Their message was that the American diplomats ought to speak the language of the country where they are posted, and ought to get out into the boondocks and talk to "the people," instead of staying in the capital and chatting with the elite.

Like us, Lederer and Burdick had been influenced by the assumptions of the American progressives. The hero of their book is an unpretentious, ugly American engineer with dirt under his fingernails: "Listen, you damn fools, it's a simple problem. Let us engineers solve it. . . ."

In those days we had faith in engineers—and in an ahistorical form of rationality. As we saw it, America's mission was to show the world the way to a perfectly rational society. That meant America would have to repudiate, among other things, organized religion and national pride. Americans would be the first nonethnocentric ethnics. Only Americans could possibly do it!

DREAMING OF A BETTER WORLD

In the early sixties, we spent an evening almost every week with friends who shared our convictions. After gloomily commenting on the problems of the world, we all ate ice cream.

It was then that we and our friends spoke of The Other World. We were inclined to think in utopian terms, anyway, that is, in terms of permanent rather than temporary solutions, but we were encouraged in this by signs that a nuclear war was increasingly likely. The government was promoting civil defense. People were digging fallout shelters. The milk we bought was contaminated by debris from nuclear tests in the atmosphere. The famous clock on the cover of *The Bulletin of the Atomic Scientists* showed twelve minutes till midnight.

Was it any wonder that our thoughts turned to Another and a Better World? We checked charts showing prevailing wind patterns and decided that if there was a nuclear war, wind-borne fallout would be likely to miss Humboldt, California. That was where we would go. We would build log houses, plant gardens, dig wells. We would need some capital—but we were teachers; we would start a school—for the screwed-up kids of rich, despicable parents. It would be like A. S. Neill's Summerhill. Students and teachers would be free to do whatever they liked, but at the same time, we imagined that it would also—somehow—resemble the utopia in B. F. Skinner's *Walden Two*, where people got to do whatever they liked because the Planners saw to it that what they liked was precisely what was best for themselves and their community.

Talk was cheap and we were poor. We weren't really interested in establishing a city on a hill in Humboldt. So in 1963, when we got a letter from a friend who was working on the Canal Zone as a teacher, we wrote back at once for a salary schedule. We discovered we could make more money there than in Kansas City. Our house needed a new roof. Our car needed a new everything. Kansas City was familiar, stale, and unprofitable. Going to the Canal Zone would be an adventure!

5

Over the Rainbow: The American Canal Zone in Panama

THE JUNGLE

Green jungle, green lawns, green birds, green lizards—and into our hands themselves did reach—right in our own backyard—green mangos, green limes, green papayas. "It's the Emerald City," we told our daughters. And they were from Kansas, too, just like Dorothy Gale. When we saw a rainbow, we said we were on its other side, but instead of pretty little bluebirds, there were buzzards, hundreds of them, spiraling mazily overhead.

"Panamanian air force," a neighbor told us, then advised, "Say, don't let your kids break a branch of Dunb Cane. It stinks and the sap will give them blisters."

"Dunb Cane?"

Everything was faintly ominous. Everywhere things grew on, around, or out of something else. Orchids clung to branches. Vines draped leafy afghans over the leafy crowns of trees. We saw a six-foot royal palm sprouting from the fork of an elephant-ear tree and a row of fenceposts that had taken root.

We were assigned a house on the Ridge in a village called Gamboa —a place set aside for newcomers. Our one-bedroom apartment was in a dingy wooden building that accommodated four families. It was built on stilts so we could drive underneath out of the rain.

Periodically, a platoon of grass-cutters appeared and fought back the jungle with mowers and machetes, but it was always there, just beyond the cleared area. Indians lived just up the river, we heard.

Our children discovered a miserable horse tethered in a gully behind our house. Our neighbor said it was there to attract mosquitoes
for the doctors to study. We newcomers talked a lot about mosquitoes
—the bluish ones bearing jungle yellow fever, the ordinary ones
bearing dengue fever or malaria. We talked about tarantulas, too,
and the Paraponera ant, whose bite can disable a man. After the
woman next door ran her hand around the inside of her washer,
checking for stray socks, and came up with a snake, we talked
about snakes.

We never ventured far into the jungle ourselves. It limited our
vision and excited our imaginations. Overhead, thready roots dangled
from parasitic plants. Underfoot, rotting trunks, bogs, and sinkholes
were concealed by the tangled vegetation.

Some Zonians loved the jungle. Ken Vinton did. He wrote a book
about it, hoping to persuade others to love it, too. There is no reason,
he says, to fear the "lush, tangled tropical environment with its
strange swarming life."[1]

While hunting on the Zone at night, a friend of Vinton's was
knocked sprawling by a blow on the leg. The man lost his gun and
felt one leg being flopped about. A companion ran up and killed a
fourteen-foot boa that had its mouth around the man's thigh. But
Vinton reassuringly points out that "this monster boa made no attempt
to constrict the man it had attacked with such force." Boas, he says,
attack men only by mistake. Snakes, he admits, are pretty stupid, but
he insists that man's fear of the jungle is like a child's fear of the
dark. Once we understand "the vast teeming environment called
the tropical jungle," it is not, Vinton says, "sinister, terrifying, or
particularly dangerous."[2]

We weren't convinced.

There were all sorts of creatures in the jungle—or so we were told.
Not all of them stayed there. That fall, there was a tropical moth
around that gave almost everyone itchy soles. Up at dawn, scratching
our feet on a rug as if doing some primitive dance, we could see
coatimundi and ñequi in the yard and Munchkin-size deer at the
edge of the jungle. Huge iguanas climbed trees to look in at us

through our kitchen window. Spiders, ants, and cockroaches marched right inside to say hello.

THE WEATHER

There were two high schools on the Zone. We taught in the one on the Pacific side, Balboa High. It was air-conditioned by the time we got there, but because we were newcomers, we taught in the wooden, non-air-conditioned annex behind the main building. The humidity clung to us like a vague illness. When the rain slammed down, as it did at least once a day, there was no use trying to talk. Our students would sit up and look outside at the blurred landscape. The rain was refreshing—and soothing. Soon, wrapped in its steady roar, we would all be fighting off sleep—some unsuccessfully.

We wouldn't have stayed without air-conditioning. We bought an air-conditioner as soon as we found where they were sold and ran it —and its successors—twenty-four hours a day for the next nineteen years. But not everyone needed air-conditioning like we did. We met one couple who never did air-condition their quarters. They had grown up on the Zone without it, hardly noticed feeling sticky, and had learned to savor the Zone's rich variety of smells, from night-blooming jasmine to the sweetish-sick mildew smell of their mattresses. Some people, including our children, say the Zone itself had *a* smell, as well as a variety of subsmells, a smell *típica*.

Before air-conditioning, if you left your shoes under the bed for a couple of days, they sprouted beards of mold. Shoes had to be kept in "dry closets" where light bulbs burned day and night. Light blubs burned inside "dry cupboards," too, and hung on extension cords inside pianos. But neither clothes nor cereals were ever crisp, nor was anyone's piano ever in tune. Books warped and fell apart. Cameras grew flowers of mold behind their lenses.

It wasn't until 1957 that the Zone's electricity was converted from twenty-five to sixty cycles, making it possible for Zonians to install air-conditioners. At the Panama Canal Company's expense, contractors converted or replaced thousands of motors, fans, refrigerators, record players—everything that was frequency-sensitive. "It was like Christmas," sighed one Zonian. "Biggest thing around here since we switched to the right side of the road." (Until 1943, everyone on the Zone and in Panama drove on the left.)

Air-conditioning was the last in a series of changes during the fifties that transformed the lives of the Zonians. In 1950 they stopped using Canal Company coupons in the Zone commissaries and began paying in cash. That was also the first year they paid income tax. In 1951, the company was reorganized from an independent government agency to a nonprofit business corporation under a federal charter. Its functions were reduced, as was its work force. The Zone became less of a self-sufficient ministate. But it also grew less isolated. Access to the States became easier. Canal workers began shipping their household goods and cars to the Zone from the States. Also, during this time, academic credentials were gradually becoming more important for promotion.

However, the introduction of air-conditioning, between 1957 and 1960, was the most important change of all. It brought with it "New styles of architecture, a change of heart." The new public buildings resembled bunkers. They were designed to keep the cold in.

They also kept the bureaucrats in—as did the older buildings once they were converted to air-conditioning. In the old days, an administrator with a problem would go out to the field and talk to the workmen who were doing the job, obtaining not only the answer he was looking for but a lot of other information as well. After his office was air-conditioned, he was reluctant to leave it. He solved his problem with a phone call and lost touch with the overall situation. This irritated the workers. "You felt like you were battling shadows," one of them told us. He was referring both to the increasing isolation of the administrators and to their amazing proliferation during the fifties, when the company's work force as a whole was declining.

Before air-conditioning, most Zonians used furniture provided by the company—"one dining room table, square," "two dressers, varnished," "six chairs, mission." Much of the company furniture was metal. Zonians supplemented it with sheeshamwood screens, Chinese chests, and knickknacks from the Hindu stores in Panama. A few people bought solid mahogany furniture from a local craftsman. After air-conditioning, they bought a wider variety of furnishings. Both the uniformity and intimacy—the collectivism—of life on the Zone declined. No longer could you "smell everyone's dinner and hear everyone's fights."

One quiet Sunday morning, Elly came running upstairs to say there was a man outside calling for help. We thought she had been reading too many Nancy Drews but followed her down to the street and, after a moment of silence, we heard him, too: "Help, help me." The faint cries came from a top-floor apartment down the block—the only one in the neighborhood with its windows open. An old bachelor had broken his hip. He was lying on his kitchen floor, calling for help, but his neighbors, with their windows shut and their air-conditioners droning, couldn't hear him.

THE ZONIANS

At first we didn't know any Zonians; we had just arrived. But we knew all about them. They were the bad guys, and the fact that everyone was friendly and helpful didn't alter our opinion.

We took it for granted that there were two main classes of Americans: Those who had risen above ethnocentrism and those who had not—us and them. The real Zonians were "them," like the man wearing an orange shirt, orange socks, and purple shorts who stopped beside Mary as she was buying a red Panamanian fruit from a push-cart vendor.

"What's them things for?"

"I don't know. He says you peel them and eat them."

"You sure got a lotta courage. I been down here twenty-six years, and I ain't never tried 'em."

Zonians called the second set of locks on the Pacific side Peter McGill instead of Pedro Miguel, which was the way it was spelled. We took this to be a deliberate affront to the Panamanians, so we pronounced it with exaggerated correctness. We were declaring our position. No one noticed. It never occurred to us that there might be some other reason to say Peter McGill than to insult Panamanians— that it might be an arbitrary linguistic habit, or that it might dimly amuse people. We were too sensitive to consider alternatives. As soon as we learned our way around, we intended to live in Panama instead of on the Zone. We wanted to meet some Panamanians, to make friends, to become bilingual and sophisticated.

An American ex-missionary and his Latin wife lived downstairs— newcomers like us. We drove to Panama City with them for dancing lessons. We learned Panama's national dances—the *cumbia*, the *tamborito*, and others. We stamped and hopped and yelled, "Aoowah!" as we whirled and turned.

Early Sunday mornings, we went to the market and bought Boquete oranges, corbina, and turtle meat from scrawny, gap-toothed vendors who looked like pirates. We sharpened our Spanish on them while they sharpened their *cuchillos*.

The rains grew longer and more frequent. After games of mud football, boys would use a garden hose to wash themselves off while standing in a downpour. Thick mists clung to the jungle-covered hills. And we dreamed of freezing winds, heavy coats, and snow. A tall, thin, sweating black Santa walking along Avenida Central seemed like a hallucination.

The Zone wasn't like anyplace we'd seen or read about. Kipling was no help at all. Nothing about the Canal workers and their world echoed the imperial idealism or anxieties of Kipling's upper-class sahibs.

One place, though, gave us a strange sense of déjà vu—the Tivoli Hotel—four stories of latticework, verandas, and high-ceilinged rooms —222 of them, each one furnished with white wicker chairs and dressers. Everything except the floors was painted white. In front of the main entrance, a curved driveway passed under a portico. On the veranda, ladies sat rocking the balmy days away, while inside, ceiling fans revolved slowly above lines of potted palms in the empty ballroom.

The Tivoli was built in a hurry in 1906 for Theodore Roosevelt's visit to the Canal—the first overseas trip by an American president—and it was the center of social life on the Pacific side of the Zone until the day it was torn down in 1971. Panamanian politicians fled there when their opponents seized power. Once there were four ex-presidents of Panama there at the same time![3] We fled there after school for a beer, and sitting in its bar, we could imagine ourselves in any of dozens of much-loved movies. *That* was where we'd seen the Tivoli before—not it, specifically, but its ambiance—at the movies!

A West Indian school administrator on the Zone invited us to a Christmas party at his house in Panama. It seemed so bare. Where was all his furniture? We drank sticky punch and danced to salsa music in the sticky air. Our host beckoned us to his balcony. He gestured at the neighborhood with pride. Every house, fence, and wall was outlined by strings of multicolored Christmas-tree lights. We smelled jasmine. And in the distance a fake-looking coconut palm was silhouetted against the fake-looking moonlit sky. The movies again. Everywhere we turned, we kept walking out of reality into a movie set.

Except at the high school. Balboa High was all too familiar—all too "real." Every classroom had its flag. Teachers led their homerooms in the Pledge of Allegiance every day. Students sometimes tattled to the principal if a teacher "forgot." There were rules, rules, rules. Rules about posters, rules about bells, rules about what to do when it rained, rules about paperbacks. (Students couldn't carry them around; they were "trashy.") And of course, there were rules about clothes. No T-shirts, no thong sandals, no shirttails hanging out, and girls could wear jeans only on Friday.

For the first two weeks—two weeks!—of school, the English teachers were supposed to drill their students on parliamentary procedure—*Robert's Rules of Order.*

The ROTC unit was the school's pride and joy. Squads of uniformed students were forever tramping through the halls on their way to raise or lower the flag outside. Some of the uniformed students were Zonians, but most were from military families. There was no Department of Defense school system on the Zone, and 50 percent of the students at Balboa High in 1963 were from military families; 34.5 percent were from company families; the rest were from the United States Embassy, foreign embassies, the American business community in Panama, and from Panamanian families.

Our students believed the United States had never lost a war or broken a treaty. They also believed in God, so we had to be tactful about evolution and overpopulation. But most importantly for us, they believed in a Liberal Education. It was the Stairway, the Door, the Key to a Better Life. They took notes. They did their homework. They were a joy to teach.

During the sixties and seventies, there were about 46,000 people living on the Zone. There were two main groups: the military and the Canal workers. The military amounted to about 10,000 active duty personnel plus 20,000 dependents and civilian Department of Defense families. All of them lived and worked mainly on their bases—zones within the Zone. Most of them stayed only a few years.

Some of the Canal workers stayed only a few years, too. Others spent their whole careers with the company. A few settled in Panama when they retired. The company employed about 3,500 Americans, who had roughly 6,500 dependents.

There were about six thousand other workers and dependents living on the Zone. They were Panamanians, more or less. Some called themselves "forced Panamanians." They were black West Indians, the descendants of men and women who had come from the islands to help dig the Canal. They lived in their own communities, segregated from the Americans by race. But their race, their language—which was English—their culture, and the fact that they lived on the Zone also separated them from the other 8,700 Panamanian employees of the Canal Company who went home to Panama each night.

So much for the big picture; a closer look shows that all was not so clear-cut. Many American Canal workers were married to Panamanians—or to Costa Ricans, Chileans, Colombians, and so on. Many West Indians and a few American Canal workers lived in Panama. Some Latin Panamanians lived on the Zone. The person who, for many years, was our downstairs neighbor, was the brother of the man who became the second president of the revolutionary government of Panama. He was a Canal Zone policeman—undeniably a Zonian, but not the kind of person one usually thinks of as a Zonian. Across the hall lived the niece of a former Panamanian president, a member of the Panamanian oligarchy. Her husband was from upstate New York.

Within the company, there were the bureaucrats "up on the hill" and the workers "on the Flats." There were Atlantic Siders and Pacific Siders. And there were the dredgers. Like a separate species, the dredgers lived apart in their own town, Gamboa, a village halfway across the Canal and just beyond the Chagres River. It is at the end of the road and is surrounded by jungle—the Zone's Mirkwood. You drive out the same way you drive in, waiting each time at the curved, one-way bridge over the Chagres for the green light to tell you that it is safe to enter or leave the dredgers' misty kingdom.

Our Hobbits were the "old Zonians"—people who had grown up on the Zone, whose parents—perhaps their grandparents, too—had also worked for the company. They were the community's memory. They knew where things were and who you had to talk to to get things done. And they were more likely than other Zonians to have Panamanian relatives, speak Spanish, understand the mysteries of Panamanian politics, and have a weekend cottage in the hills or on one of the beaches up the coast.

A few Chinese from Kwang Tung Province raised produce on small farms carved from the jungle and sold it at picturesque roadside stands, but the most exotic people on the Zone were the Cunas, old Indian allies of the English buccaneers. Their villages were on islands in the Caribbean, but Cuna men stayed on the Zone for months at a time, working for the army or for clubs like the American Legion, which ran a restaurant. They are among the smallest people in the world, but are not to be trifled with. Within living memory—in 1925—they massacred twenty-two Panamanian policemen who had been sent to keep order on their islands, along with an almost equal number of their own tribe who had cooperated with the police.

In the seventies, Cuna women—wearing sarong-type skirts and mola blouses, four or five inches of tiny beads wrapped tightly around their arms and legs, and red and gold cotton scarves thrown over their short-cropped black hair—began coming to Stevens Circle in Balboa to sell their molas—brightly colored appliquéd cloth rectangles that they fashion into blouses for themselves and that they sell to tourists, who frame them or make them into pillow covers.

All day the Cuna women would sit under the trees across from the post office, giggling and sewing, and ducking away from tourist photographers aroused by the sight of elvish Indian women with gold rings in their noses.

LOCAL VARIETIES OF ENGLISH

We could hardly wait to learn Spanish. We thought knowing Spanish would make us different from the ethnocentric Zonians, but we discovered there were local varieties of English that were more important to learn first.

The West Indians spoke Bajun. It was an English dialect, but that doesn't mean that Americans and West Indians always understood each other. Herb telephoned the Housing Office shortly after we arrived on the Zone. Unable to understand the man he was talking to, he explained—in halting Spanish—that he was a newcomer and that his Spanish wasn't very good. Was there someone in the office who spoke English?

A long pause—a *very* long pause.

"Mon, hi hahm aspeakin' HINGlish."

The phonology and accent of Bajun differed from mainstream American English: "Hit fat you" (It fits you); "De tilet she COUGH, but she no swalLOW!" So do its grammar and lexicon: "Chut, mon, she don' ripe enough for a good maid"; "De nex' mango, he don' there"; "When you go to a sihop carri me a bread come." An umbrella is a "shower-stick," a "keep-dry," or a "house-in-hand." An injured person is "mash up good." When a flower blooms, "Hit hyatch."[4]

The dialect was an important part of the West Indian's group identity, but few of them were sentimental about it. Handicapped by prejudice toward blacks both in Panama and on the Zone, the ambitious West Indian could not afford to be handicapped by his language, too. Being able to speak mainstream Spanish or English did not guarantee that he would get ahead, but if he was unable to speak a fairly correct version of one or the other, his options were very limited. Within the West Indian communities on the Zone, the ability to speak "correct"—that is, mainstream—English was always associated with high social status. So was education. It is not unusual for an elderly West Indian who worked all his life as a helper on the Canal to have a son or daughter with a doctorate in literature or a master's degree in engineering.

The American Canal workers, on the other hand, spoke pretty standard American English. Nothing so grand as a local dialect ever developed, but there were distinctive local expressions. Men drove electric locomotives called "mules" on the locks. Old Zonians asked for "a jitney" when they wanted official transportation. Cars were repaired at "the Corral"—which had once been a corral. Company headquarters was known as "The Building," as if there were no others. Zonians ate at restaurants called "clubhouses" and bought lumber and whatever used items the company had "surveyed"—i.e., decided it could do without—at "Section I." And "old Zonians" spoke of living *on* the Zone rather than *in* it.

On the Canal itself, men spoke a lingo that could be incomprehensible to outsiders. They mixed standard nautical expressions with expressions specific to the Canal. For instance, a lockmaster might refer to a "sixteen-wire, clear-cut, daylight vessel." There were four-, eight-, twelve-, and sixteen-wire ships. "Wires" are the cables that are attached to the towing locomotives, "the mules." "Clear-cut" vessels, those with over ninety-foot beams, are too large to pass another ship in "the Cut," the narrowest part of the Canal. All transits are scheduled around the need for those ships to reach the Cut alone. The largest ships can transit only during daylight hours, which adds still another constraint to the scheduling. Tugs may be lashed "cut-style" to the stern of a ship and used as a rudder.

Normally a rowboat is sent from the locks to receive a rope from an approaching ship. The rope, or line, is used to thread the wires.

Sometimes a tug comes in so far that its wash makes it impossible to send out a rowboat. In that case, the lineman must do a "wing fling" from one of the wing walls of the locks. The locks have "soft noses" and "jaws." A ship between the approach wall and the side wall is "in the jaws." When a ship's bow passes the nose of the center or approach wall, its boatswain calls the control tower of the locks with that announcement, and the lockmaster says something like "Arrive on the east at thirteen," meaning at thirteen minutes past the hour. The teletype operator relays this information to Marine Traffic Control. The time the ship clears the locks is also recorded, so that if there is an accident, an investigator can deduce the ship's speed.

Approaching the locks, a ship may "take a shear" if it hits a "mixing current." When the locks at either end of the Canal are "spilled down," fresh and salt water mix. Fresh floats on top of salt. On the Pacific side, where the tides are high, the "spilldown" may create a four-knot current one way while there is a four-knot tidal current twenty feet lower going the other way.

THE LAY OF THE LAND

Slowly, we began to get oriented. Slowly—because like so many other things about the Zone, its geography mocked our expectations. We expected the Canal to go east and west. Instead it goes north and south. People talked about the west bank and the east bank. We were living on the east bank. To drive to the States—people did that in those days—we would have to cross to the west bank and drive southwest for a while. If there were a road through the jungle to Colombia, which there is not, it would go northeast.

Panama is shaped like an S laid on its side. Its right loop puts an expanse of the Pacific to the east of the southern entrance to the Canal. As a result, a person can stand beside the Canal on part of the North American land mass and watch the sun rise over the Pacific.

Balboa was the Zone town at the southern entrance, right across Fourth of July Avenue from Panama City. At the northern entrance, the Zone town was Cristóbal—right across Front Street from Colón.

At Colón and Balboa the Zone was narrower than elsewhere. Generally, it extended for five miles on either side of the Canal, which is fifty miles from deep water to deep water. But the Zone also included a river and two artificial lakes that extended beyond its five-mile border—Gatún Lake, which forms the top level of the Canal; the Chagres River, which replenishes Gatún Lake; and Madden Dam and the lake behind it, which controls the flow of the Chagres—558 square miles of land and water. By way of comparison, New York City covers 365 square miles.

When we decided to go to Colón on the Atlantic side to look around, we drove through the Zone's forest preserve into Panama, then around Gatún Lake on the Boyd-Roosevelt Highway. We drove past towns half-erased by the weather, past buildings painted confectionary pink or turquoise, past lone *campesinos* walking from apparently nowhere to nowhere. When we were almost to the Atlantic coast, the road turned and we reentered the Zone.

Just as the Zone divided Panama, Gatún Lake divided the Zone. A person who wanted to go from coast to coast without leaving the Zone could take the company railroad, which crosses the lake on a causeway, or he could hitch a ride on a transiting ship. He could not drive. The road stopped at Gatún on one side of the lake and at Gamboa on the other.

A transit by ship takes about eight hours. From the Atlantic side, it sails south to Gatún Locks, where it is raised eighty-five feet in three stages to the level of the lake. It turns southeast, crosses the lake, and enters a channel between jungle-covered hills. At the mouth of the Chagres, it passes Gamboa, where the dredgers live. Farther on, at Pedro Miguel, it is lowered thirty-one feet. At Miraflores, it is taken down the rest of the way in two stages. The lock gates at Miraflores are the largest on the Canal, because the Pacific tides can run up to twenty-two feet, some nineteen feet higher than those on the Atlantic side. Sailing on, the ship passes Balboa, where the Canal Commission's headquarters is located, goes under the Thatcher Ferry Bridge, and enters the Pacific.

6

Symbols, Sovereignty, and Social Engineers: The Flag Riots of 1964

MAKING BELIEVE

Late in the afternoon of January 9, 1964, at the Gamboa commissary, a strange woman seized Mary's wrist. "Ship's in," the woman said—meaning, "Buy while you can." Her message delivered, she pushed her cart on down the aisle. Mary met her again by the cake mixes. "Hi," they both said. In produce, they met again. By this time, they were old friends. "There's going to be trouble," said the woman, squeezing a tomato thoughtfully.

"Trouble?"

"Uh-huh, at the high school," and the woman spoke in tongues of what had happened that day at Marine Traffic Control, and of *Arnulfistas, Rabiblancos,* Communists, the *Chiriquí Guardia,* and of the flagpole—especially of the flagpole.

Mary came home and said, "I've just had the strangest conversation."

There was already trouble, though we didn't know it. A couple of hours later, our friend from downstairs came pounding on our door, telling us to come listen to the radio with her and her husband. He translated for us simultaneously, as overwrought voices shouted in Spanish—a feat that amazed us almost as much as what he told us the voices were saying: American troops and tanks had invaded Panama! Buildings were on fire. American civilian deformatives hidden in the Zone's Episcopal Church were shooting at Panamanian children. North American aggressor-assassins were machine-gunning

53

Panamanian patriots who were resisting with sticks and stones. Patriotic *Guardia* were joining the people. To the streets! Defend the nation's honor against the bastards of the earth. Yankee hypocrites to the wall! Kill Americans!

We turned to the American Armed Forces station: "Silent Night" was followed by "Hark, the Herald Angels Sing," which was followed by "White Christmas." We looked at each other. Besides, Christmas was over!

Whatever was happening had to do with what had been going on at the high school for the past week—something about the flagpole. Busy teaching, we hadn't paid much attention to the flag business. We knew someone had ruled that wherever an American flag flew on the Zone, a Panamanian flag was to fly beside it. Someone said this was because the United States had only the right to act *as if* it were sovereign on the Zone, while Panama retained "real" sovereignty—without the right to do anything. Very confusing. But at almost a dozen places on the Zone, both flags were flying side by side —had been in some places since long before we arrived. We thought that was fine—something that should have been done long ago. Five more dual flagpoles were slated to go up, but at some of the places where the American flag had been flying, Governor Robert J. Fleming, Jr., had decided to fly no flags at all. During the year, several flagpoles had been removed.

Two of the places where there were to be no flags at all were the two American high schools on the Zone. Some Panamanian newspapers said the governor should fly dual flags at those locations. He did not agree. On December 30, he ordered full compliance with the dual-flag policy to begin on January 2, 1964.[1] When the American students returned from their Christmas vacation, they found that their flags had been removed—but the flagpoles were still there.

On January 3, students at Balboa High circulated a petition to President Lyndon Johnson, protesting the removal of their flag. The petition was confiscated by school authorities who weren't going to put up with any nonsense. Later, nervous higher authorities returned it to the students.

The situation continued to simmer for three more days.

On January 7, before school started, approximately seventy-five students, watched by hundreds of others, raised an American flag on the empty pole in front of Balboa High School. (There were 1,851 students enrolled at Balboa High that year.)

When school started, the students went inside the building, and the principal and two of his superiors emerged. They removed the flag. Half an hour later, six junior-college students and one high-school student raised another flag. That one stayed up all that day, was lowered that night, and was raised again the next morning. Some twenty-five students remained on watch at the pole all night. Adult sympathizers provided them with food and blankets. Similar protests took place elsewhere on the Zone.

On January 8, the Pacific Side Civic Council asked the governor to postpone further implementation of the dual-flag policy until Congress could examine it. He replied that he was implementing an established policy. None of our students was enthusiastic about the dual-flag policy. A few were vociferously opposed to it and were encouraged in this by adults. But the general sympathy the protestors enjoyed at the high school was not based on their opposition to dual flags but on their opposition to the removal of the American flag.[2]

On the afternoon of January 8, about 200 American students marched around the flagpole, carrying signs, singing, and shouting.

On January 9, about 200 Panamanian students, accompanied by some adults, marched into the Zone carrying a Panamanian flag that was "stained with the blood of martyrs of the Student Federation of Panama." Zone police stopped them a block away from the American students, who had gathered around the single flagpole. The Panamanians wanted to hold a ceremony in front of the now famous pole. The police escorted five of them through the American crowd. They were greeted cordially by the president of the Balboa Student Association—who was jeered for this courtesy by his constituents. Americans and Panamanians began arguing in Spanish.[3]

The Panamanians decided they wanted the American flag lowered so that they could raise their flag. The police told them it was time to go. They refused. Enough police were present to remove them without the use of damaging force. Once among their fellows, however, the five Panamanians declared that they had been beaten by the American students, that their flag had been "clubbed" by a policeman, and that "many hands pulled and tore" their flag.[4]

Much shouting! The Panamanians ran as if pursued. They threw rocks at houses and overturned trash cans as they ran. When they were back in Panama, they told reporters that Zonians shot at them from houses along the way.

That night, ten American policemen on Fourth of July Avenue retreated before some three thousand Panamanians who upset and burned several unoccupied cars. The police halted them with tear gas, but seven policemen were injured by stones. Part of the mob began burning and looting the Ancon Freight House. Several hundred rioters headed toward the Little Theatre, where a rehearsal was in progress, and toward a housing area. The police were out of tear gas. They were given permission to fire over the heads of the mob. It isn't clear whether shots had already been fired at them from Panama, but the shooting started. Canal officials repeatedly asked the government of Panama to send its well-trained riot police to the scene. Panama refused and ordered its police to allow the riots to continue.[5]

About three thousand Americans fled from Panama City into the Zone. Most were families of servicemen but among them were the families of Canal workers and of embassy and AID personnel. Many were escorted by Panamanian friends or by details of *Guardia*.

When it was all over, hundreds of Panamanians were hurt. Twenty-four were dead. Some looters had died inside buildings in Panama that other rioters had set on fire. Other Panamanians had been shot. Four Americans were dead—three soldiers and a civilian working for the army.

A friend of ours helped write an article called "What Really Happened" for the Canal Company newspaper.[6] She scoffed at our suspicions that maybe, after all, the Zone police might have been just a little rough on the Panamanian students and might accidentally have torn their special flag just a little bit.

"They didn't touch that flag. I saw it. They didn't let any American student within ten feet of a Panamanian, either. Why, that old flag of theirs—I went to that school—to the *Instituto*, sure. That flag was always torn. Say, you should have seen the first version we wrote—the one the governor wouldn't let us print. He made us take out all the quotations from the police reports. 'Don't upset the Panamanians,' he says. Oh, sure, but then what we wrote wasn't the whole truth, was it?"

That made us think. We had assumed that the official American version would make the Americans look as good as possible without actually lying. But if, instead, it had been vetted so that it would not offend the Panamanians . . .

"And those military types! We wanted to announce what was happening over the radio. Doesn't that make sense? There were Americans in Panama who should have stayed there. Trying to come home across Fourth of July—that was where they got into trouble. Well, a delegation—some of the younger officers—went to see the general. 'Play Christmas carols,' that's all he would say. Whatever happens, we mustn't upset the Panamanians. Ha! I'd say they were pretty upset already."

We had to agree to that.

"It was a put-up job, right from the start. The Communists had it all planned out ahead of time."

Oh-ho, we thought, discounting all the disturbing things our friend had said, for we realized that she was one of those Americans who believed in the fictitious menace of international Communism.

But it turned out she was right.[7]

As evidence mounted of the Communist role in the student demonstration, the initial rioting, and the subsequent agitation, we reluctantly had to concede that Communists and Communist plots actually existed. They were not, as we had supposed, mere "projections" of right-wing paranoids.

However, Panama's president, Roberto Chiari, denied that the Communists had played a significant role in the riots: "That is the most brazen lie I have heard and seen," he said of such allegations.[8] The Communists had to disappear, because the riots had been directed against not just the Americans but the government of Panama. *"Abajo el gobierno"* was the message on a wall in the middle of the riot area. The government, however, outmaneuvered the Communists by endorsing their riot and depicting it as a patriotic uprising. Thus, Chiari hoped to bolster his party's chance of winning the next election. When the *Panameñista* party, led by the popular Arnulfo Arias, attacked the Communists for inspiring and directing the riots, Chiari and *Radio Tribuna* attacked the *Panameñistas* for echoing the coarse accusations of the North American newspapers and seeking applause from foreigners.[9]

Arias' popularity worried Panama's oligarchs, its Communists, and many Americans. An ardent nationalist, he was widely perceived during the Second World War as a Fascist sympathizer.

Chiari also boosted his party's chances by persuading the State Department that *negociaciones* was the Spanish equivalent of "discussions." So the Spanish text of the joint communiqué that followed the riots used *negociaciones*, and the Panamanians announced that their heroes had not died in vain while resisting the aggressor; the Americans had capitulated and agreed to negotiate a new Canal treaty. Apparently shocked, the State Department assured the American people that it had done no such thing.

During the riots, hundreds of shots were fired into the Zone from populated areas in Panama. At first, the American commander would not let his troops fire back, for fear of hitting innocent people. Finally, he permitted selected soldiers on the Atlantic side to respond with shotguns loaded with bird shot, and on the Pacific side, he sent marksmen with rifles to the top of the Tivoli Hotel. Later, we talked to one of those marksmen. He mentioned that a Panamanian had been shooting at the hotel with a tommy gun.

"You mean a carbine?"

"They had those, too," he replied. And he confirmed what we had heard elsewhere about men from Panama sneaking around in front of the mobs—exposing themselves to the Americans—and firing back into Panama to make it look as if the bullets were coming from the Zone.[10]

"Why didn't you . . . ?"

"Our orders were not to shoot at anybody who wasn't firing at us, and there were a lot of officers around to make sure we didn't."

All this was hard for us to take in. Everybody was playing make-believe: The Communists were making believe that they were Americans; the Panamanians, that they were victims; the Americans, that they were sovereign; the government of Panama, that the Communists did not exist; the American general, that the riots did not exist— "Play Christmas carols." And these, we discovered later, were only some of the games of make-believe that were being played on the Isthmus.

PLAYING FOR TIME

American journalists jumped to the conclusion that the flag riot was a dispute between American high-school students, who were defying the law, and Panamanian students, who were responding with righteous indignation. However, from where we stood, the Panamanian students and their adult advisors clearly interposed themselves between the original disputants and thereby changed the focus of the whole affair. A person didn't have to sympathize with the Zonians—and in those days, we didn't—to see that the flag protest was directed against the American government. Ex-president Harry Truman and Senator Barry Goldwater, men who did not normally agree, both said that the American students had been right to raise the American flag on the empty pole.[11] That should have caused some media pundits to reconsider their assumptions, but it didn't. Truman's and Goldwater's opinions were discounted as coming from emotional men who were not likely to weigh both sides of an issue evenly. The vanity of the new establishment that had formed around President Kennedy and had been inherited by Lyndon Johnson was that it could. It saw itself as particularly able to judge issues rationally and objectively and, thus, as able and entitled to intervene in everybody's best interests at home or abroad.

Such assumptions did not prepare the Kennedy-Johnson team to discover that the team itself was part of the problem. But that was the case in regard to the flag riot. What was bothering the Zonians was more fundamental than whose flag was to fly where. After the riot, the governor met with the high-school teachers, and the first question one of them asked him was, "Last night in your message on TV, you said our government was a government of laws not men. Do you mean that the people exist for the state and not the state for the people?"[12]

What a nut, we thought. As hard-boiled pragmatist-contextualists, we knew *this* was no time for a bullshit question about political philosophy. But that was what the flag protest had been about. It was an argument between the people and the executive branch. The involvement of the Panamanians was secondary.

Specifically, the Zonians were concerned about the extent to which the executive branch could commit the nation to a foreign policy that was not approved by the legislature and not understood by anyone. Presidents have always found it easier to make foreign policy than to explain it. Repeatedly, the foreign-policy establishment has asserted that ordinary people are too stupid to understand it. Not explaining avoids controversy. However, what our leaders do not have to explain to us, they often fail to make clear to themselves.

The dual-flag policy on the Zone went back to President Eisenhower, who ordered that one pair of dual flags be flown on the Zone as "visual evidence of Panama's titular sovereignty." By making this symbolic gesture, Eisenhower thought he could satisfy the "emotional" needs of the Panamanians, while he satisfied their "real" needs—their bread-and-butter needs—by offering them a multimillion-dollar aid package. Thus, he would avoid controversy with Panama. And when the House prohibited the use of company funds for the display of dual flags, Eisenhower provided special funds, thus avoiding controversy with the House.[13]

In 1962, President Kennedy's assistant secretary of state announced that dual flags would fly at three more sites on the Zone, and in 1963, Kennedy and Chiari appointed a joint commission to discuss the issues that divided Panama and the United States. Quickly, the commission conceded to Panama many of the demands it had made to no avail during the 1955 treaty negotiations, including the demand that wherever an American flag was flown on the Zone a Panamanian flag would be flown beside it. By agreeing to Panama's demands, Kennedy hoped to avoid controversy with Panama, and by authorizing his concessions by executive fiat, he hoped to avoid controversy with the Senate, whose ratification process he was bypassing.[14]

Neither Eisenhower nor Kennedy intended to give the Canal to Panama. To them, the display of Panamanian flags was merely symbolic. Both the Zonians and the Panamanians had a better grasp of the way symbols can shape reality. One Zonian sought an injunction against the display of dual flags on the Zone, and although his petition was denied, the judge who denied it commented prophetically: "The flying of two national flags side by side in a disputed territory for an undeclared purpose is a position of weakness that can lead but to further misunderstanding and discord."[15]

The Zonians who believed that something important was going on that had not been considered by their representatives in Washington had reason for that belief. But anyone who objected to the dual-flag policy was accused of emotionalism.

On the morning of January 9, before he left for Washington, Governor Fleming taped a television address that was shown that evening. In it, he explained that the flag agreement was "a valid commitment of our government." He said that all of us had "an obligation as citizens to support that commitment regardless of our personal beliefs." And he urged everyone to avoid "emotionalism."[16]

Later, he would try once more to persuade the Canal workers to rally around not the flag, but the "valid commitment." Having already used the appeal to duty—"an obligation as citizens"—he now invoked the secret knowledge of experts: "I can assure you that the decisions made by people in foreign policy are based on a thorough knowledge of facts and a thorough analysis of the potentials of the actions that can be taken as a result. Such information is not usually available to the people who are most vocally critical."[17]

The governor was pleading, "Father knows best"—or, to put it another way, that the people exist to further the valid commitments of the state. In this instance, the American Left agreed. It deplored the emotionalism and presumptuousness of the Zone's jingoes. However, a few years later, when spokesmen for the executive branch used the same arguments to justify America's involvement in Vietnam, anti-war liberals and radicals took to the streets. Like the Zonians before them, they were demonstrating because a coterie of management experts, without consulting the representatives of the people or making their intentions clear, had, by themselves, committed the nation to a course of action that was of profound consequence.

I WANT TO KNOW WHY

The Panamanians renamed Fourth of July Avenue *Avenida de los Martires*. They broke diplomatic relations with the United States. They rushed to the United Nations, where they accused the United States of "unmerciful acts of aggression," "inhuman actions," and mass murder.[18] They demanded an admission of guilt and reparations—millions. They called for an investigation by the International Commission of Jurists.[19] However, when that commission's investigating team largely exonerated the Americans and accused the Panamanian government of encouraging the riots once they had begun, the Panamanians ignored the report. They knew their behavior had been faultless.

Zone officials were equally sure that their behavior had been above reproach. The governor blamed Congress for failing to legislate the changes he had recommended to promote good relations between the Zonians and the Panamanians. He blamed his advisors, all of whom, he said, had recommended that he not fly dual flags in front of the schools.[20] (The governor's decision was eventually reversed by Secretary of the Army Cyrus Vance, who ordered dual poles to be erected in front of the high school. This was immediately done, and the ROTC raised both flags simultaneously every morning without incident for the next fifteen years.)

Reporters who interviewed the governor found him pacing about his office carrying a swagger stick. On his desk was a sign reading, "I Don't Have Ulcers. I Give Ulcers." To one reporter, he confided that most of the Canal workers were moderates: "But like all moderates, they're passive. Now you've also got down here 200, maybe 300, members of the radical right. They've been isolated so long, they've developed a reactionary mentality." And he said the flag protest was "the perfect situation for the guy who's 150 percent American—and 50 percent whiskey."[21]

However, in the Canal Company newspaper, he assured the workers, "I have been telling, and most emphatically, representatives of the press and radio that the American employee was not responsible for what has happened."[22]

The governor's subordinates did not believe they were responsible, either. After the governor's speech to the teachers, the director of civil affairs took the podium and said, "I think the action of the school officials was exemplary. I think that through their careful and thoughtful help the situation was depressed. I thought it was best to let the situation go on a day or two and not arrest or expel a child. In retrospect, this may not have been a good decision, but I still think it was."[23] He concluded, "We tried not to emphasize this problem we had that day, hoping it would dissolve itself shortly."

Anyone unconvinced of the wisdom of the authorities was guilty of Monday-morning quarterbacking. Nevertheless, David Baglien, a high-school counselor, called out, "I want to know why nothing was done last Tuesday when this started, why no positive action was taken at that time. . . ."

The governor answered,

I can't answer that question. I know why I didn't take any action. I did not take any action because I was desperately trying to end the incident without having to go in and take action. . . . I also knew— and I do hope that this question was not asked in a spirit of Monday-morning quarterbacking—knew that anyone down here who turned out the police against them or had the fire trucks turn on the fire hoses that the whole damned Zone would have revolted.[24]

We looked at the general-turned-governor with dismay. *Those* were the only alternatives he could think of?

"I thought Oz was a great Head," said Dorothy. "And I thought Oz was a terrible Beast," said the Tin Woodman. "And I thought Oz was a Ball of Fire," exclaimed the Lion. "No; you are all wrong," said the little man, meekly. "I have been making believe."

7
Choosing Sides

CHOOSING AMERICA

Panama's president vowed he would never resume diplomatic relations with the United States until it agreed to renegotiate the status of the Canal. Zone officials warned Americans not to go into Panama. The Panamanian press railed against the Americans who had "massacred" Panama's youth. But the 8,700 Panamanians who lived in Panama and worked on the Zone kept coming to work without incident. Before long, Americans were venturing into the Republic again.

We were more determined than ever to live over there. We didn't want to waste our two years abroad living with Americans. And, maybe, we thought it was our duty. Unlike the Zonians who obviously hadn't made many Panamanian friends, we were sure we could.

We didn't expect to make many friends on the Zone. By and large, the Zonians didn't seem to be our kind. The Zonians hadn't caused the flag riot, though. We were quite clear on that. So we shared the indignation of our friend from the Information Office when she reported that a man from the American embassy had used her phone to call a Panamanian journalist and apologize for what had happened: "I asked him, 'What the heck did you do that for?' And he mumbles, 'Uh, um, well, we could have handled it better.' 'Sure, and how about them handling it better? I don't hear any of them calling us.' I told him that."

We also shared the disgust of everyone on the Zone when an

American named Kenneth Darg, the director of the Panamanian-North American Institute, made a speech in which he said, among other things: "I feel guilty because I am a North American. I am a North American and have not used well my opportunities to help my fellow countrymen see their errors. I am and feel guilty for all the deaths and all of the damage which has taken place. I ask your forgiveness for all this. I ask for your forgiveness for my fellow countrymen."[1]

However, disgusted as we were with Darg, we also knew that we, meaning we Americans, *could* indeed have handled the events leading up to the riots better. Since we had not behaved perfectly, we were responsible. *Somebody* had to be. Panama's politicians said they were not, and we had to agree to that. Clearly, they were not responsible. That left it to America—and Americans. We were willing. In those days we were young and lusted for responsibility. Also, we figured that if America was responsible, something could be done to improve things.

Suddenly the sky was no longer close and gray but far and blue. We opened our windows. Dry-season breezes swept pictures from walls, scattered papers, and filmed everything with dust. Toward evening, the breezes died. The air thickened, filling with vegetable odors. Frogs made gulping noises. Some kind of insect split the air with "one continuous shrill tone, high and keen as a thin jet of steam leaking through a valve."[2] We woke up that night with damp air sticking all over us, shut the windows, and turned the droning air-conditioner back on.

The grass turned brown, but the jungle stayed green, its leaves fluorescing in the brilliant sun. A few trees shed their leaves, though, and as we crunched them underfoot, we were disoriented—it was March—by thoughts of pumpkins, Puritans, chrysanthemums, and football games. Distant grass fires sent billows of smoke into the sky. Bits of ash settled on our clothes. Then everywhere bushes and trees were blooming—bronze, yellow, pink, red, and purple blossoms. The jungle hills were patched with color.

We met an American couple who lived in Panama City and needed a house-sitter for the summer. Would we do it? We could hardly wait! Moving to Panama would separate us from the Zonians, who preferred the security of the company store to the adventure of living in a foreign culture. It would give us a chance to justify our view of ourselves as people unshackled by the assumptions of our society.

We stuffed our VW with clothes, toys, and books, and drove past the giant white horse galloping against the sky on top of the green apartment building just across the border from the Zone. We expected living in Panama to be a deprovincializing experience, and it was, it was—but . . .

> *Life will never go according to the Epistles.*
> *Expecting whistles—it's flutes; expecting flutes—*
> *it's whistles.*

Our house was in the San Fernando district. There were cracks in the wall. Its doors were warped, and half its light switches didn't work. Our friends had told us that the landlord wouldn't put any money into the place. That seemed crazy. The house was almost new. It had won an architectural prize. It had an inner courtyard and a bidet! Why wouldn't he keep it up? We loved it. We loved our neighbors' chickens that kept us awake at night. We would have loved our neighbors, if we had ever seen them. We loved the fences and walls around every yard, the way the trash was picturesquely dumped into the street. We loved the lack of zoning.

We saw little girls in front of the Virgen del Carmen Church dressed like pink, white, and blue angels; big girls in white with blue sashes; a brass band in blue and white and a huge gold chest on wheels with big statues of Jesus and Mary on top; a crowd of women in mantillas all around. Another time, we saw a funeral procession: taxis with huge wreaths on their roofs. We decided it was the custom for the mourners to put their own names on the wreaths—either that or a lot of people were being buried at the same time. Every day we crossed the intersection where Margot Fonteyn's husband had been gunned down by a political rival.

Out at the ruins of Old Panama, which had been destroyed by

Henry Morgan and his pirates, we tried to imagine ourselves back in time, to feel what it was like to be alive when those buildings were new in 1519. It didn't work. It was like a magic trick that we started well but kept fumbling.

Panamanian music—loud, vigorous, monotonous, and punctuated by yelps—blared from loudspeakers above the stores. Cars honked. Busses painted blue and red or green and orange and red went by. Chenille balls fringed their windshields, and under their rear windows were painted pictures of panthers, waterfalls, or Jesus. Passengers looked out from behind girls' names in Gothic script, which were painted on the windows. An old Zonian told us that there used to be a bus driver in Panama who would take only men. He prospered and bought a second bus, which followed the same policy. "Men only," he would cry as he levered open his door.

Barkers urged us to enter their stores. Salesmen slapped yardsticks on tables stacked with bolts of cloth. We had to step into the street to get around the people congregated in front of women selling lottery tickets. Trash spilled from dark alleys and narrow wooden stairs. Overhead an old woman and a naked infant watched us from a grillwork balcony where flags of shirts and underwear were drying in the bright, moist air. Here was the otherness we craved—and wanted Americans to leave alone. But at the same time, we still believed people everywhere were fundamentally the same and open to improvement by scientific experts.

The lottery, for instance—that bothered us. Gambling wasn't just an amusement that didn't appeal to us; it was an affront to our religion of rationalism. Everywhere, women sat behind rickety folding tables selling tickets. Customers would look at the tickets and frown— as if they were *thinking*. But they selected a number based on their birthdate and a friend's address, things like that. It was insane.

When the sink stopped up, the landlord came over with his daughter, his father, and a black West Indian plumber. Herb said he wanted to see what was wrong, too, and got under the sink with the plumber. Later, Mary told him that when he did that, "They—well, I had the distinct impression that you'd done something real dumb."

We had lunch with a woman who spoke contemptuously of Panamanian men. "They think the world centers on them. If you have a baby girl, the *doctor* sympathizes. It's like something *bad* happened to you."³ We wished she'd lower her voice. However, as the parents of two girls . . . But we resolutely refused to draw conclusions or be critical. We couldn't judge, we told each other, because we'd been conditioned by our own culture.

We believed every culture had its own values and had to be judged on its own terms. We wanted to be fair—but most of all, we wanted to disassociate ourselves completely from American tourists, from Zonians in orange shirts and purple shorts, and from all other "simple-minded" Americans who went around bragging about how great America was.

When we got lost, which was pretty often, we would ask Panamanians for directions, and they were delighted to help. They were friendly. Charming. But they often gave us the wrong directions. Did they secretly hate gringos?

(Years later, we responded with a blip of recognition to the truth of a paragraph in *The South American Handbook*: "Be careful when asking directions. Many Latin Americans will give you the wrong answer rather than admit they do not know; this may be partly because they fear losing face, but is also because they like to please!"⁴)

We kept wondering how things fit—the pink and blue and white angels, the lottery, the noise, the fences and walls, the general refusal to stand in line or take turns, the apparent gulf between the manual worker and the businessman, our own unexpected status as *profesores*, the climate, the language, the ruins of Old Panama. Nothing by itself was completely outside of our experience, but together—everything was strange.

The only place we met Panamanians socially was on the Zone. We found ourselves going back there regularly to get our mail, take the kids swimming, go to the library, and pick up a few things at the commie. It was a Zonian who recommended our new Panamanian dentist. Another Zonian introduced us to Elly's new piano teacher, an American woman who is married to a Panamanian musician. They lived in a tiny apartment behind the Hilton with their baby and two grand pianos. We were beginning to realize that at least some Zonians knew a great deal about Panama.

On the Fourth of July, we went back to the Zone to see the parade. There were the usual straggly contingents from the VFW and the American Legion, endless Cub Scouts, Girl Scouts, and Boy Scouts, and the Knights of Columbus. Shriners on minibikes tossed candy to children. There were clowns and a cavalry corps of adolescent girls from the various Zone stables. The JROTC was there and the band from Balboa High—which was good—but a moment later here came the Southern Command Air Force Band, playing Sousa. We didn't expect anything to top that, but we could hear drums approaching, and the crowd, which lined both sides of the street, was breaking into applause. With a sudden blare of horns, the *Bomberos'* Drum and Bugle Corps marched by—Panama's firemen. They wore white duck pants tucked into high black boots, black caps, and red flannel shirts!

A friend invited us to a Unitarian-Universalist meeting on the Zone. Some Peace Corps people were going to speak. Weren't they supposed to stay in the boondocks? Our friend shrugged. It was a great opportunity, he said.

They spoke with the certainty and idealism of nineteenth-century missionaries, but they preached a vague universal brotherhood rather than any divisive, sectarian form of Christianity. They boasted about how primitive life was in their villages and told us how much the people loved them. "They protected us during the riots," one bragged. Another announced, "People are basically friendly," and another began, "The trouble with the Zone is . . ." A chubby girl stood up and said she identified completely with "her people." Raising her fist, she declared that if we drove through her village and her people threw rocks at us, she would, too. She wanted us to know whose side she was on.

We had always thought the Peace Corps was on our side.

Many of its members were, of course. But the idealists who talked to us that day—like their colleagues who, a few years later, lowered the American flag from the top of the Peace Corps headquarters in

Washington and ran up the banner of the Viet Cong—were above divisive, sectarian, national loyalties.[5] They could respond to simple, abstract, universal causes and to people they perceived as simple and pure, but not to the messy complexities of patriotism.

Their attitude was disturbingly familiar. We were dismayed to realize how similar it was to our own.

Our Unitarian-Universalist friend urged us to come to his house for lunch—several of the Peace Corps volunteers were coming. "We can talk to them some more. Isn't it interesting?"

Something must have shown on our faces, because he added, "I can understand, can't you? They have conflicting loyalties."

We excused ourselves, saying we had to get back home. We had conflicting feelings, but we knew whose side we were on.

CHOOSING THE ZONE

We moved back to the Zone when our friends returned and then drove regularly the other way for Elly's music lessons, visits to the dentist, and evenings on the town. Both girls were taking swimming lessons, too, and we were all learning Spanish. We wrote the Spanish names of things on scraps of paper and stuck them on walls, chairs, tables, the toilet—everywhere. Mary wore three—*"la esposa," "la madre," "la cocinera."*

Without our quite realizing it, fall went, winter came, and our lives settled into a comfortable rhythm. Things began to lose their strangeness. We talked less often of leaving the Zone when our two years were up.

Sarah began taking a ballet class that was taught at Albrook Air Force Base by Jean Gee, a former dancer with the Chicago Opera who, it was rumored, was a friend of Margot Fonteyn. It was there that we met Mrs. Olsen. She brought her granddaughter to the class on the bus. Mary began picking them up at the bus stop. Josie Olsen was the first "old Zonian" we got to know. She was almost twice our age and had more than twice our energy. We would see her walking from La Boca during the hottest part of the day and would meet her out walking after dark. She would surprise us by stepping off a little Panamanian bus at the most unlikely places. She was always *going*.

We asked her about the old days.[6]

Things were getting pretty bad in the States with the depression coming on [the 1920 depression] and with me and my husband just married and him being jobless. We were living in Houston where he had worked as a machinist for the Reed Roller Bit Tool Company. Somebody told him that there were machinists needed in South America for some special job that was being done. He made an appointment and got the job. After he finished down there, he applied for a job here in Panama, and he got it. Then he sent for me, and I arrived on March fourth, 1920.

For entertainment, my husband and I would usually go to the movies. We had books called "Commie" books, which we used in the place of money. The two-dollar-and-fifty-cent book was white, and the fifteen-dollar one was pink.

In my earlier days here, every employee received a railroad book of tickets for the year. There were twelve tickets to each book, which allowed us one free ride a month. Trains at that time were a very important means of transportation. The little *chiva* busses [wooden, side-seaters built on a truck chassis] were used more than trains, though. They had benches along the sides, and you just crowded in where you could find room. They would tie all their chickens and wicker baskets or whatever else they had on top or around the sides of these little busses. We used them all the time to get around.

I can remember when Lindbergh flew the first airmail flight down here in 1927. He went to the swimming pool and sat in the grandstand and watched the children perform.

This used to be quite a place for swimming. Over the years, swimming records were broken right here in the Canal Zone. Two of the young people went as far as the Olympics. Admiral Byrd also stopped by here on his way down to the South Pole. We were allowed to go aboard his vessel, and a friend of ours went with him on his travels. Ruth Elder was one of the first women that tried to cross the ocean in a plane. She didn't make it, but she wasn't killed, either. She was married to one of the boys down here.

One day Mary had a cold, so she and Sarah missed the ballet lesson. The next time they went, everyone was still aflutter. Mrs. Olsen said that Margot Fonteyn had visited the class. "Margot Fonteyn!" So it was true.

By the time we had to declare our intentions for summer travel in 1965, we knew we had chosen the Zone and that we would be back— at least for two more years. We still weren't crazy about the Zone, but we had come to realize that it was a great place to work, and, like most Zonians, we found our fulfillment in our work. It was also a great place to raise kids, and we had two of them to raise.

So we planned a real vacation in the United States and asked for round-trip transportation. We bought tickets to see Fonteyn and Nureyev perform *Romeo and Juliet* in Chicago. There were alternate casts, and the Royal Ballet wasn't telling which night Fonteyn and Nureyev would perform, but Mrs. Gee knew, and she told us.

In Chicago, Fonteyn and Nureyev took twenty-three curtain calls, while we applauded till our hands hurt. We went on to New York and Boston, then back to Kansas City and then to New Orleans to catch the company ship and return to the Zone.

Had we known that before our next two-year hitch on the Zone was over, the United States and Panama would be on the brink of signing a new Canal treaty, we might have decided it was more prudent to look for work in the States than to return to Panama. But we did not know, and it was just as well, since the revolution in 1968 would set the new treaty back for a decade. We were not thinking about politics as we returned to the Zone in the fall of 1965. We were remembering the rooms and rooms of luminous Renoirs in the Chicago Art Institute, especially the *Two Little Circus Girls*, so like our own; taxis hurtling down Forty-second Street in New York and the expensive smell of the Biltmore lobby; the Old North Church in Boston and the swan boats in the Public Gardens; and the moonlit balcony scene in Kenneth MacMillan's ballet.

Gradually, we would realize that it had never been America we wanted to rise above, but Kansas—Kansas and a future of dull certainties.

8

Paternalism and Politics: How the Zone Worked

LOOKING BACKWARD

What we had actually done was to trade one set of certainties for another, for life on the Canal Zone was just about as predictable as the mind of man could make it. We had idly wished we lived in a utopia, and here we were, in a place with an uncanny resemblance to the utopia that Bellamy had outlined in *Looking Backward*.

As Bellamy saw it, capitalism was the great enemy of the good life. It forced a person to "plunge into the foul fight, cheat, overreach . . . ," and so on—in order to compete for a limited supply of inefficiently produced goods.

His solution was to merge corporation to corporation until everyone was working for one giant corporation, which he called the Industrial Army. Its commander was the president of the United States. He was an elected official, but Bellamy distrusted democracy. People were all too likely to elect someone unqualified to represent them. So, like the political bosses he despised, Bellamy fixed things.[1] He restricted the candidates to those with the right credentials, and he restricted the franchise. There were no political parties or campaigns in his utopia.

Everyone there received the same salary. Housing was comfortable but modest. The Industrial Army's treasure was lavished on what was public—parks, restaurants, schools—and on factories and equipment.

There was no class or sexual prejudice in Bellamy's utopia and, one assumes, no racial prejudice either, although he never mentions race.

On the other hand, while economic and social inequalities were

74

eliminated, other inequalities were introduced. Each citizen was routinely tested and graded. There were three grades in each industry and two classes in each grade. Each worker wore a badge signifying his rank.

Preoccupied with the injustice of class distinctions based on wealth or breeding, Bellamy did not foresee the danger of class distinctions based on tests or academic credentials. However, if his promotion system were perceived as fair and objective, it would follow that the worker-soldiers in the lowest rank belonged there. Those in the highest rank might develop an ethic of *noblesse oblige* toward their inferiors, but the lower ranks *would be* their inferiors. By eliminating unfairness, chance, and favoritism, Bellamy inadvertently eliminated the grounds for genuine brotherhood.[2]

Economic abundance was possible in his utopia because of the advanced state of technology and because the Industrial Army was so much more efficient than numerous competing businesses would be. There was no advertising, no middlemen, no product duplication, and no product innovation. If people wanted a new item, they had to petition for it.

There was almost no crime. There was no *reason* for crime, so a criminal was unreasonable—insane, in other words. He was sent to a hospital not a prison, and he did not ask for a lawyer. There were no lawyers. In fact, there were few laws in Bellamy's society. Its equality and its Religion of Solidarity made legal wrangling almost unheard of.

The Religion of Solidarity was a religion without a ritual, creed, or hierarchy. It was based upon the assumption that people could find sustaining spiritual satisfaction by working for the common good of mankind.

After work, the people in Bellamy's utopia did as they wished. No artistic establishment directed their admiration. No media elite manufactured celebrities. No government censor restricted information. People made up their own minds about everything, but universal, compulsory public education had so improved their taste that quality never went unrecognized.

Bellamy thought his system would free people from the "fret, worry, and hurry" of the American way of life. Free of all that, people would be—not unhappy and not ungood.

On the Canal Zone, that's more or less the way it was.

THE ALL-ENCOMPASSING COMPANY

The Zone's industrial army was divided into bureaus: engineering, marine, supply, health, transportation, civil affairs, and personnel. The bureau chiefs reported to the governor of the Zone, who was also president of the Canal Company. Traditionally, he was a general from the Corps of Engineers, but he wore civilian clothes on the Zone and was paid by the company.

The governor presided over some 14,000 employees: pilots, lockmasters, muledrivers, linehandlers, cable splicers, translators, carpenters, statistical draftsmen, machinists, longshoremen, admeasurers, marine traffic controllers, transit accounting technicians, divers, doctors, lawyers, merchant chiefs, butchers, bakers—no candlestick makers, but there were dairy farmers. Of all federal agencies, only the Department of Defense handled a greater variety of jobs than the Canal Company.[3]

Company meteorologists and hydrographers monitored water levels on computers, but they also paddled up jungle streams in *cayucos* to meet Choco Indians wearing nothing but body paint who turned over the sediment samples they had collected. They, too, worked for the company.

With a few licensed exceptions, the company/government ran all the businesses on the Zone, owned all the houses, and mowed all the lawns. There was one piece of private real estate. In 1921 the Panama Railroad—a division of the Canal Company—sold a city block in Cristóbal to the Masons. But that was a unique transaction authorized by Congress.[4]

The company/government had its own customs service, its own postal service (Canal Zone stamps were not interchangeable with U.S. stamps), and its own fleet: three ocean-going passenger ships, seventeen tugs, and an assortment of other vessels, from $6 million dredges to *pangas* (rowboats). The craneboat *Atlas* and the tugboat *Arraijan* were built in the company's own shipyard.[5]

Besides building ships, the company roasted coffee, baked cakes, stuffed sausage, and manufactured ice cream. Until the mid-fifties, its manufacturing division made or repackaged under the commissary label over 200 items, from pharmaceuticals to cosmetics: Bocas Mouthwash, for example, and Cree-Mee Brushless Shave, Athlene Liniment, Borymol Oral Antiseptic, and the ever-popular Menticol Cooling Lotion.

Naturally, the company provided its workers with office supplies. On every wall was the same calendar; on every desk was the same stapler, pen, and paperweight; and until a newcomer got to know them, the Zonians seemed as if they had been issued by the company, too. They were like characters in a first-grade reader: our friends the policeman, the fireman, the clerk, the dredger. But, of course, one did get to know them. That strange slogan "Socialism with a human face" was a pretty straightforward description of life on the Zone.

THE COMPANY/GOVERNMENT: A CLEAN MACHINE

In 1914, Willis Abbot, a popular journalist and author, praised the Zone for being socialistic *and* despotic *and* like Bellamy's utopia. A few years later, he visited Mussolini's Italy and praised it, too, in the same terms, and for the same reasons.[6] As far as Abbot was concerned, socialism, Fascism, and Bellamy's Nationalism were all variations of the same thing—a new and improved centralized form of government that was vastly fairer, less corruptible, and more efficient than democracy.

But they are not all alike. And if America ever forswears democracy for despotism, that despotism is unlikely to be a foreign brand. Something resembling Bellamy's home-grown Nationalism is more probable, which is to say, something resembling the authoritarian socialism of the Canal Zone.

But the intellectual socialists and social idealists of the West ignored the Zone. Some of them made pilgrimages to the Soviet Union, China, North Vietnam, or Cuba. They praised each country for realizing the communal aspirations of "the people." Paul Hollander has pointed out that every government that Western intellectuals have idealized since the 1920s has been seen as realizing communal aspirations.[7] But America's intellectual idealists never visited or praised the American Canal Zone, where the most communal technological society in the world flourished in a pastoral setting without border guards, secret trials, or political murders. In fact, the Zone was so communal that Panamanians sometimes denounced the Zonians as communists!

However, the Zone was, after all, an American place—just an American small town in the tropics, presumably. Worse, the Zonians were not alienated from their culture. To the contrary, they were patriots—and they spoke English. They were, therefore, totally unsuitable material for intellectual myth-makers, being quite impossible to glamorize behind veils of foreignness.

And that was what the intellectuals were after—material for myths —the glamor and magic of comic-book superheroes and saints. To Norman Mailer, Castro was like the ghost of Cortez on Zapata's white horse. To Abbie Hoffman, he was "like a mighty penis coming to life." Sartre believed that after the Cuban revolution, Cubans exercised a veritable dictatorship over their own needs and rolled back the limits of the possible. Angela Davis discovered that the job of cutting cane had become "qualitatively different [in Cuba] since the revolution." Susan Sontag and other intellectuals accepted without question the claims that Cubans after the revolution often worked twenty-four hours a day, several days a week, liberated from sleep as well as from capitalism.[8]

New York Times reporter David Halberstam found the material for his myth in Hanoi and, after the manner of Parson Weems, wrote, "The higher he rose, the simpler and purer Ho seemed, always retaining the eternal Vietnamese values: respect for old people, disdain for money, affection for children. . . ."[9]

Children are important to myth-makers. Heroic dictators invariably love them and are loved by them—instinctively—in return. Moreover, elitist intellectuals, no matter what their political stance, tend to see themselves and those they approve of as more mature than "the people," whom they see as the children. In her romantic assessment of the goals of the Communists in Vietnam, Frances Fitzgerald gushed, "Instead of merely trying to renew an elitist system [the National Liberation Front] was attempting to change that system and to bring the common people, the 'children,' to participate in the affairs of state."[10]

No wonder such intellectuals did not visit or write about the Zone. There were no saints or superheroes there. The Canal workers slept every night—or day, if they were on shift work. And they did not regard themselves as children, though they often thought resentfully that they were treated as though they were.

Some people will object to our assertion that the Zone was a form of authoritarian socialism. Unlike the more radical American socialist intellectuals, who do not see anything incompatible between socialism and dictatorship as long as they are magically combined into a chimera called "the dictatorship of the proletariat," or a "people's democracy," many people believe that "real" socialism means democratic socialism. Since the Zone was not democratic, they would not want it called socialistic. Goethals, for instance, chided one of the Zone's blacksmiths, "Now look here, Morrison, you mustn't say we have Socialism down here. Introduce the franchise and we'd go to pieces. It's despotism; and that's the best form of government."[11]

But it was not a Fascist or Communist form of despotism. The Zone's atmosphere was not even faintly tinged with the romantic salvationism that idealistic ex-Fascists and ex-Communists have testified was the great attraction of those political faiths. No one gave his life meaning by working for "Zonianism"!

The Zone was closest to Fascism under Stevens, who presided over an army of roughnecks and suggested that he was a man sometimes bent solely "upon smashing a way through all obstacles" and as not possessing "too deep a veneration for the vagaries of constituted authority."[12] In his day, the Zone was a raw company town.

Had it not soon become considerably more than that it would be of less interest today. The American company towns of the late nineteenth century were echoes of European feudalism. They embodied a militaristic paternalism that is fundamentally offensive to democratic Americans. There is no room in America for the paternalism of kings, czars, commissars, captains of industry, or *caudillos*.

Americans are committed to brotherhood, not paternalism, and to the idea that in some essential sense all men are equal.

Inadvertently, the government of the Canal Zone developed in a way that up to a point at least balanced a muted militaristic paternalism with what one Zonian called a "democratic setting." The Zone's governor was not just an officer. He was an engineer—a professional who had advanced in school and in the Corps of Engineers by passing objective tests and by being rated on his efficiency. He was not an aristocrat or a politician. Nor was he a businessman bent on maximizing profits.

The Zone did not simply have a management like a company, or an officers corps like the army; it had a government, complete with legal code, and—to the everlasting irritation of the State Department—its own involvement in foreign affairs, not just in Panama either, but with shipping interests all over the globe.

In all this, the Zone echoed Bellamy's utopia. In that paternalistic, quasi-military meritocracy, all men are, theoretically at least, brothers. The president of Bellamy's Industrial Army is an elected official, but he is chosen from a restricted circle of experts who began their careers by outscoring their rivals on objective tests that are "democratically" open to all the brothers and sisters. Theoretically, the citizens of his utopia are variously talented, not variously privileged. And so it was, theoretically, at least, on the Zone.

But was the Zone's government despotic? To hear Goethals' venerators tell it, it was when he was in charge. Abbot called him "an absolute autocrat," "a dictator," and said he doubted if the efficiency of despotic management had ever been so impressively manifest as it was on the Zone.[13] Moreover, according to Goethals' admirers, his despotism was universally popular. "The rough canal men," declared his biographers, "understood him."[14]

But not, perhaps, in the way his biographers think. When Farnham and Joseph Bucklin Bishop speak for the "rough men," it is well to remember that they did not belong to that group. The rough men didn't write much. In the few places where they have left a record, they refer to Goethals as "the Emperor" and to his office as "the throne room" or "the torture chamber."[15] Goethals adroitly squelched every outbreak of labor unrest on the Zone. It is unlikely that he did this without leaving some hard feelings among the "rough men."

It was Stevens the roughnecks loved. They respected Goethals— admired him, but he was different from them. They could never be like him unless they started over and went to college. Not much chance of that. When the Bishops reported that the admiration accorded to Goethals by his subordinates "assumed the proportions of a cult,"[16] we believe they were talking mainly about Goethals' subordinate bureaucrats. He was their kind of man. That was why they exaggerated his despotic power. They were dreaming that they shared it.

But Goethals was not a despot, and subsequent governors had less power than he did. Lenin defined "the scientific concept of 'dictatorship'" as "nothing more than unrestricted power, absolutely unimpeded by law or regulations and resting directly on force."[17] No Zone governor had that kind of power. In the first place, the governor was appointed for a limited term and had limited power to appoint his subordinates. In the second place, the Zone was not ruled by whim but by law—the Canal Zone Code. It was almost identical to American law in criminal cases but recognized Panamanian as well as American precedents in noncriminal ones.[18]

At first, the governor was authorized to make or change laws subject only to a confirming order from the president. Theodore Roosevelt soon limited the governor's power by providing Zonians with the equivalent of a partial bill of rights—excluding the right to trial by jury.

But the Americans on the Zone, workers and managers alike, were powerfully attached to the jury system, and in 1908, J. S. C. Blackburn wrote to Roosevelt, quoting Roosevelt's own words about "certain great principles of government which have been made the basis of our existence as a nation . . . which shall have force on said zone." Blackburn said he thought the right to a trial by jury fell within the scope of those principles. Roosevelt, conceding the point, authorized jury trials —but only for cases involving the death penalty or life in prison. However, that opened the door, and it soon became possible for either party to demand a jury trial in all civil or criminal cases.

In other ways, too, the governor's power was checked and balanced as the Zone government took shape. Early on, he lost the power to appoint judges to the Canal Zone Supreme Court, an institution that was itself soon abolished. The District Court, District Attorney, and the United States Marshall were transferred from the War Department to the Justice Department, making them more independent. The laws of the Zone were codified, and a system evolved for appealing cases to the States. Also, slowly but surely, more and more Canal workers came under the aegis of the Civil Service Act.

However, the governor remained very powerful. He had, for instance, broad powers to expel people from paradise. Every once in a while, we would look around for so-and-so and would be told, "Oh, he was shipped out. Didn't you know?"

Adultery, homosexuality, petty theft, persistent public drunkenness—anything that might interfere with the tranquility of the community (which is to say, with the efficiency of the work force) or anything that might embarrass the United States before Panama— could serve as a reason for "shipping out" someone.

However, there were no consistent standards. Some supervisors were more tolerant than others. An old-timer was harder to dislodge than a newcomer. The Zone's managers generally remained passive until someone's behavior became a public issue. A person could get by with a lot if he or she was discreet. The company, itself, for instance, in line with community standards, was willing to sell *Playboy* from behind the counter but drew a line at a publicly displayed selection of pornographic publications. One Canal executive told us that in his experience there was "less railroading out of the Zone than an overlooking of things." But in either case, the point was to keep things quiet—to preserve, one way or another, the image of the Zone as a tranquil, efficient model community.

That was not always possible.

The governor was not immune to political pressure, or to direction from the courts. To some extent he even had to consider public opinion on the Zone, since, while he could force people to leave, he could not force them to stay. Thus it was possible for dissidents on the Zone to outmaneuver the governor. One of the first to do this was Mary Hibbard. She was the chief nurse at Ancon Hospital in 1904. When her nursing staff grew, she requested "further service assistance." The governor answered, "Refused. I thought that nurses came down here to help, not to make work."

That was quite the wrong tone to take with Miss Hibbard. Her leave being due, she promptly set off for Washington. Later, she reported, ". . . within a year, all requests made by me were granted and in force, even the purchase of a piano made for tropical use."[19]

When the unions discovered they could not get pay raises through strikes on the Isthmus, they, too, traveled to Washington, the steam-shovel engineers leading the parade.

Perhaps the best known dissidents in the history of the Canal Zone were Arthur C. Payne, budget director of the Community Services Division, and Richard Meehan, president of Policeman Lodge 1790 (AFL-CIO). In 1964, shortly after the Flag Riots, Governor Fleming announced a plan to add fifty Panamanian policemen to the Canal Zone police force. Not surprisingly, many Zonians did not think this was a good idea. Payne and Meehan led the opposition to the plan. The governor charged them with making "libelous" statements and with failing to obtain clearance to issue statements with regard to government policy. They were dismissed and exiled from paradise.[20] Payne and Meehan went to court and after prolonged litigation won reinstatement and back pay. Even before that outcome, however, the example of their defiance and persistence contributed to the freer atmosphere on the Zone during the late sixties and seventies.

It was not always necessary, however, to appeal to Congress or go to court in order to contravene the Zone authorities. Even on the authoritarian Zone, it was possible to play politics—a shadowy, diminished politics compared to politics in the States, but a semblance, at least, of the real thing.

Jean Heald, who lived on the Zone during the twenties, drew attention to what she called the Zone's "democratic setting." She emphasized the governor's "democratic manner" rather than his despotic authority—and she was on to something important.[21]

The Zone's governors did not try to intimidate the populace with uniforms and swagger, or to buttress their claim to authority with ceremony and social distance. That makes a difference. It permits, as Heald says, a "democratic setting," which to some extent can take the place of democratic procedures. Because of the Zone's "democratic setting," people felt free to "kick" and complain, to argue about the governor's policies. They cornered him personally, and they challenged him through their community organizations.

For many years, the Metal Trades Council—representing most of the unions—was the governor's chief antagonist. Then, in 1937, Governor C. S. Ridley created the Canal Zone Civic Councils "to further promote democratic processes in the absence of official local self government."[22] The peculiar nature of life on the Zone encouraged that kind of double-talk. Actually, since both the councils and the unions were "special-interest groups," they were expected to leave all final decisions to the company, for it alone could see what was best for everyone.

With depressing accuracy, the Zone's Civic Councils paralleled the student councils of America's high schools. The Civic Councils could only recommend action to the real authorities, who were often the very people the councils were complaining about.

However, after lengthy investigations, much documentation, and persistent protests, the councils would sometimes bring about a change—a leash law, for example, or the reduction of some commissary prices, or the restoration of two movie showings a night. Not very famous victories but important ones, for they kept the idea of democratic politics alive.

What the Zone resembled most was a progressive muckraker's "clean" version of a big-city political machine. Some observers saw in the working of that machine a social achievement of the first order: "The Canal Zone is the best governed district in the United States," claimed a popular travel writer in 1912, and he added that until an American visited the Zone, he would not have a very good notion of just what good government means. Sixteen years later, in 1928, a Zonian made the same point in a guidebook for tourists: The Zone was "the best governed section of the United States, if not the world."[23]

However, a visitor in 1919 had had reservations. George Miller reviewed the advantages of living on the Zone and concluded that the Zonian should be "a satisfied and happy man."

> In practice, however, the American on the Canal Zone is not so contented as the external features of his lot would lead one to suppose. There is an undercurrent of petty complaint, directed at everything in general, and indicative of a state of mind as much as of evils existent. These complaints are the result of too much community life without room for individual ownership and initiative. The followers of Bellamy should come to the Zone and stay long enough to get a few pointers.[24]

Since the Zone's Bellamyite system of government did not seem to produce satisfied and happy citizens, Miller concluded that the system was at fault. Harold Martin made similar observations in 1960 but came to a different conclusion. To him, the Zonian was simply an inferior type—a person who was in the main "content with his chains" and who would "fight to draw them closer about him." He enjoyed, Martin said, living in a "pleasant prison."[25]

It is true that the Zonian liked being taken care of. It was liberating to have a relatively secure job in a safe, well-maintained community. It was liberating not to have to worry about astronomical medical bills. And certainly people are freer than they would otherwise be if they have someone to look after their houses and yards for them. The rich have servants for that. The Canal workers had the company.

On the other hand, no Canal worker really liked for the company to decide how the community would be run. "The other side of the 'You'll always be taken care of thing' is a certain amount of anger at not being able to manage your own affairs," a Civic Council member observed in 1976.[26] A State Department survey of Zonian attitudes concluded, "The single most common grievance is that Panama Canal never consults with the employees before making a decision; they feel they are always presented with a 'fait accompli,' and tells them [sic] that if they don't agree, 'there's a boat leaving on Saturday'. . ."[27] A union officer snarled, " 'Consultation'—that meant they did what they wanted then called you in and told you."

President Taft once compared the Zone to a literal machine with the governor's hand on the controlling lever.[28] It follows that the Canal workers were the cogs in that machine. That was the theory. In fact, the Zonians never resigned themselves to being cogs in a utopian social machine.

However, the indirect ways by which the workers could sometimes influence the hand on the lever were not satisfactory substitutes for direct democracy. The Zone's citizen-workers alternately despaired of influencing the company/government and grew stridently determined to do so. In 1974, a labor consultant told the secretary of the army that the Canal Company made no effort to deal with the unions until a problem had reached "crisis levels."[29] Thus, the company encouraged moderate men to take extreme positions in hope, thereby, of persuading the company that a particular problem was ripe for consideration. But this opened the workers to the charge that they lacked a sense of proportion and served to justify to the company managers the idea that the workers were people who still needed guidance and were not yet "mature" enough to govern themselves.

When the Zone's deputy executive secretary retired in 1979, he told the company newspaper that his greatest source of satisfaction during his years with the company had come from his involvement in what would elsewhere have been each citizen's private affairs.

This is the area in which we've tried to do our most valuable work and to keep the employee, his welfare, and his peace of mind, as our first concern. Our guiding philosophy is to do our very best for the employee, although it is the nature of our work that the employee cannot always see this.[30]

The condescending tone, the royal "we," and especially that last ominous clause suggest the kind of attitude that tended to develop among the nonelected, fair-minded experts who managed the Zone.

EFFICIENCY, WASTE, AND CENTRALIZATION

Did the Canal project show that centrally directed, government-controlled agencies were more efficient than private contractors? Stevens irritably dismissed such talk as speculation.[31] But he, himself, had shown that the Canal Commission could feed its men more efficiently, cheaply, and generously than the J. E. Markell Company of Omaha and had arranged to abrogate that firm's contract with the commission. And at least one businessman was glad the government had decided not to subcontract work on the Canal. With the benefit of hindsight, Arthur F. MacArthur commented dryly that had his group's bid been accepted, the result would have been "dividends of patriotism."[32]

So it is not surprising that in 1913 Willis Abbot was chortling that the Zone's "socialized" administration gave "cold chills" to those who stood in dread of that doctrine.[33] Even Ira Bennett, whose book emphasized the contributions of private industry to the construction of the Canal, freely admitted that the federal government had made a remarkable record on the Isthmus "not only in the saving of money but in setting an example of public efficiency."[34] And, in 1934, Marshall Dimock, a consultant who examined the company, declared, "In the Canal Zone one finds evidence of the falsity of the gospel that has been preached in the United States for years, namely, 'Government is by its very nature inefficient.' "[35]

However, just before he retired in 1980, a jaded Canal Zone government bureaucrat told us, "This wasn't so much a business as a welfare organization. There was plenty of money. Things were not done cheaply. It was not efficient."

Of course, efficiency means one thing when applied to a business and another when applied to a community. Since the Canal Company/Government was both, there will always be room for debate about whether or not it was efficient. However, the bureaucrats on the Zone had the same attitude toward money that federal bureaucrats have in the United States, and that attitude seems destined to undermine all efforts to create a rational, efficient society.

For instance, was it wasteful for a bureaucrat to go on a buying spree near the end of the fiscal year, as was customary on the Zone? Or is that a sign of good (i.e., efficient) management? No good federal bureaucrat wants to run over his budget, but he doesn't want to be caught with a surplus, either. If he is, he runs the risk of seeing his forthcoming appropriation cut back proportionately. A "good manager" will therefore save his bureau's money until he is sure it will last the year. Then he will spend every penny, so that he can ask for more. His subordinates are counting on him to do so. They want their agency to grow so that they can be promoted. They want their responsibilities to be expanded so that they can be more helpful and useful. And there is no end to being more helpful and useful.

We were shocked the first time we saw the principal of Balboa High arbitrarily tripling and quadrupling items on his school's book-and-equipment order to help the Schools Division spend its quota. But we took heed and thereafter kept wish lists, along with the relevant catalogue numbers and addresses. It isn't easy for a bureaucrat to spend tens of thousands of dollars in just a few days. Anyone willing to help is usually welcome.

Competition and waste do not disappear in a noncapitalist society. They just take different forms. The "conspicuous consumption" of the insensitive capitalist who snarls, "The public be damned," is replaced by the inconspicuous consumption of the sensitive bureaucrat who argues that he needs to spend more money for the poor public's good.

9

The Zone's Landscape
and Architecture

There were ten villages on the Zone during the years we were there—plus a couple of ghost towns in the jungle. The largest occupied village was Balboa. The Balboa area—including the adjacent villages of Ancon, Los Rios, and Diablo—had a population of just under six thousand in 1969. Those were all company employees and their families. There were more Americans on the nearby military bases of Albrook and Fort Amador, but while the military and civilian communities overlapped in some ways, they were not the same. They were "centered" differently.

The other Canal villages ranged in size from Coco Solo, with a population of about a thousand, to Rainbow City, with over two thousand residents.

The villages were neat and clean. Almost the first thing we were told when we arrived was, "Look, no flies! And *this* is the tropics!" But the villages were not sterile looking. As soon as the first permanent villages were in place, a company horticulturist was at work planting flowering trees and bushes: guayacans, pink cassias, royal poincianas, yellow poincianas, jacarandas, tulip trees, bougainvillea, crotons, hibiscus. The men who laid out the Zone had consciously in mind that the quality of the landscape would influence the Canal worker's satisfaction with his job, and perhaps nowhere else in the world have men come closer to harmonizing technology and nature. The Canal was our machine; the Zone, our garden.

Surrounding the villages was jungle—a giant scribble, though it looked more like a wall where it began dramatically at the end of a street or the edge of a yard. Parts of the jungle and all of the villages were webbed with concrete drainage ditches. Without them, parts of the Zone would have turned back into swamp during the rainy season. Balboa, for instance, is built on a swamp that was filled with spoil from the Canal—not the firmest of foundations. Many of the concrete apartments in Balboa have a distinct tilt.

Balboa was the "capital," so to speak, of the Zone. It lies between two hills. On Ancon Hill is The Building, the Canal Company's headquarters; on Sosa Hill is the Union Church, the largest church building on the Zone. Several denominations worshiped together there and billed themselves as an example of "the Amazing Power of Cooperative Christianity."[1]

Cooperative Christianity—that was a slogan of the religious wing of the progressive reform movement. The Union Church and The Building are both representative institutions embodying the progressive virtues of nondenominational cooperation (tcamwork) and efficiency.

On the Balboa Flats there were four rows of concrete, tile-roofed, four-family houses. They were among the earliest permanent buildings on the Zone, and, along with the terminals buildings in Balboa, the headquarters building, the control towers on the locks, and the hydroelectric station at Gatún, were designed in Italian Renaissance style by Austin W. Lord, head of the architecture department at Columbia.[2]

The company was devoted to the virtue of efficiency, but that did not mean its buildings were always plain or cheap. It expected to be operating "in perpetuity." Perpetuity justifies some extra expense. Even the Balboa furniture store—essentially a warehouse—had a pleasing pattern of relief lines that caught the shadows from different angles as the day progressed. And there were surprises, like the petal frames of the attic windows of the Balboa train station, the courtyard of the Balboa elementary school, the octagonal gas plants in the Pier 16 area, various balconies, rows of arches or columns, fan windows, diamond windows, and examples of ornamental ironwork. The mortuary gates were especially impressive. So was old Gorgas Hospital—a monument to the victory over yellow fever. Its buildings, connected by tile-roofed walkways, sprawl amid tropical trees and shrubs across acres of hill-side.

The Canal Company lavished treasure on its equipment and on some of its buildings, but not all of them. Its commissaries were un-distinguished, and some of its stores and theaters were wooden barns, as were its so-called clubhouses. Originally the clubhouses were "lib-eral" YMCAs (Goethals made them allow bowling on Sunday and admit women). Over the years, they became company cafeterias where some workers ate breakfast and a lot of schoolchildren ate lunch. There was a cubbyhole for a seamstress upstairs, filing cabinets for the Scouts, and a place for people to play bingo. Company officials, afraid that "clubhouse" suggested something like an affluent country club, tried to get the Zonians to call them Service Centers—but to no avail.

The Zone's barn buildings were too primitive and obviously tem-porary—although some were used for half a century—to be inferior from an architectural standpoint. From that standpoint, there were only two egregious structures on the Zone. One was the new Gorgas Hospital—a giant cube on stilts. The contrast between it and old Gorgas illustrates how the imperatives of technology, in this case, air-conditioning, can exact a horrendous aesthetic price. The other abomi-nation was the Goethals Memorial, a white, megalithic rectangle erected in 1953 when every architect was echoing Mies van der Rohe's "newspeak" dictum, "Less is more." It erases one of Austin Lord's best effects—a view down a palm-lined boulevard of the Y-shaped stairway leading up Ancon Hill to The Building. That stair-way was built in the days when more was more. It has the vitality of a Sousa march. But some bureaucrat with an unwrinkled brain placed the Goethals slab right in front of the stairs, so that now all a person can see from the far end of the Prado is a white blank—with The Building balanced surrealistically on top of it. A visible manifestation of how, by 1953, our specialists, both administrative and artistic, were unable to see things whole.

The housing for the Canal workers was considerably less impres-sive than the Zone's best public buildings. For years, most Zonians lived in wooden multifamily quarters built on stilts and finished with open studs. But not all those wooden houses were alike. The best had screens from floor to ceiling and eaves extending well beyond their walls. They were called French-style houses but looked Japanese-ish to us. A Zone architect called them birdhouses.

In 1945, a man from the National Housing Agency took one look at the Zone's wooden houses and called them substandard.[3] Thirty-four years later, when the Zone was turned over to Panama, many Zonians were still living in wooden houses. However, the worst of them had been torn down during the fifties and replaced by masonry duplexes. Those long-awaited "real houses" were a great disappointment, however. Their rooms were so small! "Chicken coops," the Zonians muttered.

10

The Zone's Civic Religion

But the Zone had a dimension to it that made houses like barns and rooms like chicken coops less objectionable than they would be in Panama or the United States—a sense of purpose. That sense of purpose was the Zone's civic religion. It was sustained by a "ceremony" that was performed around the clock, over a hundred times a day—the process of putting a ship through one of the locks. Every Zonian's job was related to that "ceremony." What a cathedral was to a town in medieval Europe, the locks were to the Canal Zone, and tourists came from all over the world to watch ships being locked through the Panama Canal.

On one level, locking a ship through was a no-nonsense business; on another, a symbolic drama. It evoked dreams of harmony between men and their machines and of peace among the nations.

It still does, of course. The work of the Canal goes on. Indeed, the gradual transfer of jobs and authority from the Americans to the Panamanians is an inspiring example of international cooperation and enlightened self-interest. However, as is almost always the case with progress, a balance has been altered; something has been lost. Ships are no longer locked through by members of a fraternity; the community that existed solely to maintain and operate the Canal is gone.

So is the sense that the Canal's significance went beyond its military or commercial advantages. In the February 1912 *National Geographic*, a writer predicted that the Canal would become "one of the greatest factors in the promotion of universal peace" and that upon its completion "the prophecy about swords being beaten into plough-shares . . . will have been brought nearer to fulfillment."[1] Ironically, the first ocean-to-ocean transit of the Canal took place on the day Germany declared war on France, August 3, 1914. But that did not shake the faith of the Canal Zone poet Seymour Paul. His poem celebrating the official opening of the Canal ends with these lines:

> *This is the way and the day!*
> *The day is dark with war in lands that blazed the way,*
> *But the day seems brighter for that—for*
> *This is the way*
> *For the navies of trade and the armies of work*
> *Of a world that will learn.*[2]

Big fluorescent blue butterflies often greet ships that are beginning their transits, and the ships of all nations go through the Canal non-denominationally, without regard for ideology or national alliance.

The work—the "ceremony"—goes on in near silence.[3] A tug nudges the ship toward the jaws. Two men in a *panga* row toward the ship. The *panga* trails a messenger line that is fed out by linehandlers on the lock walls. The deckhands on the ship throw a weighted heaving line toward the *panga*. The boatmen secure it to their messenger line and get out of the way as fast as they can. The deckhands haul in the line, which the linehandlers have attached to a steel cable or "wire." The wires are connected to towing locomotives, the "mules," which are tracked along the tops of the lock walls and which haul the ship into the lock chamber.

Large ships often rub against the knuckle, where the wing wall meets the side wall, so the knuckle is buffered by tires set on an axle. They roll against the side of the ship, leaving thick, black lines of rubber. "Panama Canal racing stripes," said the man who pointed them out to us.

The pilots on the Canal are not merely advisors to the captains of transiting ships, as are pilots elsewhere in the world. A Panama Canal pilot is in charge of his ship, and that means of a Russian or Cuban ship, too, as long as it is in the Canal.

But no pilot could take a ship through by himself. It takes teamwork. Inside the lock walls, machinists and electricians are hiking through tunnels, checking the starting panels and motors that move the lock gates and valves. At Marine Traffic Control, men are charting each ship's progress. In the channel, men on a dipper dredge are widening the Mamei Curve, while other men on a suction dredge are drawing silt from Balboa Harbor. On the graveyard shift, men on a drill barge will be blasting beside Gold Hill—channel-deepening tests.

At Miraflores, a maintenance crew is rebuilding a softnose that was struck and sunk by a transiting ship, while at Colón, men are replacing, one by one, the 700 dolosse, the giant concrete jacks that shield the breakwater. Meanwhile, somewhere along the Canal, crews are cleaning up an oil spill, cutting brush to keep it from overgrowing navigational aids, spraying floating vegetation, which could be sucked into the water intakes of transiting ships, herding water hyacinths through culverts to ponds for harvesting, clearing potential slides from the banks, or replacing light bulbs in floating buoys.

Those distant thumps are explosions in the Velasquez Dump, where men are excavating long, narrow drainage ditches.

In the jungle, men are fogging backwater mosquito breeding grounds, and jungle policemen are searching for timber poachers and slash-and-burn farmers. Water for the lockages, for hydroelectric power, and for the water systems of the former Zone and Panama's two largest cities is supplied by the run-off from the Gatún Lake watershed. Once the trees are destroyed the soil is subject to erosion, and the jungle doesn't recover.

Each of the locks is regularly overhauled—an event scheduled seven years in advance. The floating crane, *Hercules*, lifts the miter gates off their pintles. The gates, which weigh 440 to 770 tons each, are floated to dry dock for repairs. Their pintle casting is removed and sent to the Industrial Division for overhaul. The bearing plates, which form a watertight seal between the leaves and the side of the lock chamber and between the leaves themselves, are blasted off and the lead alloy behind them—the babbitt—is removed. New bearing plates are aligned within 5/1000 of an inch, and the space behind them is refilled with molten babbitt. Meanwhile, in the dry lock chamber, where the water is being held back by a caisson, men with air-hammers are breaking the old lock sill, while others are working on the hollow quoin plates, the pintle ball, and the yoke. A chamber is dewatered for ninety-six hours.

Sometimes startling things interrupt the work. Men thinning water hyacinths may flush an alligator. Once a golf ball landed on the deck of a transiting ship. The captain threw it back on his next trip through the Canal. Once a tarpon jumped over a *panga*, knocking the line-catcher into the water. Sometimes a ship is damaged in transit, but normally there is a peaceful dreamy atmosphere about work on the Canal. Men carry out their almost silent routines amid intermittent rain and tropical mists.

That dreamy atmosphere seems appropriate. The Panama Canal was conceived and built at least partly in response to a dream. America's eagerness to DO IT was not based on cost-effectiveness projections but on a dream of bringing the nations together—a dream of peace and harmony, which was shared by both the individualistic Americans of the nineteenth century and by the collectivist reformers of the twentieth.

However, the collectivists also dreamed of a more rational and efficient society, and after the Canal was completed, that aspect of their new vision came to dominate life on the Zone. Managerial experts devised "rational" policies that they expected the workers to accept without "irrational" protests. The workers were expected to be dedicated and efficient in return for rational rewards and recognition. Governors and bureau chiefs spent a lot of time handing out merit badges for good behavior, longevity, and even occasionally for good work. Scarcely a day went by without a dramatic photograph in the newspaper of a 14 shaking hands with a good and faithful 6. (We all had numbers on the Zone.)

But the Zonian's commitment to his job was not the result of this sort of social engineering. It was the result of the kind of job he did and of its historical implications. The Zonians were not manufacturing something silly or shoddy; they were not despoiling the environment or squeezing shippers for the last penny of profit. They were doing an obviously demanding and useful job for the glory of their country and the benefit of the world.

That idea may strike some readers as quaint—a curious historical survival—but history on the Zone wasn't simply words in a book. It was in the lay of the land. The Zone's hills and rivers had been shaped by an international army of laborers, gathered and led by Americans. What was crooked had been made straight; what was swamp had been made solid; what was hostile to man had been made livable and beautiful.

In the dusk—as the last buzzard circled over Ancon Hill and a squeaking flock of parakeets burst from the top of a royal palm, trailing through the dimness like a pale green comet—it was easy to imagine yourself back in time. Many buildings and prospects looked essentially the same in 1979 as they do in photographs taken during construction days.

In the States, "The great eventful Present hides the Past." Tax laws and an atmosphere of hustle and fashion encourage men to let buildings deteriorate, tear them down and build new ones, to write off their equipment as fast as possible and buy new. By contrast, on the Zone, a big part of the work went into preventive maintenance. The last of the original "mules"—the electric locomotives used on the locks—was not retired until 1964. The apartment building we lived in was built in 1914, as was the Dredging Division's crane boat, *Hercules*. Both have been in continuous service ever since. *Hyacinth II*, a workboat, was even older. It was built in 1882. The Americans inherited it from the French. "Hints and echoes of the life behind" were part of the fabric of every Zonian's life and work.

Of course, as members of a small American outpost thousands of miles from home, most Zonians were more self-consciously American than they would have been had they spent their lives in the States. The Canal reminded them of America's historic mission, and Panama, by numerous contrasts, of America's blessings.

However, for most of this century, the Zonians' flag-waving enthusiasm was shared by Americans everywhere. Then, in the sixties and seventies, that enthusiasm came to be viewed by some of America's "best and brightest" as irrational and obstructive. It interfered, they felt, with the exercise of a rational, flexible foreign policy, although there was nothing intrinsically inflexible or obstructive about it. It merely required that policy decisions be justified in terms that America's new elitists, vain of their rational, sophisticated outlook, found embarrassingly simple and provincial. Indeed, the fact that flag-waving patriotism was a popular enthusiasm was in itself enough to make the new elite abjure it. But we are getting ahead of our story.

11

Life on the Zone:
World Enough and Time

TIME TO STAND AND STARE

Life on the Zone involved trade-offs, and just as we were convinced that what we gave up to live there was worth less than what we got, something would happen to change our minds. Compared to the States, the Zone was a very limited place. It did not provide people with an abundance of things or with a great variety of opportunity—although we have the impression that the superstitious academic credentialism that prevails in some quarters in the States was never generally accepted by the Canal Company, and that Zonians with ability but without distinguished academic backgrounds got a fairer shake on the Zone than they might have elsewhere.

What the Zone provided instead of things and a variety of opportunity was security and time. In the States, we never had enough time. We seemed to spend half our lives on the road between places, and as a result were always juggling schedules and watching the clock. On the Zone, it was different. The Zone was small, and residential neighborhoods were not distanced from industrial areas, administrative office buildings, or retail establishments. The inhabitants of Balboa lived cheek-by-jowl with Pier 18 and the roundhouse of the company railroad. The Zone's college was located next to a tank farm and under the bridge that crossed the Pacific entrance to the Canal. One of the stanchions was planted in the school's athletic field. In front of the college was the residential district of La Boca. The Marine Traffic Control Building was located there, and around the hill less than a quarter of a mile away were the dry docks and piers, the gas plants, storehouses, electrical shops, and so on. People lived close to their work, their clubs, and their commissaries. They spent less time between places and more time where they wanted to be than most people do in the States.

The Zone's socialist simplicity was another reason the Zonians had more leisure than they would have had in the States. We liked that simplicity at first. Who needed twenty different kinds of bread or toothpaste? We were tired of the unnecessary choices that confronted us in the States; and we were weary of the importunities of intellectual and entrepreneurial hucksters, always drumming for the latest idea or gadget.

But sometimes on the Zone, we yearned disconsolately for the hubbub and excitement of the United States. Sometimes we were so bored that we set out to buy something—anything—simply to lift our spirits, although the variety of consumer goods on the Zone was limited, and for most of our stay on the Isthmus, there wasn't much variety in Panama City, either. There were some fine Panamanian jewelry stores, and some American women acquired exquisite collections of gold jewelry. However, most Zonians, after years of shopping in Panama, ended up with chests full of embroidered linens, drawers full of jade fruit, dozens of molas, and too many sheeshamwood screens.

To our surprise, we soon learned that we had been able to organize our private lives far more efficiently in the apparently wasteful consumer society of the United States, where we could choose from a wide variety of goods offered at a wide range of prices—where we did not have to "make do" with things that didn't quite fit or that weren't what we actually wanted in the first place.

Of course, efficiency is not everything. The efficiently organized life does not leave much time for reflection, exploring one's interests, or enjoying casual encounters. There was time on the Zone for all that. Some Zonians explored Panama, seeking relief from the familiar tranquility of the Zone in the unfamiliar tranquility of the interior, where they owned small *fincas*, or along the coast where they owned or rented beach houses. Other Zonians went looking for excitement in Panama City, where they went to movies, restaurants, and casinos. Some of them went looking for business partners; others, for "shameful and culpable pleasures."

Zonians spent more time on hobbies and self-improvement than they probably would have in the United States. The range and quality of their expertise was daunting. They devoted themselves to photography, painting, classical music, square dancing, bagpiping, scuba-diving, baseball, golf, hunting, sailing, and theater. Community theater was taken very seriously. Canal workers, Panamanians, and lonely American servicemen joined forces to stage elaborate and polished productions.

One Zone teacher spent his free time mapping butterfly refuge areas in Central America and kept in touch with scientists who shared this interest. A policeman who collected shells established a professional relationship with conchologists at Cornell, eventually giving the school a thousand specimens. Numerous Zonians collected plants, sending unusual ones to universities, botanical gardens, or pharmaceutical houses in the States.

It seemed like almost everyone on the Zone collected *something*: insects, pre-Columbian pottery, antique bottles, shells, guns, orchids, rocks. For forty years, Lucille Bryan, "the birdwoman," collected live birds. They flew through her house freely and would light on the shoulders or extended fingers of schoolchildren and other visitors.

Zonians restored old cars, built boats and ham radio sets. They became experts on Panamanian archeology, Indians, festivals, dances, molas, birds, snakes, history, and the lost-wax process for casting gold huacas—small ornamental figures found in Indian graves. Some Zonians wrote books and scholarly papers. And quite a few of them wrote poetry. The Zone's poets included soldiers, visitors, workmen, teachers, and administrators. Maurice Thatcher, who was in charge of civil affairs on the Zone from 1910 to 1913, wrote his autobiography in verse.

Randolph Atkin, an Englishman searching for a place where "God's earth's not rented / By an aristocracy," loved the Zone where "to be a landed lord / No advantage would afford / It's men they seek, not titles, in that land."[1]

John Hall spoke for the roughnecks in the Cut:

> *"The 'ditch' is growin',"*
> *We often hear.*
> *We can't see 't grow;*
> *We're here.*

He wrote, too, of their domestic escapades, about, for instance, the man who "Hied him away to the haunts of the Sirens / And picked out a beautiful, fancy-free maid." When this irregular situation came to the attention of the authorities, they invited him to take a vacation. He "sailed on a boat leaving next day, / This cable then came: 'Send in resignation; / We mail you to-morrow a draft for your pay.' "[2]

When the Canal was completed, Percy MacKaye hailed Goethals as a "prophet-engineer" and as a poet. (What higher compliment?)

> *For a poet wrought in Panama*
> *With a continent for his theme,*
> *And he wrote with flood and fire*
> *To forge a planet's dream,*
> *And the derricks rang his dithyrambs*
> *And his stanzas roared in steam.*[3]

Glen Ward Dresbach, proud of the job the diggers had done on Panama, proclaimed:

> *The Panama of pesthole, harlot, lout,*
> *Is now no more. She stands*
> *With young, unfettered hands,*
> *Greeting the world she lived so long without.*[4]

James Gilbert, a long-time resident of the Isthmus, wrote of almost every aspect of life there, from boring bridge games to a Frijoles washer girl, "Clad but in nature's modesty," and from the prickly heat to "the Great Socialist / King Fever is his name; / Whose leveling power none can resist."[5]

Walter Goldstein, a soldier stationed on the Zone during the Second World War, lamented, "I'm home alone with my cockroach friends. / We understand each other." He sang also of Panama's dubious consolations—the cantinas, "Burrowed in some alley wall," where

> *the juke box thumps a rumba*
> *That loosens up your feet,*
> *And the night is filled with smells*
> *Which ain't too awfully sweet.*[6]

The Canal Zone teacher Dorothy Moody wrote of the Zone's flowering trees, one of its glories. She invokes their names—"the words themselves are music"—then describes individual species:

> *. . . on Ancon Hill, some day as March is dying,*
> *Triumphal bursts of yellow appear in twos and threes.*
> *The guayacans spring into bloom as bugles call to battle.*
> *What matter if tomorrow they shatter in the breeze?*

She wonders if when "home from exile" and buried on the Kansas prairie, she will "wake one fleeting moment and know from all that distance / That bright, ethereal pageant is once more drifting by?" And she decides:

> *I shall be briefly sentient, while silent snow is falling,*
> *Or the catbird in the cottonwood performs his mimic trills,*
> *And feel again the tingling ecstasy and poignance*
> *Of fragile clouds of blossoms on the Panamanian hills.*[7]

In 1984, Bill Dunning, retiring chief of the Industrial Training Branch, summed up his forty-three years on the Isthmus in "Local Boy Blues or Gringo's Lament." It's all there, from life in a twelve-family barracks to Carnival at Chitre; from skinny-dipping at Cerro Azul to dancing at *El Rancho*.[8]

Probably the most famous Zone poem is the one Arthur Payne published in a Panamanian newspaper on January 9, 1964—which turned out to be the first day of the Flag Riots. It begins, "Where has Old Glory gone tonight / When taken from her pole?" and ends by explaining that "she fell to lies / And officialdom's endeavor."[9]

Our favorite is much less well known—L. M. Scull's laconic observation in 1947: "So now my dreams are over, the fire is burning low— / I'll never dig a Canal again, but tomorrow I'll shovel snow."[10]

The Zone's male poets worked alone, but its female poets had a club —the Penwomen. Hobby clubs and study groups were ubiquitous. Church groups studied the Bible. The Natural History Society studied Panama's animals and ecology. During the dry season, the Zone's amateur astronomers studied the stars. In 1930, a locomotive engineer wrangled a larger telescope from the navy and, with a little help from his friends, built a small public observatory.

Throughout the fifties, groups of Canal workers met voluntarily after work to kick around problems that had come up on the job and to upgrade their skills.[11]

The Isthmian College Club, founded in 1925, sponsored the most varied and longest-lasting series of study groups. The women studied everything from "Period Furniture" to "Government, Business, and the Individual." They studied Panama, too, organized field trips, and invited Panamanian poets, scientists, historians, and career women to address them.[12]

Apparently, then, the pursuit of happiness flourished on the Zone— and it did, but only in certain ways and up to a certain point. In 1937, a Zone woman, surrounded in her home by aquariums filled with tropical fish, grimly told the journalist and travel writer Negley Farson, "One must have a hobby."[13]

The non-commercial, functional atmosphere of the Zone drove people to find hobbies—frivolous, non-functional interests to nourish their souls. But a hobby on the Zone was not the same as a hobby in the States. In the States, a hobby resonates to a greater or lesser degree with possibility. On the Zone, where what led to what was carefully supervised by the company, a hobby was destined to remain just that—an amusement, a pastime.

FASHION AND TIME

The ordinary people in Bellamy's utopia were concerned only with the present. They had nothing to worry about and nothing fundamental ever changed.

There was more than a whiff of this futurelessness in the atmosphere on the Zone, especially for North Americans who were accustomed to seasonal changes marked by temperature changes. On the Zone, it was never cold and never hot, at least not by the standards of Kansas in August. Instead, it was wet or dry, but that didn't mark the passage of time for us very effectively. The vegetation was always green and there were almost always flowers. As far as we were concerned, it was always summer.

More importantly, however, there was a sense in which nothing ever happened. The local authorities filtered all the local news, and by the time that ideas, fads, and fashions from the States reached us, they were purged of most of the excitement and controversy that had attended their birth. The Zone's one anti-Vietnam War demonstration—a two-block march down the Prado and a candle-lighting ceremony—was but a ghostly echo of such protests in the States.

Zonians combated this eerie feeling of detachment by going to the States for conventions and workshops and by making the most of their biennial home leaves, but the feeling of "being in touch" was short-lived. Once they returned to the Zone, the feeling that they were living in a timeless society renewed itself.

Take fashion, for instance. There was no high fashion on the Zone, of course—no visits by Trigère or Galanos to the local specialty store. Even the fashion magazines arrived months late. Fall, winter, and spring arrived not at all. Without designers, stores, publicity, or seasonal changes, a community loses track of what's "in" and what's "out."

"Every blessed day the same; / Change is nothing but a name / In the Paradise of Fools," complained the local poet James Stanley Gilbert.

That, however, was poetic license. Actually, styles did change on the Zone. By the time we got there, women had long since stopped wearing the ankle-length, mildew-scented dresses that were fashionable in Gilbert's day, and the men had finally stopped wearing the white suits that had been popular on the Zone for half a century. They went "out" in the early sixties, just as air-conditioning came "in," making those suits reasonable things to wear, at least indoors. Nevertheless, they were replaced by the cooler, more informal *guayabera*, a pleated shirt worn outside of the trousers.

So fashion wasn't completely absent, but the utilitarian Zone certainly lacked chic. In 1957, the commissary managers sold a big shipment of dresses by reserving one day for the 14's, one day for the 12's, and so on—more efficient that way. Women were always "seeing themselves," since they all shopped at the same stores. After one Christmas, it was disquieting to know that every other woman was walking around in jungle-print underwear.

Styles on the Zone used to lag far behind those in the States— indeed, the new styles never quite emerged as a "new look" on the Zone. There was instead a gradual shift toward some modified form of what was new. In the seventies, when air transportation became common and Zonians made more trips to the States, they began to catch up, but even then it was hard to be *au courant* on the Zone. "Place-bound and time-bound in the evening rain," women were still vowing that this year they were somehow going to "get an outfit together." On the Zone, it was easy for a woman to suspect that she was letting herself go, like someone in an institution.

However, Bellamy would have approved of the Zone's lack of chic. He loathed fashion. Utopians always do, because it is socially divisive. Also in a perfect—that is to say, changeless—society, fashion, with its message that there is always a surprising new way of doing things, carries a potentially disruptive political implication. In a real utopia, no one is ever surprised, which is a good thing only if you expect all your surprises to be unpleasant. Utopias are designed by pessimists, and time is never on their side.

A GREAT PLACE TO RAISE KIDS

It was the Zone's atmosphere of suburban security that particularly oppressed Jan Morris, who wrote in *Rolling Stone* in 1976 that going from Panama into the Zone was like stepping out of reality into pretense. "Suddenly across a city street or at the end of an avenue, the Latin jumble of life evaporates, the rickety dark tenements disappear, the rubbish-strewn gutters give way to almost obsessively tended lawns and everything is plumper, richer, duller . . ."[14]

This is sentimentality. Panama City also has its "zones"—La Cresta, Golf Heights, Paitilla—where life is plumper, richer, duller, and *nicer* than it is in those rickety, dark tenements that writers of romance love to *visit*.

However, Panama's "zones" are too expensive for ordinary working people. They differ in that respect from the Canal Zone, which was a workers' paradise. Its orderliness, which visitors looking for action found dull, gave the Canal workers a degree of security similar to that enjoyed by the rich in Panama and the United States, and enabled them—again like the rich—to shape their own lives, within limits. There were, of course, limits. The workers paid a price for living in paradise.

"What was the best thing about the Zone?" Everyone said the same thing: "It was a great place to raise kids." The kids agreed. During the mango season, they fought mango wars, turning their battlefields to mango muck. During the rainy season, they played mud football or held skimboard contests on the sloshy grass. Secretly, they slid in the drainage ditches, which ranged in depth from a few inches to twelve feet. Parents did not approve of ditch games, especially during the rainy season. Occasionally, a child would be hurt in a ditch. Once in a great while one would be swept away and drowned. ("*Et in Arcadia Ego.*")

During the dry season, children slid down grassy hills in cardboard boxes—or on what was left of the box after the first trip. They used palm fronds as play horses. They squirted each other with water from the pods of African tulip trees and burned each other with "burnie beans" that looked like eyes. ("You rub them on the sidewalk, and they get real hot.") They watched as workmen draped a three-story wooden duplex under a canvas tent, preparing to fumigate for termites, or they fished from the bank of the Canal, thinking "long, long thoughts" as they took in the "beauty and mystery of the ships / And the magic of the sea."

Every neighborhood gang had its hill: Clay Hill, Chalk Rock Hill, Dinky Hill, Suicide Hill, and so on. In Diablo, some children played in "the Swamp" and "the Garden of Eden." ("Really, it was a lady's back yard with a birdbath.") Hummingbirds and honey-creepers flitted there amid the hibiscus. Beside "the Garden" was "the Path"—a tunnel between two rows of overarching bougainvillea.

At 6:15 P.M. the street lamps went on, and the children went inside for dinner. When they came back out, they played Ring-a-levio, except those who lived in Curundu. Curundu kids were ditch kids: "There's a jungle all around there, so to get to your buddy's house, you ran the ditches, kind of looping up one side and down, then jumping across and going up the other side. You could get a lot of momentum going."

When the mosquito truck came by, kids ran, yelling, to hide in the plume of white insecticide trailing behind it. After that, some of them went inside. The rest gathered to tell scary stories of *Tuli Vieja*, searching for her lost child, or of the donkeys from construction days that were supposed to be buried under that big pile of rocks back in the jungle, or of *Sal Si Puedes* ("Get out if you can"), a street of shops in Panama City where children were supposed to disappear—and diners in nearby restaurants to gag, now and then, on a toe or thumb in their won-ton soup!

We asked newly arrived students what they missed most about the States: "Good TV and Big Macs." And they complained that the Zone was "bo-ring." We could understand what they meant. A woman who grew up there told us of the long afternoons when she and her girl friends, for *something* to do, would watch the tarantulas under her house through the cracks in her bedroom floor. And certainly television and fast food were not the Zone's strongest points. The army ran the Zone's television station. Its ads touted the military life, United States Savings Bonds, and safety. Safety was big. One of the army's young announcers repeatedly warned us that holes in the floor could be dangerous!

Even after the army station was able to transmit some news and sports events live via satellite, its programs were still chiefly of historical interest. Johnny Carson, for instance, was still telling jokes about LBJ on our screen, long after the newspapers said Nixon had resigned; Bob Cummings, Dick Powell, and Peter Lawford were smoothing their beveled haircuts and chuckling at "the girls," while women in the States were campaigning for the ERA; and "Gunsmoke" kept coming around with planetary regularity.

As for Big Macs, the closest thing to that gustatory delight on the Zone was a lumpy burger sold by the concession known as the Drive-Inn.

However, the Zone's limitations were the other side of its advantages. When we asked the Zone kids what they missed most about the Zone when they were in the States, they told us about certain smells, the sound of rain, the feel of dry-season *brisas*, and of times spent at favorite places like the Causeway. On the Zone, a child woke each day to a "fruitful monotony not boredom / to be explored . . ."[15]

Everywhere a child went—the pools, the libraries, the stables, the small boat ramps, the company zoo, which was located in the company's 300-acre botanical garden—there were adults around who knew him or knew of him, and who, as a result, were inclined to look after him. We liked that. Older children sometimes found this oppressive, but it gave them a chance to know a lot of adults who were not relatives. We liked that, too.

Adults and children worked together to stage plays and parades, to organize the annual *cayuco* race through the Canal, to win baseball games, and to burn Christmas trees. In some ways, Christmas was a bigger holiday on the Zone than it is in the States. Men put a giant Christmas card on the center wall of the upper level at Gatún. It offered season's greetings in seven languages. Plywood sleighs and reindeer were displayed where passing mariners could see them. Every control tower was decorated, as were the company stores and buses. Lights were strung around houses. Some neighborhoods saw themselves in an unofficial decorating contest, but no place out-Christmased Santa Claus Lane—the folk name for a neighborhood where for years one of the residents played Santa on Christmas Day. In 1977, a teenager recalled her first Christmas in that neighborhood. She was four.

I didn't know what it was all about until I saw this big, red sleigh in Mr. Townsend's garage. All I could see then was a red cap and a snow white beard. When it was my turn, I was handed up to this big, fat man. I can remember David got a set of cowboy guns, and I got a square box containing a white tea set decorated with little red flowers. That was the last year they did that.

A much bigger Christmas project was organized about 1946 on the Atlantic side by Roland Lees and Desmond Doig. They got both Panamanians and Zonians involved, and for eight or nine years provided gifts of toys, food, and clothing to thousands of children and elderly adults in Colón. Sometimes their Santa arrived by airplane, then climbed aboard a float bearing a sleigh and reindeer for the trip through town.[16]

Every year, the company brought down a shipment of evergreens, and each house and classroom had its tree. After the presents were unwrapped, the real fun began. Children went from door to door collecting the trees. For the next week, the Zone was alive with spies and alarms as rival gangs tried to raid each other's caches. On January third or fourth, each gang took its trees to its special place. "We went to Farfan," one ex-tree scavenger told us, "for a bonfire at low tide."

There would be 50 to 100 kids there, maybe their parents. If you were a brother or sister you could come, but if you were anyone else, you had to contribute. We did this almost every Christmas. Sometimes just my family would collect 30 or 40 trees and go out and burn them ourselves.[17]

But even more than burning Christmas trees, the thing that brought adults and children together on the Zone was baseball. In the early days, division chiefs hired some men more for their skill on the diamond than for their skill on the job. The first play-off was in 1906 at the Panama Athletic Park. It featured the Has Beens versus the Never Wases, and the spectacle they made of themselves raised $1,200 for the orphans of Panama.[18] In 1916, the Twilight League was organized—so called because fans and players had to rush from work to the playing fields to get in a game before dark. In the 1930s, the big games were held at "Razzberry Park." After the war, the Twilight

League was revived, but by that time the company could afford lights, so it was really night baseball. Baseball was even available at the penitentiary. The prisoners' team was The Rebels.

The historian Gunther Barth has suggested that organized baseball, "the first urban spectator sport," helped urbanize the immigrants to the cities of nineteenth-century America. It did this, he says, by introducing them to the importance of rules within a free society, while at the same time letting them know that within that framework of rules exhilarating things could happen.[19]

We suspect that baseball was equally important to the American "immigrants" to the more bucolic Zone, but for a different reason. They, too, had to get used to "playing the game" within a framework of rules that restricted their behavior in new ways. However, baseball started out as a folk game and has never been completely sanitized by the social engineers of organized sports. Baseball is the only game where fans not only cheer and boo but "razz" and "chatter." It is the only game where protesting the ump's decision is part of the show— the only game where, traditionally, both players and fans let "them" know they need glasses! The importance of occasionally doing that to Canal Zone officials may have been baseball's most important covert lesson on the semitotalitarian Zone.

Because everyone looked out for children on the Zone, the younger ones could be allowed a degree of independence that would have been imprudent elsewhere. As they grew older, they became extraordinarily sophisticated in some ways. Most of them understood some Spanish. Some spoke it fluently. Many of them had traveled in Central and South America. Some had trekked through the jungle. Others had sailed far and wide on tuna boats. All of them took foreign faces and customs as matters of course. A good many of them, boys and girls alike, were handy with tools.

They were working/middle-class kids who grew up with advantages usually available only to children of the upper-middle class or the rich. In the States, it is standard procedure for people on the way up to invest in an impressive house. Their mortgage payments reduce their discretionary income for many years. On the Zone, people lived in rotten (literally rotten) housing, yet had more money to spend. And, of course, on the Isthmus their money went farther. They hired maids. If they gave a big party, they hired bartenders. They owned boats, belonged to yacht clubs, and went deep-sea fishing. Their children kept exotic pets—sloths, deer, or parrots. Lots of the Zone's teenage girls owned horses.

And, until the late sixties, all of the children on the Zone took Caribbean cruises every two years, when the company sent their parents on home leave. They traveled on the Panama Line, which consisted of three company ships: the *Ancon,* the *Cristobal,* and the *Panama,* which were decorated by the industrial designer Raymond Loewy, who also designed the Cold Spot refrigerator and the Avanti Studebaker, among other things. Until 1961, the ships stopped at Haiti on the way to New York, the company's home port for fifty-seven years. Children were taught the address of the Panama Line—24 State Street—and told to go there if they got lost. In 1961 the company's home port was changed to New Orleans. When the company began sending its workers back and forth on charter flights in the late sixties, the Miami airport became as familiar to Zone kids as their living rooms.

Indeed, children on the Zone had some opportunities not equally available to the segregated children of the rich—for instance, the opportunity to know people of different races, nationalities, occupations, and social positions.

Charlie Heim remembers growing up on the Zone in the twenties. He and his pals would hitch rides on the ferry to Fort Sherman. "We kids knew all the crew. . . . On Saturday, we would catch a ride . . . and eat with the soldiers in their mess halls. . . . The men always made us feel welcome and what a time we had." Charlie also hung around with the coachies who lined up their *carrometas* at the gate of the Washington Hotel in Colón, often eating rice and beans with them at the stables.[20]

Children got to know the street people: the Spanish knife-sharpeners, who rode around on bicycles and announced themselves with a high melodious whistle; the men selling fish; and the fruit vendors, like Banana Joe, who roamed the streets of Balboa in the early fifties. "Banan'!" he would call. "Get your ripe plantain!" He told the kids that when his box was empty, he put a child in it and carried him away. There were also a few harmless street crazies, like the Panamanian who came to Balboa from time to time in the seventies dressed in a Nazi costume—high boots, jodhpurs, monocle, armband, cigarette in a long holder—the whole bit. As he marched up and down the Prado, kids lined up behind him and imitated his strut. Once in a while, he would whirl, raising his swagger stick, and they would scramble, giggling and screaming.

In their teens, Canal Zone kids explored Panama. Girls bought little wicker suitcases from the Hindu shops, which they used as purses. They bought sandals and the velvet slippers that Panamanian women wear with the national costume, the *pollera*, from the cobbler at Avenida Central and J Street. Some boys and girls from the Zone went to parties at the Union Club or the Golf Club (Panamanian clubs).

They also interviewed celebrities for their high-school newspaper; entertainers and political figures were always passing through the Canal. At the Yacht Club—a glamorous name for the basement porch under the American Legion building—the Zone's apprentices and junior college students met the rich, the weird, and the adventurous, who for one reason or another were wandering the oceans in small boats.

A woman who came to the Zone from a little town in Alabama in the late forties told us that while the Zone schools were segregated at that time, just as schools were in the States, there was still a big difference between going to school on the Zone and going to school in Alabama. She was never in a classroom, she said, that was white, by Alabama standards: "We had Orientals and Europeans and exotic mixtures—exotic to me at that time, anyway. French and Persian, for instance, which I thought was fantastic. There were Jews and Arabians and lots of Panamanians—very dark, some of them."

Until some time in the late fifties, most Zonians had the general notion that the Zone—with the exception of its primitive housing—

had pretty much the best of everything: the best mechanics, pilots, engineers, cops, teachers, swimmers—everything. Doctors came from all over the world to study tropical medicine at Gorgas Hospital. Dr. Samuel Darling identified histoplasmosis there.

The Zone police handled jobs that would have been reserved for FBI or Treasury agents in the States. On many occasions, they had to conduct an investigation and make an arrest during the eight hours a ship was transiting the Canal, and a case might well involve a half-dozen different nationalities. No other law enforcement agency in the world dealt with so many nationalities on a daily basis, and none had a more unblemished record.

The Zone's junior college was special, too. In 1933, the year it was established, the children of the Canal workers studied under a faculty of seven, composed of graduates from Columbia, Harvard, Yale, Carnegie Tech, and Stanford.[21] Three of them were Ph.D. candidates, and in those days Ph.D.'s weren't a dime a dozen. One of them was an even rarer specimen—a woman Ph.D. candidate. Dr. Dorothy Moody grew up in a little house on the prairie, went east to school at Yale, then sailed south for adventure. The Zone attracted people like that.

But the Red, White, and Blue Troupe was the most visible and popular manifestation of the Zone's specialness.[22] It was a swimming troupe organized by Henry Grieser in 1919 to entertain the Allied soldiers going home through the Canal. Boys and girls dived off the tip-tops of dredges and did other stunts as the ships went by. The 1920s and 1930s were the heyday of the Red, White, and Blue Troupe. It performed at the opening of Madison Square Garden's indoor pool and went back to New York to put on a show when the pool was closed. It sent water polo and exhibition teams throughout Latin America and performed for dignitaries who came to the Zone. Members of the troupe won national swimming championships; some of them swam on United States Olympic teams. One of them, Alan Ford, broke Johnny Weissmuller's twenty-year world record in the one hundred-yard freestyle.

Children caught a sense of the Zone's specialness from adults on the Zone and confirmed it at the library. No community of comparable size had so many books written about it in so short a time as the Canal Zone. Many of the books were by Zonians themselves. Some were works of historical or scientific scholarship. Others were written for younger readers: *Panama Patty, The Pelican Tree, Christmas on the Isthmus,* to mention only a few.

Yet many parents who thought the Zone was a great place to raise kids urged their older children to "get away," as if it were a trap. Even young children were aware of the Zone's limitations. They would sometimes finish a quarrel with a dialogue that went something like this:

"Get out of my house."

"This isn't your house."

"Is so."

"Is not. It belongs to the government."

A young mother idly asked her four-year-old at Amador Beach, "Hey, who put the salt in the water?" and was sobered when the child replied, "Oh, the government, I guess."

The government did just about everything on the Zone, and children who grew up there were subject to anxiety attacks about how well they would perform in the States, where they would have "to do" for themselves. They were also haunted by a feeling that they were missing out. Much of what they were missing was, from our point of view, well worth missing, but it is one thing to reject the clamor of American popular culture and something else to miss out on it. Even at breakfast, Zone children were reminded of their remoteness. The ads on their cereal boxes invited them to send for super code rings and fancy cocoa mugs, but in the fine print was the refrain, "Good only in the continental United States." Teenagers, too, often felt insecure and provincial when they compared themselves to teenagers in the States who were casually familiar with the latest hits, brands, and catchwords.

Work experience was another thing the Zone kids missed out on. In the 1920s, Charlie Heim made a nickel every Saturday morning by sweeping the floors at Stilson's Hardware in Colón. During the

1940s, Ken Millard cleaned M-1's for G.I.'s at fifty cents each and made a small fortune. Some teenagers found jobs as lifeguards at the Zone's pools or as ushers at its movie theaters. A few Zone boys shipped out on tuna boats. The company created as many summer jobs as it could, but there were never enough to go around. Without work experience and without exposure to the variety of jobs that exist in an "irrational" society like that of the United States, Zone teenagers were often burdened by a lack of self-confidence and an ignorance of possibilities.

It is impossible to say whether the Canal Zone produced more or less destructive adolescent behavior than the United States or Panama, but it had its share of reckless teenage drivers, runaways, drug abusers, drunks, and teenage pregnancies.

It also had Corozal—a mental health hospital that would have fit right into the utopia that Bellamy described in *Looking Backward*. Parents who could not manage their rebellious adolescent could call a counselor at Corozal. If their child was admitted, he was placed on a "token economy." If he was good, he received privileges—a mattress, permission to use the telephone or to wear jeans instead of hospital garb, a weekend pass, and so on. If he was not good, he was negatively rewarded. His teachers were asked to complete a weekly report on his behavior at school. The theory was that a "scientifically" designed system of rewards and punishments would modify the child's anti-social behavior.

All this rested on a solid footing of progressive dogma—the idea that a disinterested professional elite could "engineer" good behavior. This corresponded perfectly with the Zone's progressive government, in which politics was replaced by administration and emotion by reason.

No adults were sent to Corozal to have their behavior modified. Adults who didn't fit into the Zone's paternalistic system left the Zone voluntarily or were "shipped out." But had those options been unavailable . . .

12

Class and Social Status on the Canal Zone

BRAINS, SNOBS, AND ROUGHNECKS

Some outside experts arrived on the Zone with the fixed idea that it was a colony. "Colony" brought to mind England, and "England," class distinctions. Paul Theroux told the readers of his *The Old Patagonian Express* that on the Zone, "There is a pecking order, as in all colonies; it is in miniature like the East India Company and even reflects the social organization of that colonial enterprise: the Zonian suffers a notoriously outdated lack of social mobility. He is known by his salary, his club, and the nature of his job. The Company mechanic does not rub shoulders with the Company administrators. . . ."[1]

To the extent that this was true, it is true of any place. It was less true of the Canal Zone than of most places. Everyone rubbed shoulders there. The Zone was not big enough for its administrators to have their own stores, churches, schools, dentists, and dancing teachers, as the rich do in Panama and the United States. Moreover, many Zone administrators were promoted from the rank and file, and were not a great deal richer for their elevation. Indeed, many pilots were richer than many administrators.

In 1978, Dr. Renata de Arboleda, the director of the Zone's mental health hospital, told a reporter, "If the director of a hospital anywhere else lived in the kind of house I do, well . . . they would think I was crazy! Here, you don't keep up with the Joneses. There is

117

no status. You can drive an old car, dress the way you want. You can do away with the outward sham."[2]

That gives a more accurate general impression of life on the Zone than Theroux's tendentious analogy does, but the Zone was not a classless society.

Sham, it is true, was almost nonexistent, but that was because status was so well-defined. There is not much scope for sham in a community where what counts is rank, and everybody's rank is known. Seniority, family, your golf game, even your personality, might have added to your status on the Zone—but not much. On the Zone there was very little of that creative interaction of pretense, potential, and reality that enlivens social relationships in the United States.

On the other hand, while the Zone was a status-conscious society, its status differences were relatively slight. The Zone was far more equalitarian than Panama or the United States—or the Soviet Union or East Germany, for that matter. (Of course, the Zone was a racist community for many years, and the West Indians were an underclass. But American-style racism and classism are best understood separately. We discuss the Zone's racism in Chapter 14.)

During the construction era, some of the Zone's administrators lived on "Brain Hill" in Culebra. By the time we arrived, many of them were living in Ancon, on what was sometimes called "Snob Hill." That shows an important change in perception but should not be taken to suggest a growing social gulf. In fact, the opposite was true. As the years went by, manners on the Zone grew more informal; college degrees, more common; and wage differentials, narrower. In 1905, John Stevens was hired as chief engineer for $30,000 a year, about $100,000 a year less than he figured he could earn in private business in the States. The lowest-paid West Indian laborers made ten cents an hour—approximately twenty-five dollars a month.[3] So, Stevens made about a hundred times as much as the lowest paid worker.

In 1970, the lowest-paid full-time Canal worker made $3,492 a year. The governor made almost exactly ten times as much—$34,214. By contrast, in the supposedly classless societies of East Germany and the Soviet Union, the differences between maximum salary and minimum wage in the late seventies were 50:1 and 30:1, respectively.[4] Moreover, those figures do not reflect the even greater non-income privileges of the Marxist elite. It has access to special stores, schools, medical services, and travel, which magnify its distance from the proletariat.

The Zone's elite had no comparable privileges, except preferential housing. They went to the same hospital and shopped at the same stores everyone else did. Their children went to the same schools as the children of the Canal workers. It was that way on the Zone from the beginning, even though there was a far greater social distance between classes in 1904 than there was later. Rose van Hardeveld remembered how she enjoyed "seeing tall, stately Mrs. Goethals and small, dainty Mrs. Gaillard going by in the official Brain Wagon or on the observation platform of a train. I knew that if we had an almost inedible, tough roast for Sunday dinner, so did they, for they bought from the same shipment we did; and if my husband got wet and muddy and cross, very likely theirs did, too; and it pleased me to think that the wives of those high-salaried men found their duties right by the side of their husbands, just as we all did."[5]

Of course, all the Zone's governors had chauffeurs and entertainment budgets, but they had some pretty onerous entertaining to do. Nobody begrudged them money for that.

However, when the American community on the Zone was abolished in 1979, a wide range of economic inequalities appeared in the Canal Area, as the former Zone is now called. The cost of living for the Panamanian Zonians, mainly West Indians, went up 50 percent overnight, with further increases in the offing. New hires came in under new rules. The Zone's American teachers were all transferred to the Department of Defense, and their wages were re-scheduled so that they would gradually come into line with the much lower wages that DOD sees fit to pay its other teachers. The Canal pilots, on the other hand, "put it to" the new Canal Commission. They demanded and got a whopping, unbudgeted increase. In 1977, a top pilot was making $42,000 a year. In 1980, after the Canal community disappeared, a top pilot made well over $100,000 a year.

Naturally, a person's rank and salary were linked to his or her status on the Zone, as they are elsewhere. Nevertheless, "society" was a pretty nebulous concept. In 1921, A. Hyatt Verrill noted that on the Zone all the social "sets" he examined, including the governor's, contained people who in the States would be as socially separate as antipodes: "A mechanic, a boiler maker, a carpenter or any other working man is greatly restricted in his opportunities for social life in the United States, for even in our so-called democracy, class distinctions are pretty sharply drawn. But not so in the Canal Zone, or at least not so obviously or strictly."[6]

The governor didn't socialize with muledrivers, but his children might pal around with a muledriver's children if they were in the same class at school. When Elly was in fifth grade, she went to a birthday party for the governor's son and came home all excited. Yes, she'd had a good time, but her news was, "Momma, they have lids on their toilet seats!" Such was the quality of status symbols on the Zone.

Houses were the primary outward manifestation of status on the Zone. They were assigned on the basis of seniority or privilege, and the endless quest for better housing divided the Zonians into Newcomers, Old-timers, and Others. Newcomers did not get much house. When we arrived in 1963, housing on the Zone was better and more plentiful than ever before, but we spent fourteen months in a one-bedroom apartment. Our children slept in the living room.

Each week, people applied for the houses and apartments that were "up." But some old-timers, to the dismay of the newcomers, amused themselves by moving from house to house, "busily seeking with continual change" the perfect residence. "Y'know that three bedroom was up last week?" sputtered our neighbor, a newcomer like us. "The people-who-got-its service date was 1931! That's before I was born!"

When the pilots made up a cock-and-bull story about deserving a five-year head start in the competition for housing, people were furious and said so at Civic Council meetings.

Then there were the Others—people whose rank or profession entitled them to preferential housing. Not all the houses set aside for them were superior to the houses that were available to old-timers in the rank and file, but they were set aside, an important distinction.

To facilitate maintenance and social harmony, the company tried to keep the variety of Zone housing to a minimum, and for a while it succeeded. In the 1930s, when Amy McCormack went to the commissary, she left her daughter's red trike in front of her house so that when she came back, she could tell where she lived. However, there were differences even in houses built at the same time and according to the same plan. Often, the slighter those differences were, the more difference they made to people—a point the planners of utopias ought to bear in mind.

However, what the Zonians wanted was not uniformity. It was more space—the particular kind of space that suited their particular needs. So they complained until the company agreed to let them make improvements, and as the years passed, the Zone's houses became less and less uniform. Zonians added rooms, patios, stairways, carports, even, in one case, a swimming pool.

As for Theroux's idea that a Zonian was known by his club! In the first place, Zonians belonged to *clubs*, not to *a club*. A man might belong to the Gamboa Golf Club, the Legion, and the Elks, for instance, all of which had bars. Mechanics and administrators not only rubbed shoulders, they bent elbows side by side. Chances are, a Zonian was also a member of a hobby club such as the Gem and Mineral Society or the Diablo Camera Club, and of a church, and of a union or a professional organization. All such groups drew members from a variety of levels within the company. Before the Second World War, which dampened enthusiasm for parties, a Zonian probably belonged to one of the numerous dance clubs, too. Dancing and baseball held the Zone together in those days.

The voluntary associations on the Zone were no different from those in the States. They were more numerous, however, in proportion to the population. Two hundred nonprofit community organizations were listed in the 1979 Canal Zone phone book, including sixty-three church groups, thirty-six fraternal orders, and forty-seven recreational clubs: the Boy Scouts, the Girl Scouts, the Jewish Welfare Board, the VFW, the Legion, the Elks, Masons, Knights of Columbus, and so on.[7] There were still others that did not aspire to the dignity of a line in the phone book: the Diablo Spinning Club, the Sweet Adelines, the Police Wives, the San Juan Hunt Club, and the Fat Fighters, for example.

Voluntary associations were more numerous on the Zone than they are in the States because they were more important to the community. Alexis de Tocqueville, the French aristocrat who toured the United States in 1831 to study its new and curious form of government— democracy—pointed out that "In ages of equality, every man naturally stands alone; he has no hereditary friends whose cooperation he may demand; no class upon whose sympathy he may rely: he is easily got rid of, and he is trampled on with impunity."[8]

He went on to say that Americans counter this development by banding together in voluntary, unofficial organizations. And he concluded that if equality is not to lead to tyranny, "the art of associating together must grow and improve in the same ratio in which the equality of conditions is increased."

On the Zone, where authority was more centralized than it is in the States, and where there was far more equality of condition, the need for voluntary associations was correspondingly greater.

The overlapping but restrictive brotherhoods and sisterhoods of the Zone mediated in a variety of ways between the individual and the company/government, humanizing what was essentially an impersonal, rule-bound welfare state. They promoted a sense of fellowship—something a centralized welfare state threatens to extinguish. A benevolent central government can do many things for its citizens, but, as Tocqueville remarked, "Feelings and opinions are recruited, the heart is enlarged, and the human mind is developed, only by the reciprocal influence of men upon each other."[9]

Of course, the associations looked out for their own. In the 1930s, a government consultant visiting the Zone was impressed by the way the Canal Zone Women's League went about "bearding officials in their dens."[10] But usually the associations tried to resolve things without a confrontation. A religious leader would have a talk with a company official about one of the faithful, or a couple of boys from the lodge would put in a word for a brother who was in a jam.

Moreover, in a community where democratic politicking was forbidden, the voluntary associations kept alive a familiarity with democratic procedures and political skills. The associations sponsored community projects. The company didn't do *everything*. And with their different buildings, social events, parades, and moneymaking projects, the associations added some color and variety to the utilitarian drone of the Zone.

Still another thing they did was to serve as information centers, an especially important function on the Zone, where there was no free press. And those associations that were affiliated with national or international bodies connected the Zone to the larger world and thereby diminished its isolation and provinciality.

The voluntary associations did a great deal to make the Zone's peculiar system work, mainly by bringing Zonians face to face with the people their decisions or workmanship affected. That kind of intimacy could be maddening, but it had the incalculable advantage of promoting caution, diplomacy, and cooperation.

A man who, though active in civic affairs, was never enchanted by the Zone told us,

> The best thing about this place was that you could get things done— things for the community—that would be impossible anywhere else. You'd talk to somebody in Transportation or Electrical and if they didn't know you, they knew somebody who did, and if there was some snag, you could always find somebody who could appeal to a fellow Elk or to somebody from their church, and—it'd get done.

In a sense, just living on the Zone made us all members of the same club. We shared the same hassles with Housing, Transportation, and the commissary. We had the same problems with the climate. And all of us were a long way from home. Chances are that no matter where a Zonian retired, he or she joined the Panama Canal Society of Florida, which has members in fifty states, the District of Columbia, and fourteen foreign countries—an association formed "to preserve American ideals and Canal Zone friendships."

Nevertheless, while united in many ways, Zonians were divided into distinct subsets. There were three only semicompatible American institutions on the Isthmus: the military, the embassy, and the company. The soldiers and Canal workers lived on the Zone. The diplomats lived in Panama, but the soldiers and diplomats traditionally regard the world outside the United States as their turf; consequently, they both regarded the Canal worker as an interloper, although he was the permanent resident of this particular piece of foreign turf, not the officers or the gentlemen.

Reflecting on the antagonism between the diplomats and the workers, a Zone administrator emphasized to us that the company had a pattern of promotion that sent blue-collar people to the top: "The embassy thought this showed the Zone was ingrown. Also, they saw people—blue collars—whose salaries, according to their view, were way out of line. They thought they [the workers] were promoted to positions of responsibility that they didn't have the background for in terms of education."

However, except when using the company commissaries, the embassy people generally kept their distance from the Zone. The Zonians had a much closer relationship with the military. On one level, that relationship was cooperative and affable. Canal workers and military personnel hunted and fished together and belonged to the same clubs. But they also came into conflict in a number of ways.

Some of that conflict was institutional. The military resented the fact that the Zone police, not the MPs, had jurisdiction on the Zone. Furthermore, like the diplomats at the embassy, some officers were irked by the company's involvement in Panamanian affairs, especially when the company's interests did not correspond to the military's.

The Zone's governor had a foot in both camps. He was at the head of a civilian agency, not an army corps, but he was also a military man. And while some governors were more popular than others, all of them were inclined to appoint fellow officers as bureau chiefs. In 1976, four of the seven bureau chiefs were active duty or retired military men. Some Zonians resented that.

Also the parents of daughters were naturally suspicious of single men in barracks who were only temporary members of the community—and Zone boys did not relish competition from more experienced and solvent men. Hence, even during the Second World War, when the Zone's patriotism was especially fervent, a Pan Canal girl who dated a military man—even an officer—was known as "rap bait," and was not invited out by the local boys.

The commissaries were another source of contention. The military commissaries and PX's were off-limits to the civilian Canal workers, but the military were free to shop at company stores. On holidays, when the military commissaries ran out of many items, as they invariably did, military wives would flock to the company stores. But supplies were limited there, too, and Pan Canal women would ask each other resentfully, "Why don't they shop at their own stores?"

One Zone schoolteacher grew angry all over again as she told us about a Parents' Night at her school when a local general and his wife visited her class. "He kept calling me by my first name, and his wife went on and on about how hard it was to work with a domestic staff that didn't have its *heart* in its work. Was I supposed to feel sorry for her? I think I was supposed to be impressed and flattered—I think."

A. Hyatt Verrill noticed the same attitudes back in 1921. He said the military set on the Zone was "as overbearing, as supercilious" as it was elsewhere "and with as little reason."[11]

The company itself was divided into bureaucrats and workers and, perhaps more importantly, into Atlantic Siders and Pacific Siders. It rained more on the Atlantic side. Cristóbal, the Canal town there, was small and relatively isolated. Its Panamanian sister town of Colón didn't offer much in the way of family entertainment. All the good Panamanian restaurants and theaters were in Panama City, on the Pacific side. When Margot Fonteyn performed, it was in Panama's Javier Gymnasium, on the Pacific side. Moreover, the Atlantic Siders were convinced that their fellow Americans on the Pacific side got first choice of all Canal Company equipment and supplies. As a result, Atlantic Siders developed an intense community and union loyalty. They expressed themselves forcefully on civic issues, as if afraid of not being heard.

Another major social division on the Zone had to do with the nationality of a man's wife. As soon as the Canal mechanics arrived on the Isthmus, they began marrying Panamanians. One of the earliest Zone poems is about "Spickety Bill,"[12] the steam-shovel man, who met Juancita on the side of a hill "and the love that they knew never died." A Panamanian complained to an American sociologist that "from a political point of view, intermarriage is one of the surest ways the U.S. has for conquering Panama."[13]

Some Americans married white, upper-class Panamanian women who spoke fluent English. Others married darker women who spoke little or no English. Invited to dinner by one newly married couple, we discovered they couldn't understand each other! But perhaps it helps if a newly married couple starts out *knowing* that they don't understand each other. Two sociologists who studied international marriages on the Zone in the early fifties concluded that American men and Panamanian women were often very happy together.[14]

Those sociologists, John and Mavis Biesanz, added that on the Zone a man who married a Panamanian might find that advancement in his job or a higher status in his lodge was blocked by his marriage.[15] But clearly this was not always the case, for many men with Panamanian wives or mothers rose to high positions in the company, as in some cases their sons or sons-in-law did after them. Moreover, American-Panamanian families tended to stay on the Isthmus, and in any organization the old-timers form a separate and influential fraternity.

However, especially during the first half of this century, international marriages called into question what it meant to be an American. No one was quite sure. Consequently, many international families were neither completely accepted nor rejected. On the Pacific side, some of them lived in semisegregation on "Squaw Hill" or in the townsite of Curundu—known before 1943 as "Skunk Hollow" or "Jungle Glen."

"Oh, Curundu," people would say, "where you can't tell the wives from the maids."

"But *we* could, of course," an ex-resident assured us sardonically.

We are told that in the 1950s, the husbands of Panamanians tended to join the VFW, leaving the Legion to the vets with American wives. However, that was not true while we were there.

Until the late 1960s, the darkest wives were often left on the Isthmus when their husbands went on home leave. This suggests that even during the first half of the century, the Zone's tolerance of racial and cultural ambiguity, although very far from perfect, was higher than that found in many parts of the United States.

If the children of these international marriages were dark or spoke English poorly, they were sometimes taunted in school. However, they were not automatically or universally rejected. Looks, personality, brains, and athletic ability all influenced how an individual was treated. "We always had the best basketball players," bragged an ex-resident of Squaw Hill. And the Curundu kids stuck together, no matter what. Their fathers were civilians who worked for the army, and the Curundu kids defined themselves in contrast to the Canal kids, whose fathers worked for the company.

Of course, racism influenced the attitudes of Americans toward Panamanian-American families, but so did class differences. Some American men married their maids—sometimes with perfectly good motives, but other times merely to appease the company, which would not tolerate a situation in which a single man's live-in maid was bearing his illegitimate children. Such men rarely wanted their wives to learn English or to become Americanized.

Even under the best conditions, a lower-class Latin woman married to an American was likely to remain an outsider on the Zone. Her skin might be white and her neighbors friendly, but she faced an intimidating cultural and educational gulf, which she had no compelling reason to cross, since her access to Panama was so easy.

In 1969, the population of the American towns on the Zone was 10,573. Of this number, 7,808 were born in the United States, its territories, or Puerto Rico, and 2,765 were foreign born—26.1 percent. Virtually every Latin and European nation was represented, as well as countries in Asia and the Pacific. Of course, the contingent from Panama was the largest—1,832.[16]

COURTIERS AND EQUALITARIANS

A Zone administrator once remarked that the Zone "had some of the elements of a military post, but its general character was more diversified and democratic because of the presence of many civilians. The disturbing rule of precedence held slight and uncertain sway, seldom ruffling the calm surface of good-fellowship which close association in a common and inspiring cause naturally engendered."[17]

However, a hierarchical society is bound to produce courtiers, and the hierarchical society on the Zone was no exception. Its courtiers doted on rules of precedence—invented them if they didn't exist— and liked to exaggerate the top officials' awful powers of retribution. However, a hierarchical society is fundamentally un-American. Free and equal is the American ideal, and the hierarchical system on the Zone exacerbated equalitarian sensitivities. As a result, there were always some Zonians quite willing to ruffle the calm of good fellowship when they felt "crowded" by the social pretensions of their "betters" —the man, for instance, who defiantly brought a Panamanian bar girl to the genteel Sunday brunch at the Tivoli after a night on the town. Men like that were one reason the rule of precedence was uncertain.

Actually, while the saponaceous courtier and surly equalitarian were identifiable types, most Zonians did not appear to fall into either category. The courtiers and equalitarians were the visible manifestations of psychological divisions that affected nearly everyone. On the Zone as in the United States, a man who wanted to be promoted behaved to some extent like a courtier while at work, but in the States, a man goes home to a larger and different world. Not so on the Zone, where there was no line at all between company and community affairs.

Thus, eager courtiers would rope off seats for the panjandrums at community celebrations. Often the panjandrums would not show up or would grace the event with their presence for only a short time. The seats would remain empty, as if occupied by ghosts. The courtiers would also hold back the proles so that a chief could board a company ship first, or would assign a chief to the first-class compartment on a company charter flight—a petty thing, since everyone got first-class service on those flights, but irksome, nevertheless. By contrast, an equalitarian told us, "Yeah, they always told me to rope off seats. I always said, 'Sure,' and then never did. It didn't bother anybody."

The conflict between the courtiers and the equalitarians appeared early. In 1913, the Tivoli Club gave a dance for Helen Taft, the daughter of the president. Afterward, a letter appeared in an English-language Panamanian newspaper, congratulating the club for having the sense to "fix" her dance card in order to prevent any "roughnecks" from dancing with her.[18]

The writer explained that on the Isthmus, it was "a common sight to see the daughters of the highest officials and the ladies of Camp Otis and Camp Elliot dancing at the Tivoli with men of obscure lineage and position." The writer went on to comment that the club's "more common members" had a habit of rushing into the dining room in advance of the highest officials: "This lack of social coordination often results in the most distinguished persons not being able to get a seat at the tables."

A Zonian who was there said he had "known of nothing that aroused such deep resentment and keen displeasure" as that letter.

Of course, there were disputes in the States, too, about the dance card of the president's daughter, but they occurred among members of the same social class. In the States, no roughnecks were even on the same dance floor as the president's daughter. On the Zone, however, where people of different backgrounds mixed more intimately than in the States, the dispute about Helen Taft's dance card immediately declared itself a class conflict and brought up again the endlessly debated question of what it means to be an American.

There is something un-American about extending the privileges of rank earned in one context into other unrelated contexts. It smacks of aristocracy or the military, but it is bound to happen in a place like the

Canal Zone where society is a single, seamless whole. Solidarity begets aristocracy.

And aristocracy begets stagnation.

The aristocracy on the Zone was based on credentials, not class. But aristocracy is by nature reductionist; rank is all that counts, and it is permanent. Earls and dukes have their blood; bureaucrats, their tenure. And there is always an automatic preference for the conventional—the tried and true—over anything new that might upset the status quo.

THE SHOCK OF RECOGNITION

The kind of society that developed on the banks of the Panama Canal was prophesied with uncanny prescience by Alexis de Tocqueville. After studying the United States, he concluded that there was a natural tendency in a democracy toward ever-greater centralization and equality and a tendency for people to sacrifice their rights as citizens in return for tranquility. He did not see this as inevitable but believed that individual independence and local liberties would always be "the products of art" in a democratic nation and that centralization would be its "natural government."[19]

If the natural tendency of a democracy toward centralization were ever allowed to run its course in the United States, Tocqueville said that the result would be a species of oppression "unlike anything which ever before existed in the world." Words like "despotism" and "tyranny" were inappropriate, he said. There was no name for it.

It would be an oppression of a "regular, quiet, and gentle" kind, seldom forcing men to act, but constantly restraining them from acting. It would be a society with a network of small, complicated rules through which the most original minds and most energetic characters would be unable to rise above the crowd. The government would not drive men to resistance but would cross them at every turn. "Such a power does not destroy, but it prevents existence; it does not tyrannize, but it compresses, enervates, extinguishes, and stupifies a people, till each nation is reduced to be nothing better than a flock of timid and industrious animals, of which the government is the shepherd."[20]

The government's authority, Tocqueville prophesied, would be like that of a parent, except that its object would not be to prepare men for manhood but to keep them in perpetual childhood.

The Zonians resisted—sometimes deviously, sometimes sullenly, sometimes contentiously—being reduced to the level of timid and industrious animals, but anyone who ever lived on the Zone will experience a shock of recognition upon reading Tocqueville's words, for there the future he predicted came close—too close—to being realized.

PART TWO

THE PANAMA CANAL ZONE – CULTURAL VALUES AND CLASS CONFLICT

13

The United States: A Society
in Search of a New Direction

The Flag Riots of 1964 were the beginning of the end for the Zone,
but it lingered for fifteen fairly placid years—placid, at least, in comparison to those years in the States, where raggedy, long-haired
evangelists were preaching love and marijuana; the Reverend Martin
Luther King and others were preaching civil rights; and still other
preachers and preacher-types were urging Americans to oppose the
war in Vietnam.

During the sixties, the progressive-liberal consensus broke down,
and Americans once again began to reevaluate their national goals, to
reinterpret their history, and to seek a new national direction. The
debate over the Panama Canal needs to be understood as an episode
in that larger, less-well-defined controversy about where America is
going and where it has been.

In the early 1960s, the liberal elite was jolted by a rebellion of its
juniors, the liberal cadets. True to form, the liberals asked the rebels
—the radical-purists—to avoid emotionalism and discuss the issues
rationally. The radical-purists responded with hoots and jeers, and
the flustered liberals declared that the young people didn't make sense.

Making sense is what being a liberal is all about. Liberals are
problem solvers—poor negotiators because what they see as problems
other people see as contests, but great organizers. Their favorite epi-
thets are "amateur" and "redneck."[1]

The young radical-purists rejected the liberals' intellectual values.
Complexity, they said, is a liberal excuse for half-measures. They

135

exalted the heart over the head. They did not, however, reject the achievements of the old liberals, nor all of their goals.

So far, every American crisis of faith, while producing new national goals, has also reaffirmed some goals from the past. One goal the radical-purists reaffirmed was the liberals' commitment to equality. However, the radical-purists realized that equality required more than the reorganization of society. It required a change of heart. The liberals had reorganized the army in 1948 to get rid of its segregated units. In 1954, they got legal permission to reorganize the schools for the same purpose. But the liberals' plans did not cause the scales to fall from the eyes of America's racists. To make that happen, the cause of racial equality had to be taken to the people, and it was—by the evangelical radical-purists of the sixties. Some of them took up the cause of sexual equality, too, and in an amazingly short time, they produced a new national consensus on the desirability of racial and sexual equality— pockets of bigotry and the failure of the ERA notwithstanding.

The purists and the liberals also agree about the desirability of class equality, but that is a more delicate matter, for both purists and liberals consider themselves elites.

Up to a point, however, both groups have worked to diminish class barriers. The liberal organization men, for their part, made a virtue of necessity. Both world wars required compulsory military service. The liberals welcomed that. Every platoon would have its Irishman, Italian, Harvard, Okie, and Jew, who would all get to know each other and become buddies.

In the 1890s, Bellamy had actually called the army "a school of democratic ideas."[2] To him, democracy wasn't a process but an attitude of comradeship. Thus, he saw no contradiction in supposing that his utopia of absolute equality could be run by "the most perfect aristocracy."[3] Neither did any of the other turn-of-the-century progressives or the liberals who succeeded them, for this perfect aristocracy would not be an artificial aristocracy based on wealth or royal whim but a natural aristocracy of "the best and the brightest."

It was up to the schools to identify the new aristocrats. The schools were central to the progressive-liberal program of national reform.

Education was their Great Panacea, so it is not surprising that when the progressive-liberal consensus came apart, the schools were centers of antiliberal agitation. Radical-purist students refused to be programmed. "Do your own thing" was their slogan.[4]

In order to do their own things, the apprentice experts in "tracked" classrooms and on "career tracks" jumped the tracks and joined "the amateur ranks of the human beings."[5] They abandoned the conventions of the middle class. They dressed like migrant workers, but they continued to think of themselves as an elite—an elite, moreover, that was above working for a living. As a result, they were ostracized by ordinary Americans who saw that by refusing to compete, the radical-purists were declaring themselves a superior class.

John Taylor notes that competition has been a unifying force in America. It is through the struggle for status that we demonstrate our allegiance to the equalitarian ideal: "In striving to outstrip your neighbor, you implicitly acknowledge him to be your equal . . . since no ranking member of a hierarchy willingly measures himself against his inferiors."[6]

"Intolerance of the noncompetitive," says Taylor, "is the hallmark of egalitarianism." And intolerance of the unauthorized is the hallmark of an aristocracy. The aristocratic shibboleths of the radical-purists had to do with age, music, hair, drugs, the war, and sex; those of the progressive-liberal compromisers, with culture, credentials, merit systems, and immunity—through tenure, Civil Service regulations, and "peer review"—from dismissal.[7]

The liberals told themselves that they were increasing equality of opportunity with their merit systems—and they were, in some ways. But in other ways they were reducing it. They were reducing the number of avenues to success. They were insisting that everyone who wanted to succeed had to be authorized—had to go the same route, play the same game, had to be, in other words, like them.

The liberals' credentialism contributed to the divisiveness of the war in Vietnam, which was authorized by the credentialed elite but fought, mainly, by Americans with other and, in the eyes of the elite, lesser skills. As that fact sank in, the general public grew more receptive to the anti-war sermons of the radical-purists, even though the attitude of the purists toward the ordinary Americans doing the fighting could not have been more contemptuous. The purists' attitude reflected their opinion of themselves as a moral elite—a notch above the liberal intellectual elite.

The liberals stood for the old consensus about America's mission—which had to do with persuading people everywhere that they were not predestined and with showing them the way to democracy, efficiency, and prosperity.

The old consensus went back to the early nineteenth century. At the end of the nineteenth century, that consensus broke down. The progressive reformers rejected their predecessors' individualistic ethic for a more collectivistic one and their predecessors' traditional pieties for critical thinking. They did not, however, reject their predecessors' belief in America's mission.

The old individualists and new collectivists worked together to Americanize the immigrants. They placed small American flags in each classroom and a large American flag in front of each school building—including, of course, those on the new American Zone in Panama. And Francis Bellamy, Edward's cousin, wrote the Pledge of Allegiance, first recited in a classroom in 1892.

Abroad, the old traditionalists and new critical thinkers fought side by side to free Cuba from the king of Spain. They worked side by side to dig a canal through the barrier Nature had placed in the way of "trade, acquaintance, friendship, and peace." They fought "Kaiser Bill" to save the world for democracy; they fought Hitler to save the world from "the Master Race."

Underlying the interventionist élan of the progressives and their liberal heirs was the belief that conflict is caused by misunderstandings or by special interests. The solution was to help "the people" set themselves free and then to bring them together so that they could become friends.

After the Second World War, Americans hailed the coming of "One World" and of "A New Moral Order." They took the lead in organizing and financing the United Nations, where they were sure the world's sovereign states would learn to work as a team and eventually form a federation, on the model, naturally, of the United States.

Then, in 1950, Americans went to Korea to save an authoritarian regime from a totalitarian one, and in the 1960s, Presidents Kennedy and Johnson, on the advice of the best and the brightest, sent American troops to Vietnam to rescue another authoritarian regime. It wasn't the same as saving the world for democracy.

The radical-purists thought the United States was saving Vietnam for the "special interests"—a corrupt Vietnamese elite. The purists weren't wrong about that, but they thought the Communists would be better—more equalitarian and idealistic. About that, they were wrong, although few have admitted it. The systematic repression in Vietnam, Laos, and Cambodia; the massacre of millions by the Communist idealists; and the stories of the boat people and the refugees in Thailand are ignored by the purists, who continue to argue that America is the main impediment to peace, and that its mission to promote democracy and progress has always been a mask for imperialist exploitation.

However, the purists' claim to moral superiority was badly damaged by their naiveté about Communism, just as the status liberals' claim to intellectual superiority was damaged by their prideful belief that they had risen above self-interest and could see what was best for everyone, even in Vietnam, where they presumed to remake the texture of Vietnamese national life, while using the statistically validated, least possible necessary force on the battlefield. Nation-building, they called it.

By the time America withdrew from Vietnam, many of the old liberals had been converted to the radical-purists' point of view. Those liberals who had not been converted either became neo-conservatives or "took to the hills," so to speak, to work for the long-term reform of the Democratic party along traditional liberal lines. Then, in the mid-seventies, the new amalgam of converted liberals and radical-purists found a foreign policy issue they thought they could use to reassert their superior status—the Panama Canal. Taking the lead in the fight for ratification, they presented themselves as the moral and rational alternative to the blue-collar "rednecks" on the Zone, who were blinded by patriotism and opposed to progress.

The reason the debate over the Carter-Torrijos treaties was so intense was that it was a battle in a "class war." The weapons of that war are ideas—ideas about the character of the American working/middle-class, the value of American popular culture, and the role in a democratic society of a credentialed, intellectual elite.

No question was better suited for bringing that "class war" out of the shadows than the question of what Americans should think about their Canal adventure. As a workers' paradise, the Canal Zone provoked revealing comments from those who think they are superior to the working class. As an American community in the middle of a foreign country, it provoked slurs from those who were embarrassed by its unequivocal Americanness. Finally, as a profusely documented, apparently successful manifestation of America's traditional national mission, the Zone and the Canal provoked fits of invective from those skeptics whose superior status is based on their claim to see through America's myths. However, sometimes those who habitually take a skeptical view of their society's intentions and achievements fail to examine the assumptions that provide the foundation for their own visions.

14
Three Cultures at
the World's Crossroads

THE MYTH OF THE GLOBAL VILLAGE

One myth that sustains many American critics of American society is the old progressive myth that people-to-people friendships can prevent the "senseless" clash of national interests. From its inception in the late nineteenth century, progressive thought involved a rejection of the real world's complexity. It assumed that the confusions and conflicts inherent in national, racial, ethnic, and social divisions were misunderstandings that would resolve themselves as people came together in the image of a tribe—a universal tribe.[1]

This myth was partly responsible for sending American engineers and roughnecks to Panama in 1904. The Canal would, of course, serve American national interests, but it was also intended to bring the people of the world closer together and to contribute to global harmony.

However, conditions on the Isthmus during the construction of the Canal were such that the men in charge of the project did their best to prevent the intermingling of the Americans on the Zone and the Panamanians. In fact, the proclivity of many Americans to go into Panama City or Colón on their days off was regarded as almost as dangerous to the success of the Canal project as "some epidemic disease."[2]

Goethals thought he could keep his American workers on the Zone by bringing their wives down to look after them and by providing them with "rational amusements."[3] First he established the Bureau of Clubs and Playgrounds. Then he went to Congress. Upon hearing his request, the chairman of the appropriations committee expressed dismay: "A 52,000 dollar club house?"

"Yes, sir," Goethals replied. "We need a good club house because we should give them some amusement and keep them out of Panama."[4]

Clubhouses were duly built and stories were written about how the Canal workers were happily bowling and drinking milkshakes on the Zone instead of carousing and whoring in Panama. The Bureau of Clubs and Playgrounds kept statistics to prove that it was winning the war against immorality. In 1908, for example, there were 95 shows by imported entertainers on the Zone; 131 shows by local talent; total attendance for all shows was 43,321; there were 147,098 games of billiards and pocket billiards played; 64,247 games were bowled; 880 calls were made on members confined to hospitals. The statistics go on and on—and leave no room for doubt.

After the Bureau of Clubs and Playgrounds got in gear, no Zonian could say, as one had earlier, "All the entertainment I had was holding my breath."[5] But for all its activity, the Bureau could not keep the Canal workers out of Panama.

Nor could their wives, and before long many of them stopped trying. An old Canal hand who had worked many places around the world said in 1914: "Of all the places I have been . . . the Zone is the only one where the wives accompany their husbands on Saturday night 'bats,' sit beside them while they 'stew up,' and finally go home with their sodden wards; and apparently enjoy it."[6]

OPERATION FRIENDSHIP

By the late 1950s, however, the progressive social engineers had changed their minds. Instead of wanting the Canal workers to stay out of Panama, they were blaming them for not going over there more often. According to the social engineers, the lack of harmony between Panama and the United States was the result of a lack of individual friendships, not of any fundamental divergence of national interests. In 1962, General Theodore Bogart proposed a solution: Operation Friendship.

"The idea behind the project is simple," revealed a reporter for the *Washington Post*, "promote understanding between Panamanians and residents of the U.S. Zone."[7]

Bogart's solution—to promote understanding through association and friendship—was a popular one at the time. America was going to win the Cold War, not just by being tougher than the Russians, but by being nicer—more likeable. For many Americans, the competition for allies and influence was a popularity contest.

But obviously what Bogart had in mind was not friendship, that very private and idiosyncratic relationship. It was social engineering—friendly persuasion. The Zonians were supposed to "promote understanding" by learning about Panama from the Panamanians, who would then learn from the Zonians the need for continued American control of the Canal.

Operation Friendship rested on the assumption that American foreign policy had risen above special interests—that is to say, mere national interests. What was good for America was good for the world. Since all men were rational, all men would accept American policies if they understood them. It was simply a matter of communication!

As it turned out, Operation Friendship was a great success—but it didn't work. In 1963, the *Washington Post* reported that Operation Friendship had "proved so successful" that "it was thought of as a pilot project, as an arm of the Alliance for Progress." Less than a year later, the Flag Riots broke out. That should have led American policy-makers to give up the idea that the existence of numerous personal friendships would eliminate international conflicts, but it didn't. The idea that people-to-people contacts could bring us all together in one great tribe was too entrancing. If only the "rednecks" could learn to be thoughtful and considerate, there would be no need for the diplomats to endure the unpleasantness of hard bargaining or the embarrassment of unseemly displays of national power. So the liberal heirs of the progressive reformers continued to believe that Operation Friendship *should* have worked. Someone was to blame.

ASSIGNING THE BLAME

It comforted them to believe that the Flag Riots were the result of the "redneck" Zonians' unfriendliness. Besides reinforcing their sense of moral and class superiority (they were sure they could have carried it off), it enabled them to continue to dream that communities need not have outsiders, that all people shared the same "basic goals" and had the same "universalistic concerns"—and that people in close association *would* be friends.

After the 1964 Flag Riots, Norman Cousins condemned the Zonians for not *making* the progressive-liberal dream come true:

> What has gone wrong is that we have attempted to superimpose a policy of economic and military aid on a flimsy psychological base. We have never really convinced the . . . Panamanians and all the others that we were genuinely interested in them, or that we profoundly respected them, or that we had any curiosity about their books or music or art or any of the things that give them pride and a sense of achievement. . . . As nations they may be small alongside the United States, but their aspirations and their sense of dignity are large. No amount of material aid we give will make up for genuine friendship unless we also give respect and the things that go with respect.[8]

Countless similar sermons during this century contributed to the decline of American provincialism. They helped teach a continental people who maintained no continuous relationships with other nationalities to think more deeply about the nature of elsewhere.

But to berate the Zonians for not convincing the Panamanians that "we" are genuinely interested in "them" is to abandon the old ideal of being a good neighbor and to impose in its place a therapeutic relationship that reeks of the "progressive schoolroom" and that is immensely patronizing and condescending to Panamanians. It also reminds us in some way of the serape/wooden shoes approach to foreignness taken by our childhood geographies, where other cultures were inevitably treated as curiosities. When Americans and Panamanians became friends (and as we shall see, they *did*), it was not because the Americans set out with a determination to respect Panamanian culture, but because they were both interested in music, golf, acting, farming, hunting, making money, or a host of other activities—which is very different from "us" taking an interest in "them."

THE DIFFERENCES THAT WON'T GO AWAY

It is fashionable today to minimize cultural differences—to assume that the world's peoples are all basically alike—brothers and sisters under the skin. Surely that is true on some very fundamental level, but differences there are, and it is a mistake to ignore them.

Characteristic costumes and food and music are not what we are talking about. Rather, it is the hidden expectations and moral imperatives of a culture that impede friendship and understanding, because more often than not they annoy and disgust us, striking as they do at our most closely held beliefs about the world and our place in it. Left unexamined or denied, they fester and forever keep us apart.

What is wanted is an awareness of our most basic differences and a willingness to get on with the business of being friends in spite of them. It was mostly in this spirit that individual Panamanians and Americans on the Isthmus lived side by side, became friends, and sometimes married. As British journalist Jan Morris observed, they knew each other very well.[9]

No society chooses its ghosts—they are the products of history. Panama is haunted by a hero-type that belongs to a nonworking class of patrons—an "officers' class." Actual military officers may or may not belong to this class. (There is a good deal of discreetly expressed contempt in Panama for the *Guardia* officers as a group. They are alleged to be crude and boorish.) It is the ideal officer-type, not the actual officer, that is admired.

A society's hero-type is not immutable, of course. Nor is it universally admired. In Panama, some people scornfully reject the ideal of the proud officer-type. Even many of those who admire the virtues it represents do not necessarily take it as a model they should emulate. However, in one way or another everyone in Panama is affected by the idea of the officer-type.

More often than not, he is a civilian. He is a man of means and has an aura of authority. He dresses well, is intensely loyal to his friends, and does not work with his hands. Nor does he stew and fret over details and numbers—or concern himself with maintenance. He gives orders, is respectful to his superiors, loyal to his "regiment," courteous to everyone, and very proud.

In 1953, two American sociologists asked their students at the University of Panama what they were most proud of about Panama. By far the most common answer was, "Its national pride." The surprised sociologists concluded, "They are proud of being proud!"[10] It is a trait that provides its possessor with an easy sense of achievement, an endless appetite for slights, and an excuse for avoiding self-criticism.

The Panamanian hero-type does not stand in line. As he grows older, he is dignified and mysteriously powerful. At moments of crisis, he is magnetic and magnificent. He is not accountable.

Nor is he democratic. "My people are peasants, not ready for democracy," explained a Panamanian leader in 1964. Fourteen years later, in 1978, the ever-popular Arnulfo Arias—*El Hombre*—told an American reporter, "The Panamanian people are like oxen. You have to keep prodding them with a stick to keep them moving."[11] These are the Panamanian "officers" speaking.

Because of the existence of this ideal, the Panamanian middle class, which emerged after the Second World War, is not a middle class as Americans understand that category. To Americans, the middle class is the best class. Beneath it is an underclass that does not work; above it is a tiny class whose members have inherited enough money so that they do not have to work. For different reasons and in different ways, the American middle class looks down upon both. And while the middle class itself is divided into subclasses that sometimes find themselves in political and social opposition, they nonetheless share the same basic values and attitudes.

In contrast, the Panamanian middle class emerged from a system that traditionally has had only two tiers. At the present time, many of its members seem to identify success with the style and privileges of the traditional oligarchy, in much the same way that the emerging bourgeoisie of Europe identified success with the style of the aristocracy. Many middle-class Panamanians do not see themselves as members of a dominant American-type middle class, but as members of a lower upper class.

The American hero-type, like his Panamanian counterpart, has faults that are the price of his virtues and that cannot be corrected without altering those virtues as well. He can seem childishly optimistic and naive to people who live in cultures that inculcate a more fatalistic attitude toward life. He always thinks he can "do something about it"—whatever it is—an attitude that is not always justified. He has a lust for responsibility, which is sometimes overbearing and intrusive, and a casual disregard for social custom and traditions, which he sees as superficial. He is a person who crosses social boundaries: the detective, the smart athlete, or the businessman who goes from the bottom to the top but can still work with his hands and doesn't forget the old neighborhood. For example, we know a Zonian—a professional who works behind a desk in The Building—who says he dreams of buying a small garage when he retires, a place, he says, where he can get his hands dirty. That dream, whether ever acted on or not, reflects the influence of the American hero-type.

The American hero-type knows every tool in the shop. He has all the numbers in his head. While willing to go it alone, he tries to get people to work together. He does not make things come true. He makes the system work. He obeys the law. He is accountable.

But he is not subservient to authority. Thus, the American hero-type defines himself partly by talking back to the big boys. Take Mike Mitchell, for instance. He was the Canal Company stationmaster at Monte Lirio. When President Taft toured the Zone, Goethals introduced him to Mitchell. Taft, with unthinking condescension, said, "They tell me you are quite a big shot around here."

Unabashed, Mitchell replied, "You bet your big, fat stern I am."

Taft laughed. As a politician in a democracy, he knew he'd better.

Goethals squirmed and bit his lip. As an officer, he could not approve of such unmilitary sass.[12]

But the American hero-type just doesn't cotton to the idea of a condescending officer class: "A man's a man for a' that," or as the Zone poet John Hall expressed it in a poem about the Canal workers:

> *Call them "roughnecks," call them "huskies";*
> *Call them that which means a "man,"*
> *And they'll be your friends forever;*
> *For they're built on Nature's plan.*[13]

In Panama, on the other hand, signs of the regimental plan are everywhere. In the ambiguous name of the president's residence—the Presidential Palace. In the way the salesgirls stand dutifully one pace behind you and the cashier refuses to look at your identification as he accepts your check, giving you to understand, thereby, that we are all officers and gentlemen here. You see it in the uniforms worn by the women in all government offices and some private ones. Each office has its own color combinations and styles.

Clothes, uniforms—appearances—are important in a regimental society. In 1912, a Zonian remarked that the Panamanian could not rid himself of the conviction that "a man in an old khaki jacket who is building a canal must be of inferior clay to a hotel loafer in a frock coat and a tall hat."[14]

Panama's dress code has grown increasingly informal, but it has always been more formal than the dress code of the Americans. One of the first things the *Guardia* did when they took over the Zone in 1979 was to make American joggers and men walking to the swimming pool wear shirts. In the States, you can't tell a book by its cover, but in Panama, covers—or the lack of them—count.

Panama's regimental dream is also reflected in its marketplace. In the United States, workers fought to achieve a decent wage, then pursued social security and welfare benefits. In Panama, the workers were given social security benefits—by Arnulfo Arias, incidentally—but their wages were kept low. As a result, they have little positive incentive to work hard, little disposable income, and many of them invest their hopes in the national lottery.

As a group, the wealthier Panamanian businessmen prefer monopolistic concessions or distributorships to businesses that require unseemly competition or risky innovations. Commercial competition does not fit easily into the hierarchical ideal. Neither the Panamanian business sector nor the government has done much to stimulate the local economy. Panamanian businessmen and politicians are gamblers, plungers who dream of big hits—like a new sea-level canal, or of the Cerro Colorado mining project that would cost $2 billion and provide only two thousand permanent jobs.[15]

The regimental dream also affects attitudes about what is public and private. Panamanians have a finely honed disposition to keep their private affairs away from the prying eyes of outsiders. To some extent this disposition is shared by Americans who are in a constant dither lest their government use phone taps and computers to monitor their investments, movements, or friendships. However, Americans have more control over their government than the Panamanians do of theirs. Hence, Americans trust their government more. They are ruled by law and rely on the law to protect them. Thus, they can risk forming alliances with acquaintances or near strangers. Panamanians are less likely to do this. Americans have a confidence in their political and legal rights that no Panamanian can have in his. For Americans, influence helps, but the law is their main defense. In Panama, there is more reliance on influence and connections.

Compared to the people of Panama, North Americans tend not to have many secrets or to build many fences. We see this, for example, in discussions of such topics as "quality orgasms" on the "Phil Donahue Show," in the way the lawns around American houses are likely to run into each other, and in the way Americans easily join organizations to save the whales or the neighborhood.

In Panama, the typical house has a wall or an ornate iron fence around its yard. Loyalty is owed to the family and its allies, not to impersonal, impermanent public associations, and the boundaries between one private social sphere and another in Panama suggest what the world was like when it was organized around clans, households, and lords.

The dream of the regiment shows up most clearly in Panama's *Guardia Nacional*, a combination army and police force. A *Guardia* has the authority to arrest people for disrespect; therefore, public criticism of the *Guardia* is very rare. *Guardia* officers are free to function as magistrates, both in minor cases, as when they order their men to shave a hippie's head, and in major ones, as when they order their men to surround the legislative chambers until the politicos see reason.[16]

"Governments in Latin America fall not because they are bad, but because they are weak," explained Panama's strongman, Omar Torrijos, by way of justifying his decisions to deport his opponents, curtail civil rights, and raise taxes.[17] Panamanians are ruled by authority, not law. In America, the law knows no boundaries. Hence, we have public records, public investigations, and public accountability —even of presidents. American governments do fall because they are bad.

Next to the *Guardia*, Panama's bureaucracy is the most obvious manifestation of the regimental dream. Every office is overstaffed with cast-off mistresses, poor relatives, and the children of friends—the obligations of an officer—and every task is minutely divided to give each of them something to do.

Ex-Zonians still working on the Canal have complained about how long it takes to get things done now that Panama has taken over, but Carlos Lopez Guevara, a former Panamanian ambassador to Washington, has brushed aside their complaints by pointing out that there is red tape in America, too. The ex-Zonians, he says, are just being forced to live in the real world for a change.[18] Rather than compare the efficiency of the American and Panamanian ways of doing things, the ex-ambassador compares their reality, by which he seems to mean their inefficiency. Since Panama's way is more inefficient, it is more real, which is somehow better.

In 1976, American Canal workers freely admitted the competence and diligence of their Panamanian co-workers to John L. Jackley, who was preparing an unofficial study of the Zone under the supervision of the United States Embassy's political counselor. But these same Americans doubted the ability of Panama to run the Canal. Jackley called the workers' attitude contradictory. However, they were merely making a distinction between the Panamanian system and particular people—tradition and the individual talent.

There is a tradition in Panama of a public rhetoric which does not necessarily correspond to reality. Popular support or protest is easily manufactured. There is no investigative reporting. Reporters are loyal junior officers of the regiment. They quarrel among themselves, of course, about who should be promoted or who should lead the parade, but they do not grub around for facts that might disgrace the regiment before outsiders. As they see it, a journalist's job is not to map the world but to direct the troops.

When asked about the heavy censorship of the press under Torrijos, the Panamanian newsman Jorge Carrasco replied, "Never mind that, let's talk about the facts," by which he meant Panama's grievances against the United States.[19]

As far as most Panamanian politicians are concerned, the preeminent "fact" of Panama's national life is that everything bad that has ever happened to Panama, from a local electrical outage or a drought to the existence of poverty, has been the fault of the United States, and whatever goes wrong in the future—that, too, will be the fault of the all-powerful United States—the result of something it has done or failed to do.

Some Panamanian politicians seem to actually believe this. Others will joke about "political necessity" with American friends or acquaintances. Of course, many Panamanians find this stance absurd and embarrassing, but it is hard for individuals to publicly repudiate traditional political patterns without paying an enormous price— especially in a society where there is no tradition of dissent or of a loyal opposition.

There is no admiration in Panama for the man who steps forward and takes the blame. He is simply a fool. A banner displayed at the

University of Panama quoted Torrijos as saying that the only thing wrong with Jesus Christ was that he didn't go down fighting.

Jean-François Revel exaggerates when he says that Latin American civilization may be the first ever to avoid self-criticism entirely,[20] but many other observers have noted this tendency.

Octavio Paz emphasizes Latin America's historical relationship to Catholic orthodoxy, as opposed to North America's relationship to Protestant dissent. Orthodoxy, he points out, is defensive; it does not encourage criticism. Dissent, on the other hand, does. Paz goes on to point out that "when one talks of criticism, one is talking of change."[21] America is oriented toward change, toward improvement, and Americans are always living for tomorrow. Panamanians, with a zest for life and an officer's disdain, are more likely to live in the present and sometimes to act as if there were no tomorrow. The Zonians, lost somewhere between their private American dreams of tomorrow and the Zone's public commitment to yesterday, lived in a time-warp.

DISCRIMINATION ON THE CANAL ZONE

The summer of 1963 was a high point in the campaign to abolish racism in the United States. In August, more than 200,000 people gathered in Washington to march on behalf of equal rights for all Americans. That was the month we left for the Zone. When we arrived there, we were assigned an apartment in the town of Gamboa, just up the road from Santa Cruz—an all-black community.

We didn't know what to make of the segregation on the Zone. In the States, the federal government was forcing reluctant state governments to desegregate schools and public facilities. But on the Zone, blacks were carefully segregated in their own communities, and although there were a few American blacks in attendance at the high school, it was clear that two separate—and unequal—school systems existed on the Zone. All this in spite of the fact that the Zone was a federal enclave wholly under the control of an appointed officer of the federal government. We could not understand why company officials were not taking steps to integrate the Zone's housing and schools, why there were no public and vocal demands for them to do so, and why the judge of the local federal district court was not delivering ultimatums to the civil authorities. True, the Zone was no longer the hard-core segregationist community it had once been. All public facilities had been desegregated, and a gradual intermingling of the races at the swimming pools and clubhouses was taking place. However, in important and fundamental ways, segregation persisted on the Zone almost to the end of its existence.

What were the circumstances that enabled, even encouraged, Zone authorities to maintain these discriminatory policies? First of all, the overwhelming majority of black company employees who lived and worked on the Zone were not United States citizens; they were Panamanians. However, since the Canal Zone was not United States territory, they were not considered resident aliens. But their native language was English, and for a variety of racial and cultural reasons they were discriminated against in Panama. For racial reasons, they were discriminated against on the Zone. While they worked persistently to improve their status on the Zone through their unions and Civic Councils, they did not have the kind of secure base—neither United States citizenship nor support from Panama—that would have permitted them to risk the confrontational politics that drew attention to racial inequalities in the States and speeded up their demise.

It is sometimes argued that the policy of segregation on the Zone was "really" continued because the Zonians were such racists that they would not countenance its elimination. There is no evidence for this. To be sure, there were racists among us, but in every respect the Zonians were as representative a group of Americans as can be found. They came from all over the country and held the usual variety of views about political and ethical questions. Some were comfortable with racism; others definitely were not. Some were bigots, but some were fervent social idealists. If the Zone really had been simply an American small town in the tropics, as journalists looking for an easy analogy liked to assert, if it had been a democracy, if the people who lived there had been permanent instead of long-term temporary residents, and if the blacks on the Zone had been American citizens, the story of segregation on the Zone would have been very different.

As it was, however, most Zonians felt they had only a limited stake in the community. They were renters, not homeowners. They might stay on the Zone for twenty years, but they always had "one foot on the boat," as the saying went. Moreover, the company insisted that it alone was responsible for community affairs and did not welcome interference from below. As a result, most white Zonians who elsewhere would have been disposed to join in a clear-cut campaign for civil rights remained passive.

Finally, just as the campaign for civil rights was sweeping across the United States in the late fifties and early sixties, administrators on the Zone saw that radical changes in the Zone's political status were in the offing. After the 1964 riots, the handwriting was on the wall—literally—and indeed, a new treaty between Panama and the United States was almost signed in 1967.

As a result, while taking measures to secure the full civil rights of black United States citizens on the Zone, the company did not act with decision and dispatch to extend those rights to the Panamanian blacks on the Zone. If the Zone were soon to be turned over to Panama, the rights of the black Panamanians would become the responsibility of the government of Panama. Thus, company officials largely ignored the unfinished state of integration on the Zone— until the publicity surrounding the treaty debate in the mid-seventies and trips to the Zone by United States congressmen brought the problem into the light and made it impossible to ignore any longer.

THE HISTORICAL BACKGROUND

When the American Canal project got started, about 50,000 black West Indians looking for work came to Panama from islands in the Caribbean. A few were French, but most were British citizens. The largest group came from the island of Barbados—about a tenth of its population at the time. The West Indians spoke English, had a strong sense of decorum and respectability, were black, and in those days were, on the average, physically larger than most Panamanians.

As the West Indians poured onto the Zone, the Americans organized a segregated society on the pattern that prevailed throughout the United States at that time. It was unlike anything the Panamanians had ever seen: separate and inferior black schools, housing, commissaries, payrolls, toilets, and drinking fountains.

It is sometimes suggested that racism on the Isthmus was concentrated among the American huskies who did not have the benefit of a liberal education.[22] That was not so—neither early nor late in the history of the Zone. In the early days, all American Zonians were racists, from the man operating a steam shovel in the Cut to the kindly Dr. Gorgas.[23]

Gorgas believed in the theory of evolution, which showed he was an advanced, progressive thinker. However, he had his own crackpot version of that theory. Both men and germs, according to Gorgas, evolved in the tropics, but men, because of their superior powers of locomotion, were able to spread through the tropical regions faster than the germs. Thus, some men were always healthy. Eventually, however, the germs caught up with everyone. Men became diseased and stopped evolving. At that point, a small group of superior men invented fire and clothing and migrated north, where the cold killed the germs and men began evolving again. By eradicating yellow fever and malaria, Gorgas thought he was making it possible for the superior white race to return to its tropical homeland.

Mad scientists and wicked scientists can be dismissed as anomalies. The kindly, astute Gorgas was a more subversive figure. He was not mad or wicked, but prejudiced and wrong, just like many a nonscientific layman.

As racial attitudes on the Zone changed, they changed unevenly throughout the whole community. They did not change first among the academically enlightened who then tutored the workingman and taught tolerance by example. The racial attitudes of some of the American workers, a few of whom married dark Panamanians early on and all of whom worked side by side with West Indians every day, changed more swiftly than the attitudes of some of the more educated Canal bureaucrats, who had little contact with the West Indians. One official in the Schools Division was still embellishing his speeches at *despedidas* (farewell parties) with a watermelon joke in the late seventies.

However, the Americans were never the only bigots on the Zone. The Canal diggers consisted of:

> *All mixed up together*
> *In welt'ring perspiration,*
> *Men of all religions,*
> *Sons of every nation.*[24]

The two things they had in common were the Canal job and racism.

Right off, the Americans wanted to form a constabulary of West Indians and Panamanians under American supervision, but they abandoned that plan because the European workers "would not tolerate arrest by policemen whose skins were darker than their own."[25] Color was also immensely important to the West Indians. They were accustomed to making a distinction between blacks and coloreds, the latter being "fair" or "clear" persons.[26] They made geographic and class distinctions as well, the artisan from Jamaica having little use for the laborer from Barbados.

> *Nine Barbadians live in one room,*
> *Not enough money to buy a broom;*
> *What the Bajun peoples them call a spree*
> *Is one pint of sody divided by t'ree.*[27]

And neither of them got along with the French-speaking blacks from Martinique.

A few of the West Indians were educated and able. "Men of ability," Thomas Grier, a white American, called them.[28] But most of them were pick-and-shovel men who had never seen a railroad or heard about explosives. Their work habits appalled the Americans. John Stevens watched two of them fill a wheelbarrow, then hoist it onto the head of a third, who carried it away.[29] West Indian straw bosses sometimes turned up for work wearing formal clothes—starched shirt, striped trousers, a tailcoat, and spats.

An American who supervised West Indians complained to his wife, "Hurry! I wouldn't ask them to hurry if I could only get them to move fast enough so I could tell which way they were going."[30]

Such work habits seemed to confirm the racial stereotype that white Americans held of blacks, but along with their racism, the Americans brought with them the contradictory idea of equality—with liberty and justice for all. In the midst of American racism—stupid and hurtful as it was—was a yearning to be fair, to be just.

Stevens decided that the reason the West Indians were so slow was that they were not eating right. He saw to it that their traditional rice and yams were supplemented by corned beef, bread, sardines, and —since this was an American project—ice cream. He predicted that the West Indians would learn rapidly if given a chance.[31] They proved him right, and the American in charge of Labor and Quarters wrote in his final report that many of them had developed into "first class construction men."[32]

The historian David McCullough concluded that the claim that the Canal Company took better care of its employees, citizens and aliens, officers and laborers, than was ever dreamed heretofore was "unquestionably true, despite all the obvious inequities of the system..."[33]

But obvious inequities there were. When a foreman appointed one of those "first class construction men" to a white job, the white unions complained to Goethals, who ordered, "Don't let a Jamaican touch another tool."[34] Yet, according to many West Indians, Goethals was scrupulously fair and sympathetic in other dealings with them. At his famous Sunday morning counseling sessions, it was first come, first heard.

Everywhere else on the Zone rigid racial distinctions prevailed. A few of the company's schools started out with a mixture of black and white students, but the company soon separated them, establishing a regular Jim Crow system. However, as an American who was working for the company noted, "Uncle Sam" could not "openly abjure before the world his assertion as to the equality of all men by enacting 'Jim Crow' laws."[35] So, instead of putting up offensive signs that said "White" and "Black," the company put up squeamishly hypocritical signs that said "Gold" and "Silver."

At first those signs did not quite mean "White" and "Black." "Gold" referred to men and women on the "Gold Roll," who were paid in gold coin and were, with a few exceptions, white Americans. "Silver" referred to men and women who were paid in Panamanian silver. These consisted of common laborers of various colors and nationalities.

However, as soon as the Canal was completed, the white common laborers either chose to be repatriated, went into business in Panama, or found their way onto the American Gold Roll. When that happened, "Gold" and "Silver" came to mean "White" and "Black," and there was no getting around the fact that the Panama Canal Company discriminated against its employees according to color.

Yet, the West Indian Employees Association and Civic Councils repeatedly asked the company to allow all of its West Indian employees to live on the segregated Zone rather than forcing them to live in Panama, where there was no public segregation.[36] Discrimination in Panama took other forms.

Inferior as black schools, houses, and jobs on the Zone were in comparison to those of the Americans, they compared favorably to those available to most blacks in Panama or elsewhere in the Caribbean. And while the Gold and Silver system was reminiscent in many ways of the American South, there were important differences. There were no lynchings or Klan atrocities, for instance. The Zone was law-and-order country. Even in the early days when racial prejudices were at their worst, an American who struck a West Indian was fined twenty-five dollars[37]—almost a week's pay for a five-dollar-a-day man, and many Americans did not make that much. (Police privates made eighty dollars a month.)

For blacks, however, the advantages of living on the Zone made the Zone's racism even harder to bear. Better off than they would have been in Panama, they were worse off than they should have been had their careers not been stunted arbitrarily by racism.

THE DECLINE OF RACISM ON THE CANAL ZONE

The decline of racist policies on the Zone began in the forties when equal pay for equal work was given to all United States citizens, white and black. In 1946, the monolithic pattern of public segregation on the Zone began to be eliminated,[38] though the swimming pools were not integrated until 1963. In 1947, Panamanians—both Latins and West Indians—were allowed to take United States Civil Service Examinations, the first non-United States citizens who were allowed to do this. In 1954, West Indians began attending the Canal Zone College. (Latin Panamanians had been doing so since it was established in 1933.) Local-rate—i.e., black—housing was improved in the fifties, but not desegregated. By 1957, the United States wage scale was applied to citizen and noncitizen alike. And beginning in 1975, the "Latin American" schools on the Zone were phased out. The company offered a choice to all non-United States Canal workers— West Indian and Latin—who lived on the Zone. They could send their children to school in Panama or to the "American" schools on the Zone. Either way, the company would reimburse them for all expenses. Almost all the West Indians chose the "American" schools. After the treaty, those schools, which had been run by the company, were transferred to the Department of Defense. They became schools for the children of United States military personnel and did not accept any new foreign students, though the foreign students already enrolled in them were allowed to remain in the system until they graduated. An exception was also made to the law requiring Department of Defense schools to hire only teachers with United States citizenship. Thus the non-U.S.-citizen teachers from the company's "Latin American" schools who had been transferred to the company's "American" schools along with the West Indian students could keep their jobs. Finally, shortly before the 1978 treaties went into effect, all company housing was made available to all employees.

However, when the treaties went into effect, the West Indians on the Zone lost many of the benefits they had acquired over the years. "It shouldn't be, but now we feel more discriminated against than we ever felt under the Americans," complained a West Indian community leader to an American reporter.[39]

Twelve years earlier, in 1967, the black Panamanian publisher George Westerman, who is a leader in Panama's West Indian community, told a British writer, Richard West:

> Panamanians, like other Latins, like to condemn the United States for social intolerance, but in too many instances, they, too, are guilty of rank prejudices based on race or skin color. Because Americans admit that racism exists in their country and that it is a grave social ill, they are making every effort to eradicate it from the American society. Because Panamanians are not willing to admit the existence of racism in their society, they have difficulty in its removal from the Panamanian social system.[40]

It is essential to remember, however, that Westerman is talking about the American society in the United States, not the one on the Zone. The Zone might well have become more of a racist backwater than it was had it been left to itself, for it was politically and culturally moribund. Theoretically, social reform should have been easier on the Zone, where everything was controlled and directed from the top by an enlightened elite. It was not. Reform occurred on the Zone only in response to distant reforms originating in the *democratic* ferment of the United States. In the case of desegregation, it was a long time coming.

DISCRIMINATION IN PANAMA

Some North American visitors assumed that the racism they observed in Panama was there because the Latin Panamanians were copying the racism of the Americans on the Zone. In 1947, a pair of relentlessly debonair travel writers (they referred to the *bomberos* as the "fire laddies") explained, "One of the most unfortunate aspects of the elaborate governmental Jim Crow in the Canal Zone was that it was gradually encouraging the Panamanians to go and do likewise."[41]

However, there was racism in Panama before the Americans arrived. Power was in the hands of the *Rabiblancos*—the "white-tailed birds." Shortly after the Canal project got going, one of them confided to an American how unpleasant it was to attend receptions along with American nurses. Their willingness to care for black laborers offended him.[42] In conversations with us seventy years later, some upper-class Panamanians were still anxious to disassociate themselves from blacks. They referred to "us" and "them" and disparaged kinky hair. *"El color es accidente, pero el pelo no miente."*

Discrimination in Panama is not easily understood by a North American who expects racism to be accompanied by a clear-cut social difference based on skin color. Discrimination in Panama is relative to an interacting, variously weighted set of characteristics and social factors that include the shade of a person's skin, the degree of curl in his hair, his facial features, his language, the amount of money he makes, the kind of work he does, and his family connections. Dark skin alone is not an important social handicap. It may even be regarded as attractive, though José Quintero says he never forgot that his father disapproved of him because his skin was darker than anyone else's in his upper-class Panamanian family.[43] And Mavis and John Biesanz, who studied Panamanian racism in the 1950s, noted a number of ways that at that time *"El color le ofende"*—a man's color held him back.[44]

Racism in Panama is further complicated because Panamanians distinguish between "our Negroes" and the "Antillean menace." The first are descendants of slaves from colonial days; the second, the black West Indians. Panama has a long record of discriminatory legislation against the latter. Many Latins refer to the West Indians as *"chombos"*—the "niggers" from the Antilles. The West Indians came to Panama to work on the American Canal project and soon made up over half the Canal work force, which at its peak consisted of 53,679 men and women. (During the construction era, Panama had a very small labor pool, and only 357 Panamanians were on the company's books during the eleven years it took to build the Canal.)[45]

As the years passed, many of the company's foreign workers became Panamanians, and more native-born Panamanians sought work with the company, but the American habit of classifying most Latins along with the West Indians as local-rate or "Silver" workers was a constant source of friction. Nothing was more insulting to a Latin than to be classed with the *"chombos."*

In 1941, after the election of the xenophobic Dr. Arnulfo Arias as president of Panama, the legislature simply took away the citizenship of all blacks of West Indian descent. It was returned to them in 1946, after Arias had been removed from office. However, the irrepressible Arias, who once announced that sexual union with the Antillean Negro "drains the strength from the race,"[46] and who told FDR that each Jamaican man slept with three women every week,[47] is without a doubt the most enduringly popular man Panama has ever known. He led a successful coup against President Juan Demosthenes Arosemena in 1931 and was elected president himself in 1940, 1948, and 1968—although the *Guardia* has never allowed him to finish a single term in office. Many observers believe he also won in 1964, and that only considerable fraud gave the presidency to Marcos Robles.[48] (In 1984, at the age of eighty-two, the charismatic Arias again ran for president. The election commission took a suspiciously long time to count the ballots. Finally, it announced that the *Guardia's* candidate, "Nicky" Barletta, had won a narrow victory. Barletta, a former World Bank official in Washington, D.C., had never run for office before. After his election, American newspaper stories revealed that the AFL-CIO had contributed $20,000 to his election. The money was an unrestricted grant to the labor organization from the National Endowment for Democracy.)

In the second half of this century, racism has become less widespread and virulent in Panama, just as it has in the United States, but it has not disappeared in either place. Panamanians say their discrimination against the West Indians is based upon cultural not racial characteristics. They remind their critics that there has never been public segregation in Panama, and they point to prominent black businessmen and politicians.

It is true that there have never been the kind of hard-and-fast color lines in Panama that were once found throughout the United States. Public segregation—the separate-but-equal delusion—made sense to racist North Americans because they knew that there was no way to keep blacks "in their place" if they were ever *publicly included* in a society haunted by the dream of equality—that very complicated word. But in Panama, in a regimental society, racist sentiment did not require public segregation based on color, because blacks were already segregated by class and rank. The public sector was given over to the lower ranks, and, naturally, blacks were excluded from the private society of the officers' corps.

Panama's racial discrimination is similar in some ways to the pattern of class discrimination that exists in the United States. And just as some Panamanians refuse to admit that racial barriers exist in their society, so some North Americans refuse to admit that there are serious class barriers in American society. Such denials have a surface plausibility. Just as there are no hard-and-fast racial lines in Panama, so there are no hard-and-fast class lines in the States. Numerous lower-class Americans make it big, but social classes and social discrimination exist nonetheless.

OF LOST CAUSES AND IMPOSSIBLE LOYALTIES

The Zone's West Indian blacks resented American racism, yet had a strong affinity for American culture. They spoke the same language as the Americans and shared the same values. West Indian men were less macho and West Indian women more assertive than their Panamanian neighbors. The West Indians marched in parades on American holidays and bought turkeys on Thanksgiving. Their daughters became cheerleaders. Their sons played basketball and baseball and followed the Big League careers of Rod Carew and Rennie Stennett, both West Indians who grew up on the Zone. The West Indians were joiners, just like the Americans. The men

organized golf clubs and lodges for mutual aid. The women organized garden clubs. West Indian families laughed at Archie Bunker
on the Southern Command television channel. And the young West
Indian male who misbehaved could expect a virtuoso tongue-lashing
from his mother and maybe a belting from his father. This is at
the farthest remove from Latin households, where the male child en-
joys the prerogatives of a young lord.

During the construction era, the Panamanian authorities had
neither the desire nor the resources to provide schools for the despised
"*chombos*." The British consul in Panama insisted that the British
West Indians would be happier if they remained illiterate, and
American union leaders argued that the United States government
should not spend tax dollars to educate foreign nationals to take the
jobs of Americans. Nevertheless, when the Canal Company established a school system, it provided schools for the children of all its
employees—segregated, to be sure, but schools. The classroom language was English, which suited both the English-speaking Americans
and the English-speaking West Indians.

However, as the years went by, it became apparent that the West
Indians could not remain in limbo as British citizens residing on the
American Zone in Panama. Reluctantly, Panama agreed to grant them
citizenship if they could prove they were "spiritually and materially
incorporated" into the national life of Panama—in effect, if Spanish
became their primary language.

Most West Indians did not want to speak Spanish. They wanted
to speak English and to live and work on the Zone. Amos Blades, a
second generation Zonian who was active in West Indian community
life, illustrated the attitude of many older West Indians when he
proudly told a reporter in 1976 that he had spent "never a day of
[his] life in Panama."[49] But there were a limited number of jobs on
the Zone. The children of American Zonians could go to the States to
find jobs. The children of the West Indians had to go to Panama.
They were unlikely to find jobs there unless they could speak Spanish.

By the mid-fifties, events in the States were also putting pressure on
the Canal authorities. The Supreme Court was about to strike down

the separate-but-equal fiction that had sustained segregated schools in the United States. When that happened, the segregated schools on the Zone would have to be integrated, too. But the black students on the Zone were not United States citizens.

Accordingly, plans were made to switch the curriculum of the West Indian schools on the Zone to the Panamanian model. The language of instruction would henceforth be Spanish.[50]

The new curriculum for the "Latin American" schools was designed to integrate the West Indians into Panamanian society. The alternative—to offer them American citizenship—would have caused major problems. (Why just West Indians? Why not all the employees of the company—Latins, too? How would Panama have felt about that?) However, the majority of West Indians were not committed to the idea of their children becoming part of the national life of Panama. Many of them clung to the idea that someday, somehow, they would become Americans.

The hasty and autocratic imposition of the new curriculum, plus the West Indian community's lack of commitment to Spanish as the language of instruction, permanently impaired the effectiveness of the West Indian schools. Many able students came from those schools to the Canal Zone College, but it was as a result of their own determination and character and in spite of the deficiencies of their formal education.

For years, older West Indians held on to the values and customs of the old country—in their case, the British Isles of the Caribbean. They supported a cricket league, turning out in whites for long, leisurely games that were interrupted for tea in the late afternoon. They played dominoes and rounders. And they ate traditional foods—souse (cucumbers, onions, and pickled pigs' feet), bacalao (dried cod), bun (dark bread and candied fruit), and sorrel (a ruby red Christmas drink made from a flower)—while at the same time developing a taste for being Americans.

But the Zone was a place where Americans could only pretend to be sovereign. Thus, it was a place where the West Indians could only pretend to be Americans. West Indians born on the Zone were

Panamanians. They knew, however, that the Panamanian foreign minister who denounced the Americans for "having the mentality of whites in South Africa" was not interested in bettering the lot of his black fellow citizens on the Zone. He was interested in seeing to it that the government of Panama secured control of the Canal. So during the treaty negotiations, the black non-United States citizens on the Zone looked to American congressmen like Robert Leggett and Ralph Metcalfe to protect their interests.

The majority of the West Indians on the Zone were not in favor of giving the Zone and the Canal to Panama. Some were very outspoken about this, but their leaders had to be careful what they said in public because they were Panamanian citizens. When Metcalfe's Panama Canal subcommittee held public hearings on the Zone, Nick Nonnemacher, a committee staff member, asked a group of West Indian community leaders whether they thought they would lose their jobs if Panama took over the Canal. When no one answered, Nonnemacher observed, "I see I am treading on delicate ground," and made arrangements to talk to the men privately.[51]

After the 1978 treaties were ratified, American congressmen included a section in the Panama Canal Act of 1979 that provided a temporary—until April 30, 1982—"special immigration" status for Panamanians who had lived on the Zone for at least a year prior to the time the treaties went into effect. This was meant to help the West Indians, but few of them were able to take advantage of their special status.

As of June 1980, out of nine hundred applications, the United States Embassy had approved only seventy-seven.[52] Some applicants were rejected for health reasons; others, because they could not prove residence on the Zone. (They had been living in a house officially assigned to a dead relative.) A few older West Indians still had British citizenship and were ineligible because the legislation mentioned only Panamanians. Ironically, some of the visas that were granted went to Latin Panamanians, including some doctors, who would not otherwise have qualified for immigration to the United States.

The West Indian leader George Westerman told a visiting scholar from the States that the American treaty negotiators made sure that the fringe benefits of the American Canal workers were protected, but nobody protected the rights of the Panamanian employees.[53] The American Canal workers would not agree that the treaty negotiators protected their interests. They worked hard to protect their benefits themselves, feeling certain that their interests were not an important concern of President Carter's negotiators. But at least the American workers had ways to do this. The West Indians had no similar means to influence the Panamanian government.

The West Indians' determination to become Americans remains strong. More than 90 percent of those interviewed in a 1980 survey indicated that they hoped to emigrate to the States in the near future.[54] Many have relatives there who acquired United States citizenship as alien volunteers in the armed forces during the Second World War.

Father Dennis Josiah, an Episcopalian priest in the West Indian community, summed up the black ex-Zonian's plight: "Sometimes we're inclined toward the United States, sometimes toward Panama, sometimes toward the West Indies. But I think the young people are different. They're more Panamanian, but many want to emigrate to the United States. It's rather strange."[55]

15
Seventy-five Years of Association and Friendship

Almost from the moment the first American mechanics arrived in Panama, there was trouble about sex, money, class, race, politics, and language—but not about religion. Having expected all the gringos to be Protestants, the Panamanians were pleasantly surprised to find that so many of them were Catholics.

However, the Panamanians were unpleasantly surprised by the American commissary system. They had expected the Canal workers to patronize Panamanian stores—and pay the special prices for foreigners. Also, neither the upper- nor the lower-class Panamanian could figure out the social position of the American workman. He didn't fit into their social system anywhere.

The American workers, on the other hand, were astonished by the small stature of the Panamanians, their lack of education, their contempt for manual labor, and their generous admixture of Negro blood. Moreover, the American mechanics had been taught by their intellectual betters that Spaniards were cruel, greedy, haughty, religious fanatics. The Spanish were the least favored nationality in nineteenth-century American textbooks. The president of the University of Wisconsin, reflecting general opinion, told its graduating class in 1898 that the Spanish were cruel and incompetent and had

168

contributed so little to civilization that it was hardly worth mentioning.[1]

With that foundation to build on, Americans and Panamanians settled down to being neighbors on the Isthmus.

It was a relationship characterized by contradiction from the start. Two dapper American school administrators wrote in 1912 that the better class of Spanish residents in Panama was composed of "refined, cultivated, and intelligent people," among whom "the Canal builders" found "intimate and interesting friends."[2] However, writing of approximately the same period, the wife of an ordinary American worker recalled:

> The people of the new Republic of Panama considered us an uncouth race. . . . To their way of thinking, we had no finesse, no savoir faire. We were not ceremonious enough about important people and affairs. . . . In short, we made too little fuss. They made sporadic attempts to show us by celebrations how it should be done, and we were asked by Zone officials to go to these parties whenever possible.[3]

Meanwhile, the Americans were transforming Panama and brooking no interference, ceremonious or otherwise. They paved the streets, stamped out yellow fever, and established a public-health system. Inadvertently, they also changed the character of Panama's population.

Panama had not been homogenous for centuries, but during the early years of the construction era, it was less heterogenous than the Canal Zone. "In the Canal Zone," an American remarked, "one finds a most cosmopolitan people, gathered together from the four corners of the earth . . ."[4] But when the Canal was completed, the company repatriated all of its foreign workers who wished to go home and sent most of the rest into Panama. Panama became a more cosmopolitan and the Zone a more distinctly American place.

TALKING TOGETHER

For forty years there were few signs in Spanish on the Zone and few Spanish-speaking Zonians. Some Zonians did not learn Spanish on principle. Others kept putting it off because they intended to stay only two years—and then only two more.

Most Zonians had no real need to learn Spanish. They didn't often need Spanish at work. The West Indians spoke English, and the officers of the ships transiting the Canal were likely to know some English. The Zonians didn't even need to know Spanish very often in Panama, except in the interior. As residents of "the crossroads of the world," the Panamanians in the Canal's terminal cities have a powerful motivation to learn English. Because of international tourism and commerce, and because the business of the Canal is conducted in English, the Panamanian who can speak that language has always been at a distinct advantage in the job market.

But there were always some Zonians who wanted or needed to learn Spanish, and they did. One of the first things the American women's clubs did in 1907 was to sponsor Spanish classes. American men studied Spanish after work at the YMCA. Spanish was the only one of the "Y"'s night courses "to go," partly, no doubt, because an employee of the company who could pass an examination in Spanish "had a better show of getting promoted in the service."[5] When the company established a secondary school in 1909, Latin was the required foreign language, but Spanish—along with French and German—was offered as an elective.[6]

Also, over the years a great many people on the Isthmus grew up in families where both English and Spanish were spoken and were, as a consequence, truly bilingual. Most of the rest of us had one native tongue and managed in the other language with varying degrees of expertise (if at all).

However, even people who were completely monolingual found themselves "speaking Spanish" or "speaking English" as they used borrowed words and expressions that had made their way from one language to the other. Monolingual English speakers would ask, "Who's picking up the *cuenta?*" or *"Que pasa?"* or they'd say, *"Me voy,* see you *mañana."* They wore *guayaberas* and bought *billetes* from the lottery vendors. They formed *comparas* for Carnival. They ate *ceviche, salchichas,* and *arroz con pollo.* Their children exclaimed, *"Chuleta!"*

when surprised—literally "porkchop," but meaning, "Oh, no!" the same way "Hot dog!" means, "Oh, boy!"

Monolingual Spanish speakers would *taipiar un reporte*. Women bought *pantis, peticots, lipstic,* and *champu*. They had *bebis*. Men played *softbol* and bet on a *yoki*. They wrote *cheques* or paid in *coch*. A man would *parquea* his *caro* at the garage, where the mechanic would check its *breaques, bompers, esprings, buchins, guinshil,* and so on.

It was not uncommon on the Zone or in Panama to hear people speaking both Spanish and English in the same conversation! Having begun a sentence in one language, they might finish it in the other because of the limitations of their vocabulary. A question posed in one language might be answered in the other, as conversational partners accommodated themselves to the need both to understand and to make themselves understood.

Many Panamanian schoolteachers were distressed by the extent to which the local Spanish had borrowed from English. Some politicians and nationalists agreed with the teachers, so periodically, most recently in the early seventies, the Panamanian government reminded the people that according to *"Articulo 7o."* of the constitution, *"El Español es el idioma de la Republica,"* and urged them, *"Habla con orgullo tu idioma! Defiéndelo!"*—"Speak it with pride! Defend it!"[7]

Such exhortations are notoriously ineffective in changing language habits, and Panamanians insouciantly continued to go to *nait clubs* and *coctel partis* and to order a *sandwiche para lonche*.

It is impossible to say what percentage of Zonians spoke Spanish. We knew Zonians who insisted that they did *not* speak Spanish because while fluent and accurate in familiar situations, they had small vocabularies. They couldn't talk about the space shuttle or agriculture, for example. On the other hand, some Zonians who advertised themselves as Spanish speakers and were not afraid to talk about anything did not seem to know that Spanish verbs had tenses and habitually committed what one Zone Spanish professor characterized mournfully as "brutal errors."

Some Zonians were satisfied to be able to respond to introductions and greetings, ask for directions, apologize, and "catch the drift" of what was said to them in Spanish. Others could participate in simple social conversations, and some Zonians took advantage of their residence in Panama to become proficient Spanish speakers.

OFFICIAL COOPERATION

From 1904 to 1960, the Zonians—and North Americans in general—were far more undiplomatic, overbearing, and racist than they have been from 1960 on. But, paradoxically, the earlier period was the one in which individual Zonians and Panamanians may have found it easiest to become friends. Looking back on those days, a Panamanian complained to an American reporter in 1960, "They [the Zonians] used to be so friendly. Once we were like a big family. The Americans came over every night. The bars, the clubs, the restaurants were full of them, mingling happily with the Panamanians."[8] The speaker assumed it was the Americans who had changed, but so had the Panamanians and so had the world.

During the first half of this century, Panama was a distinctly under-developed country. It needed help, which many Americans were eager to provide. They were proud that the United States was bringing "progress" to Panama. In 1913, an American enthusiast announced, "Indeed, the more one studies Panama . . . the more one is convinced that all that is necessary to make the country a rich and prosperous one . . . is the application of capital, labor, and systematic management. . . ."[9]

There you have it. "Systematic management"—the progressive reformers' universal solution! But that was, in fact, exactly what Panama needed during the first half of this century, and the company on the Zone served as an example of such management. Moreover, because for many years it was responsible for public health in the Panamanian cities adjacent to the Zone, the company had a direct role in the development of a modern municipal infrastructure in Panama's largest cities. Indeed, the company helped perform tasks in Panama City and Colón that were similar to those that individual members of the Peace Corps helped perform later in outlying Panamanian villages. It paved the streets, installed sewers and a water system, built and maintained an asylum for Panama's insane and a community for its lepers. The Canal Company helped supervise and finance the enlargement and modernization of Santo Tomas Hospital. It trained Panamanian workmen and technicians. Until 1953, it handled the garbage and trash collection in Panama City and Colón, and until 1955, it ran public-health offices in those cities. Americans, in cooperation with Panamanian doctors and municipal officials, supervised markets and food-handling plants, directed fly and rat control programs, and vaccinated the populace.

When polio struck Panama in 1948, American and Panamanian doctors worked side by side to control it. In 1949, they roamed the countryside together in order to eradicate jungle yellow fever, giving 425,000 inoculations. When fire wiped out great sections of Colón in 1915 and again in 1940, Americans and Panamanians worked together to prevent epidemics. Zone firemen helped fight the big fire in San Miguel in 1958, and Zone officials cooperated in the relief and cleanup program afterward. A letter of appreciation spoke of "a reaffirmation of our high opinion of the sense of humanitarianism of the North American people."[10]

Zone firemen and Panamanian *bomberos* sometimes trained together. The Zone police and the *Guardia* sometimes competed in pistol matches. The company sent exhibits to agricultural fairs and donated heifers from its dairy herd as prizes. It provided part-time jobs for Panamanian students during their school vacation.

PERSONAL ASSOCIATION

After work, Zonians and Panamanians met each other not only in their quest for entertainment, but also as members of civic, charitable, and professional organizations. In the early years of the American presence on the Isthmus, there simply were not enough people of similar backgrounds and interests to enable all of them to find companionship solely among those of one nationality—or indeed of one social class. Shortly after the dirt started to fly, a University Club was organized—thirteen Americans, twelve Panamanians. But an old-timer recalled that "when the club was organized, the requirements were to be four years' college; they then decided two years was enough—then High School was approved—so finally the suggestion was made: how about letting people join if they WISHED they'd gone to college? Another man said, 'Let's let 'em in if they can write—especially their name on a check.' "[11]

The Incas, a Zone club for men who had been on the job since 1904, turned Goethals down when he applied for membership. He had come too late. But Don Francisco de la Ossa—Don Pancho—the mayor of Panama City, was a member.[12]

In the United States in 1920, the progressive enthusiasts scored one of their greatest legislative triumphs—the Prohibition Enforcement Act. Its purpose was to compel Americans to be sober, just as the laws mandating compulsory school attendance were meant to compel them to be smart. On the Isthmus, prohibition also furthered another of the progressives' goals—international harmony—for it drove the Zonians into Panama in search of a drink.

The drinkers formed three social clubs in the Republic: the Century, the Chagres, and the Miramar. Some of the more polished Zonians found refuge in Panama's exclusive Union Club or helped found Panama's Golf Club. Others joined the Strangers Club in Colón.

Less clubbable Zonians and Panamanians met at Happyland; Sloppy Joe's (*José El Abandonado*); Max Bilgray's Tropic Bar; *El Limite*; Pablo Paz's Lido; the Hotel International; the Florida, which deployed a hundred or so Blue Moon girls in its heyday; or Kelly's Ritz, where Zez Bennett played an endless series of rags. They rubbed shoulders and bent elbows as they watched Jade Rhodora do her Beauty and Beast routine, known locally as "The Rape of the Ape," or Gloria Grant dance with an indifferent boa constrictor. They mingled in beer gardens opened by enterprising Panamanian breweries.

It was in the Balboa Beer Garden in 1938 that ex-President Harmodio Arias gave a champagne supper for Helen Lawrenson, a vagrant New Yorker well known for writing a magazine article called "Latins Are Lousy Lovers." Instead of making her unpopular in Latin America, it made her a challenge: "Her lethal quality is that indefinable something which causes a man, even when out with his wife or the Number One Girl Friend, to stop dead in his tracks and drool," burbled the Panamanian press.[13]

Some Zonian men found Panamanian women equally attractive, which did not please the American women. In construction days, Rose van Hardeveld saw a laundress "laying her hand possessively on each man's arm" and murmuring, *"Este es mi amigo."* Rose said, "As she touched each man she glanced in my direction, but she did not claim me as her friend. It was all I could do to keep from making a face at her." At a dance, Rose watched Panamanian women "ceaselessly prinking and preening." Many of them were lovely, she had to admit, but she noticed their mamas trying to attract the attention of "our men toward their daughters," and said, "I resented this."[14]

In spite of such resentment, Panamanian women and American men often married and came to live on the Zone, and they continued to do so throughout the history of the Canal Zone. To some extent these marriages were encouraged by the complementary cultural stereotypes Panamanian women and American men held of each other: the Panamanian woman as more submissive and passionate than the American woman; the American man as more responsible and faithful than the Panamanian man. However, since Americans and Panamanians were neighbors on the Isthmus for most of this century, there was plenty of time for the limitations of those stereotypes to be widely understood and for the glamorous foreignness of both cultures to be sensibly discounted. The happy international marriages on the Isthmus cannot simply be attributed to cultural determinism. They were also the result of the long-standing, friendly intermingling of the Panamanian and American communities, which encouraged individuals within those communities to discover mutual affinities.

In 1949, a long-time American resident of the Isthmus conceded, "When the Panamanian, his country, customs, and multitude of faults come up for reprehension [on the Zone], the defense witnesses are amazingly scarce."[15] Veiled by the uneasy archness of that observation lie countless unrecorded acts of unthinking arrogance and conscious contempt. But ethnocentricity, bigotry, and jingoism were not exclusively American faults. And an academic visitor, not particularly sympathetic to the Zonians, admitted in the early fifties, "The Zonian conforms quite easily to Panamanian norms when he crosses over into the republic."[16] Panamanians were equally adept at conforming to American norms when they crossed into the Zone, and in spite of a degree of ethnocentrism on both sides, Zonians and Panamanians managed to develop close relationships and even friendships.

For decades, trolley cars, *carrometas*, *busitos*, and *chivas* shuttled Zonians and Panamanians back and forth. Zonians went to *retreta* at Cathedral Plaza to watch the girls and to the Paitilla River to watch the *caymenes* (alligators). Several Panamanian newspapers were published in dual-language editions.

On the Third of November (Panama's Independence Day), Zone veterans' organizations, high-school bands, and Boy and Girl Scouts marched along with the Panamanians in Panama; on the Fourth of July, the *Bomberos'* Drum and Bugle Corps highlighted the American parade on the Zone.

Panamanian tuition students went to school on the Zone, and a few Zonians sent their children to private schools in Panama. Many Zonians sent their children there for piano or dancing lessons. Zone high-school students held proms in Panama and roamed the city soliciting ads for their yearbooks and newspapers.

Prominent Panamanians came to the Zone to address holiday crowds, professional societies, and students. In 1951, the Fastlich family of Panama made a major contribution to the establishment of a teenage baseball league on the Zone. It bears their name and was still going strong in the Canal Area when we left the Isthmus.

Blue and white Carnival flags used to go up on the Zone, and Zonians formed *comparsas* and elected queens. Panama's National Symphony performed in the Balboa High School gym. The Balboa High Glee Club performed at the *Instituto Nacional*. A community chorus from the Zone sang the *Messiah* in the ruins of the cathedral in Old Panama.

Panamanians and Zonians met at the Theatre Guild, the C. Z. Art League, the Isthmian Historical Society, the Archeological Society, and the Friends of the National Museum of Panama. Amateur archeologists from the Zone gave artifacts to Panama's National Museum. In the late twenties, Karl Curtis traced the gold ornaments that had begun showing up in Panama City to a village in the interior and from there upstream to Sitio Conte, which the Peabody Museum excavated between 1930 and 1933. Another Zonian, Phil Dade, discovered fragments of bone and pottery on Venado Beach in 1949. He consulted with Professors Mendez and Castillero and once again the Peabody was called in.

Zonians contributed time and money to Panamanian orphanages and homes for the elderly. For over fifty years, the Cristóbal Women's Club and the Inter-American Women's Club of Colón distributed food and clothing to Colón's needy. During the twenties, the women also sponsored a free clinic.

Numerous ties existed between Catholic organizations on the Zone and in Panama. The Zone's Protestant churches stayed in touch with their denominational brethren in Panama and helped support medical missionaries. Rabbi Nathan Witkin nurtured a close relationship between the Jewish communities on the Zone and in Panama, and people from both nations attended services at the Greek Orthodox and Baha'i churches.

Civic organizations—the Rotary and Lions clubs—also had binational memberships. In 1959, the Canal Zone Lions played host to a regional conference at the Tivoli that brought Lion delegations from nine Panamanian cities together on the Zone.

Hunters from the Zone made friends with Panamanian "hillbillies." Weekend farmers from the Zone cultivated both their papayas and their Panamanian neighbors. Naturally, women from the Zone shopped in Panama and warded off attacks of cabin fever with trips to Panama's waterfront market. Some of them went a good deal farther than the market. Evelyn Rigby Moore served on Panama's National Library Board and helped the University of Panama with both its library and its landscaping. In 1947, she published the first book of Panamanian short stories in any language, and she wrote articles for both American and Panamanian newspapers. On the Zone, Moore founded the College Club and the local branch of the Penwomen. She was one of a number of Zonians over the years to receive the Order of Vasco Nuñez de Balboa from the government of Panama for contributions to the quality of life on the Isthmus.[17]

THE END OF AN ERA

However, by the time Moore left the Isthmus in 1953, a newcomer could not expect to have a career like hers. Her achievements would not have been possible had she not been unusually able, but she was also in Panama at the right time: she was needed, and she wasn't competing with anyone.

During the fifties, Panama's population was becoming more skilled, self-sufficient, and numerous. Panama City's suburbs were farther and farther from the Zone. The gringos and their Zone were becoming abstractions—ideas. Moreover, the growing number of skilled and educated Panamanians made it increasingly difficult for an outsider, no matter how friendly, to help them without offending. Panama still needed United States assistance, but its relationship to the United States was becoming like that of the stereotyped adolescent to his parents. (After the 1978 treaties went into effect, Panamanians spoke of Panama "putting on its long pants.") It was this new stage in United States-Panamanian relations that was at the bottom of the 1962 demonstrations about the name of the new bridge across the Canal. Apart from its utility, it was to symbolize "the idea of unity among the American nations." It was named the Thatcher Ferry Bridge, which conformed to the standard practice of retaining the names of historic ferries and also honored Maurice Thatcher, the last surviving member of the original Canal Commission, an ex-congressman, and a man long active in Isthmian affairs.

However, precisely because the Panamanians had contributed nothing to the construction of the bridge, many of them felt they should at least be able to name it. It was, after all, in their country, even though it was on the Zone. By demanding that it be called the Bridge of the Americas, they were asserting their dissatisfaction with their dependency, which was not exactly the same as declaring their independence.

Scores of minor unreported incidents in the late fifties and early sixties also reflected the emergence of this new stage in United States-Panamanian relations. For instance, in 1960, a Zonian who was related to the manager of a Panamanian brewery suggested to the Zone's Theatre Guild that a Panamanian theater group could use some help in setting up on the brewery's outdoor pavilion. A couple of Americans went to the pavilion and offered to help, particularly in regard to stage lighting, where the need was obviously greatest. But Anita Villalez, Panama's *primera actriz*, told them firmly, "We can handle this ourselves." After standing around a bit and being friendly, the Americans left. A similar incident may have occurred when the United States ambassador to Panama, Joseph Farland, suddenly resigned. Farland was a popular figure in Panama, made many public appearances, and had many Panamanian friends. He resigned, according to the historian Walter LaFeber, partly because of Washington's "insensitivity," but mainly because of the Zonians' criticisms: "With Farland's scalp on their belt, the Zonians . . ."[18] This is implausible. No diplomat fretted over the fact that he was unpopular with the "rednecks" on the Zone. Zone gossip had it that Farland was forced out because Panamanian officials were weary of his intrusive popularity and of his "expert advice." The last straw was said to have been Farland's attempt to tell them where to put a road they wanted to build between Penonemé and Colón—a project they wanted the United States to finance.

The relationship between the United States and Panama was further complicated during the fifties by changes in the class structures of both nations. In the States, the expansion of the college population after the Second World War was reordering American society into the degreed and the nondegreed. Panamanian students coming home from American colleges announced that they had learned that the Zonians were an inferior breed of American,[19] meaning that they had learned that American workers were different from American college teachers and students, the latter group being far more congenial to the Panamanian elite.

And in Panama, the postwar emergence of a growing but economically insecure middle class was altering many aspects of traditional Panamanian society. The new middle class was ardently nationalistic and anti-American. So, of course, were some members of the old oligarchy, but the oligarchs did not see themselves as being in competition with the Americans. The new middle class did, and its members enviously eyed the white-collar jobs on the Zone.

Attitudes on the Zone changed, too, after the war, especially during the fifties. Like their compatriots in the States, the Zonians became less racist, less ethnocentric, and less monolingual. They read *The Ugly American* or books and articles bearing a similar message. They became more sensitive to the need for good international relations.

However, they were also increasingly threatened by Panama's reiterated demand for control over the Canal. And Panama City was fast becoming just another crowded modern city. As it lost its absolving picturesqueness, the contrast between Panamanian and American ideas about civil rights, women, manual labor, democracy, and self-criticism stood out more sharply.

Moreover, during the 1955 treaty negotiations, the American diplomats had insisted that the soldiers and workers on the Zone get a 75 percent tax discount on packaged liquors purchased in Panama. That made it cheaper for the Zonians to buy liquor in Panama and consume it on the Zone rather than going to clubs in Panama. When air-conditioning and television came to the Zone, people had even more reason to stay home.

However, there was no general withdrawal behind national borders. Too many associations had been built up over the years for that to happen. Indeed, some kinds of association increased in the 1950s, associations between American and Panamanian women, for instance.

For decades there had been little social intercourse between them. A British visitor commented in 1913 that Panamanian women were not intellectual, "whilst many of the Americans strive after culture with an ardour which is frenzied."[20] "Serious" would have been a better term. The Americans were serious, middle-class women who, in those days, did not usually work outside the home. So they took up self-improvement. Aristocratic Panamanian women could hardly join so earnest a group, nor could a Panamanian laundress.

There was some association over the years between the College Club women and the University Women's Club of Panama, but it was not until the Inter-American Wives Club was formed in 1946 that the women of the two countries worked together extensively. However, the dramatic growth of Panama's population and its social transformation as Panamanians acquired new skills and ambitions plus the irresponsibility and opportunism of the Panamanian government and the temporizing and vacillation of the American government brought this era of association between Zonians and Panamanians to an unexpected and bloody close.

On Tuesday, January 7, 1964, Amy McCormack, a member of the Isthmian Historical Society, took ninety American newcomers around Panama City on a tour of points of historical interest. On Wednesday, she went to a meeting of the Inter-American Wives at the Union Club in Panama. On Thursday, the Flag Riots began.[21]

"Hey, don't you guys know what's happening?" a Canal Zone biology teacher asked a pair of *Guardia* officers who were enjoying themselves on the Zone in the bowling alley behind Balboa High School. Many Americans in Panama were similarly unaware. Panamanians helped them slip into the Zone and put Panamanian license plates on the cars they left behind, in order to conceal the fact that the cars belonged to Americans. But not everyone got the news in time. Driving back to the Zone from a movie in Panama, Bob Sander and his fiancée were attacked by rioters with rocks and iron bars. Sander managed to break through, but the doctors were unable to save his left eye.[22]

A LEGACY OF GOODWILL

After the riots, Panamanian parents called the Zone's schools to ask if their children were still welcome. They were, of course. There was never an incident between the students of the two nations who attended the Zone schools. Conversely, the Zonians gradually discovered that they were still welcome in Panama. But things had changed.

Zone high-school students no longer solicited ads in Panama for their publications. Panamanians in government circles were reluctant to socialize on the Zone for fear of compromising themselves with Panama's jingoes. Zonians who arrived in the sixties found it more difficult to establish connections with Panamanians living outside the Zone. "It was much harder to have a social exchange here than in Germany," a Zonian who had worked in both places told us before he retired. Another remarked that though he had often had his Panamanian co-workers to his home, he had never been asked to theirs. "We went to business parties at clubs and hotels. That was it."

Nevertheless, some Zonians and Panamanians with mutual interests continued to find each other, and their friendship and respect for each other endured in spite of the quarrels between the governments of Panama and the United States. No one ever studied these friendships. They could not possibly exist, according to some United States Embassy officials, newsmen, and politicians. Some writers announced that the only contacts between Panamanians and Americans involved Panamanian oligarchs and top company officials.[23] Other writers, while acknowledging that some friendships existed, took it for granted that they involved only Americans with liberal educations who were free of prejudice.[24]

That wasn't right. Neither years of education nor liberal views correlated with a person's involvement in Panama. Some conservative American men were more comfortable in the relatively formal, male-oriented Panamanian society than their liberal counterparts.

A Zone educator told us, "It was the professional and educated people who sat around complaining that there was nothing to do in Panama, because there was nothing there that interested them. But the blue-collar people went to Panama." The speaker, however, was his own counterexample, for he was a professional who spent a lot of time in the interior. Our impression is that there was no pattern. Zonians of all types went to Panama regularly; Zonians of all types found reasons to stay on the Zone most of the time.

But even those who generally stayed on the Zone often formed friendships with their Panamanian maids and their families. In 1964, a reporter found the idea that a person could be friends with his or her servant preposterous,[25] but on the Zone, it was sometimes true.

During the years we lived there, the only people we knew who had "servants" were, with one exception, Latins. Our friends, with that one exception (a natural aristocrat if there ever was one), were not cut out to be masters. They were working/middle-class Americans who were uncomfortable with the whole idea of giving orders to an "inferior." Many of them did not hire maids. Those who did considered themselves bosses, not masters. Their employees were "the help," not servants. And while the boss and the help don't usually become pals, they may become friends in the encompassing, democratic, American meaning of that word. As one Zonian said to us, "My maid is a person with a future, too."

Another thing that affected the relationship between domestic servants and their employers, making it different from similar relationships in the States, was the fact that both Panamanians and West Indians were foreign nationals with their own cultures just across the street or up the road.

Paradoxically, the Zone's commissary system also helped forge international friendships. Only Canal employees who lived on the Zone were authorized to enter the commissaries. The government of Panama supported this arrangement because they wanted Panamanians to spend their money in Panamanian stores. When a Panamanian *was* stopped at the door, however, the Panamanian government howled discrimination. The Panamanian government also wanted the company to enforce the laws against contrabanding, but tolerated vendors in Panama like the one in front of Hogar Ideal who displayed his contraband milk and bacon on the sidewalk, and, as they dripped in the sun, shouted, *"Commisariato! Commisariato!"*—a name that signified quality.

The street vendors were supplied by professional contrabanders, but the professionals were only a small part of the problem. When a Panamanian relative or friend asked a Zonian to buy a toy for a child or groceries for a fiesta, few of them refused. A commissary manager told us that each year it seemed to him that every man, woman, and child in Panama received a commissary ham for Christmas. Bags of onions were another item in great demand. Onions are almost as necessary to the Panamanian diet as rice, but for some reason they are often unavailable. When that happened, Zonians picked up an extra bag and passed it on to their friends. Some Zonians who started out buying CheeWees for their Panamanian friends progressed over the years to color TVs, bicycles, and refrigerators. Had American diplomats and liberal politicians consulted the commissary managers or someone from Canal Zone Customs, they might have revised their ideas about the supposed exclusiveness of the Zonians and their unwillingness to have anything to do with Panamanians.

And had those diplomats and politicians thought harder about the possible consequences of international friendships, they might have been less anxious to promote them. The most fiercely anti-treaty Zonians we knew were people married to Panamanians or people with children who were married to Panamanians. They had local ties and a complex stake in the situation that we, for instance, did not. On the other hand, the smoothness of the transition, once the treaties were ratified, must also be partly credited to the existence of those international marriages and friendships.

In 1976, John Jackley pointed out:

> To even ask the question of "What are the attitudes of the CZR's [Canal Zone Residents] towards the Panamanians?" implies that a recognizable difference exists between them, and this is not always the case. There has been so much inter-marriage, so much social and cultural osmosis over the years that the "WASP, all-gringo Zonian" is

well below 50 percent of the total group. . . . The popular image of a third or fourth-generation Zonian, who has nothing but contempt for the Panamanians is false because it is contradictory.[26]

At about the same time, a British journalist visited the Isthmus and, recalling her nation's effort to maintain control of the Suez Canal, observed that on the Isthmus, the American and Panamanian cultures overlapped as the British and Egyptian never did.[27] An American geographer who studied the transition of the Zone from American to Panamanian control came to a similar conclusion.[28]

All this mixing contributed to a degree of intergroup harmony but at the cost of individual confusion. Some people weren't sure what group they belonged to, and neither were their friends and co-workers. A newly arrived American liberal was shocked to hear a dark Panamanian speaking contemptuously of blacks. "When he's one of them!" the American exclaimed. However, the Panamanian just had dark skin—which didn't make him a black, not in Panama. A second-generation American Zonian was disconcerted when her neighbor began complaining bitterly about the Panamanians, since his mother is a Panamanian, his wife is a Panamanian, and he keeps a vacation house in his wife's village in the interior. That man knows the best and worst of both cultures. He could have chosen to belong to either; he deliberately chose to live betwixt and between—but that choice brings with it its own exasperations and contradictions.

When a friend of ours married a Panamanian, he asked us to start calling him Roberto (not his real name) and took to wearing his shirt unbuttoned to display a gold cross on a chain. A year later, still married, he had buttoned up and was back to being Bob again, at least temporarily. Some Panamanians were equally ambivalent. A Panamanian woman who worked for the American Canal Company reminisced for us about her school days at the *Instituto Nacional*, a hotbed of anti-American sentiment. For her, the periodic student demonstrations against the American specter were a kind of game—a rite of passage. The anti-American slogans she and her friends shouted did not prevent them—after their demonstrations against the government of Panama—from fleeing across the street into the Canal Zone, where the Americans would protect them from the *Guardia*. Nor did the expression of anti-American sentiment in her youth prevent her from acquiring many American friends over the years. She is rather proud of her classmates who have become influential, sometimes anti-American, politicians, but she is appalled by the anti-Americanism of a Communist professor she knows. "Somebody should do something about him."

In general, because the Panamanians were permanent residents of the Isthmus, they—at least those in the terminal cities—had to come to terms with the gringos in their midst and with gringo values and ways of doing things. Some Panamanians decided they liked almost everything about the United States. Others were scathingly contemptuous of the philosophical shallowness of the gringos and their lack of social flair. The Zonians, on the other hand, as temporary residents, were free to choose the extent to which they explored Panama. We knew one man who chose not to explore it at all. He never crossed the street into the Republic except on his way to the airport.

But there is statistical evidence that refutes the idea that the Zonians lived in ethnocentric isolation from the Panamanians. During the 1970s, private residents of the Canal Zone spent about $40 million a year in Panama. (The total income flow from the Zone to Panama, including purchases by private organizations and the company, was much greater—$253,130,000, for example, in 1975.)[29]

There is also a good deal of testimony to the effect that the picture of the Zonian promoted by the diplomats at the United States Embassy was incomplete—to put it diplomatically. Ted Wilber came to the Zone in 1925 when he was in the navy. He went to work for the company in 1929 and lived on the Zone until 1968. Since then, he has been living in Panama City. In 1982, after observing the local scene for fifty-seven years, he wrote,

> In all that time, I always felt that the citizenry of Panama and the Canal Zone got along pretty well. They enjoyed the company of each other: Panamanians were members of the Fort Amador Golf Club and the Amador Swimming Club, they came to the Canal

Zone for participation in many areas. The Panama Government participated with the Canal Zone Government in each annual Carnival; the Canal Zone Government used to furnish the Carnival Committee of Panama with about 100 trucks, with drivers and gasoline, and entered floats from the CZ Government and the Army, Navy, and Marine Corps. In general, there was a good feeling between the peoples of both nationalities regardless of the Panama Government in power at the time.[30]

Fernando Manfredo, deputy administrator of the Canal Commission, reported that President Aristides Royo had "fond memories" of participating in programs sponsored by the Canal Zone YMCA when he was a boy,[31] and Claudio Vasquez, one of Latin America's most distinguished pianists, gave his first public performance in the auditorium of the Canal Zone Jewish Welfare Board.

Demetrio Lakas, president of the revolutionary government of Panama from 1969 to 1978, took note of the contribution made by the Canal Zone schools to the creation of lasting friendships between Panamanians and Americans when he addressed the 1979 graduating class of the Panama Canal College—formerly the Canal Zone College. He had himself graduated with the class of 1946, whose members called him Jimmie or Greco, voted him the treasurer of the Student Association, and named him the friendliest in the class. He played guard on the football team, left field on the baseball team, and sang in a barbershop quintet.[32]

After reminding his audience that "many people in high and responsible positions in both the United States and Panamanian Governments" had attended the college, Lakas said:

My next point is more important, it seems to me, than the results of a successful educational program. Through the years, the Canal Zone school system, with its College, has been an important source of good will and friendship between the U.S. and Panamanian citizens and families. . . .

Even though the school system was established for the benefit of children of American citizens, the schools and the College have always been open to Panamanian students. There has always been a willingness to share with others what you Americans had here as leaders in the field of education. There were Panamanian graduates in the first class to graduate from this college. Dean Murphy tells me that of the 115 members of this class of 1979 that 38 are Panamanian citizens.

I would also like to express appreciation to the officials of the Canal Zone who have made it possible for the thousands of Panamanian students who have entered these halls of higher education. My reason for this is that with each Panamanian who studied here, additional lasting friendships were established and more good will was created. In addition, many Panamanian students have received scholarships through the years to attend this College, and this made it possible for many to receive a college education who could not have done so without this financial assistance.

You can be sure that these Panamanian families have a profound feeling of gratitude towards the College and its administration. However, such feelings of appreciation also extend to the highest levels of our government. When you take time to count your blessings and I feel we should all do that from time to time, you will find that you have many friends and supporters in the Republic of Panama.[33]

But while the popular image of the Zonian as a person with nothing but contempt for the Panamanian was not true, it was once *part* of the truth. It tells us something about the Zonian as he was between roughly 1904 and 1960. Interestingly, the stereotype was not often mentioned by the American press until the late fifties. By then it represented a smaller part of the truth than ever before and as a total picture of the Zonians was seriously misleading.

During the next eighteen years, from 1960 to 1978, the government of Panama promoted this stereotype as an accurate picture of the American Zonian. It had a reason for this. In order to portray Panama as oppressed, it was necessary to have an oppressor. The Zonians were an obvious choice. However, some American diplomats, politicians, and journalists also promoted this stereotype. Their reasons are less obvious and more interesting.

16
Critics of the Zone: From Ladies and Gentlemen to Aristocrats of the Spirit

THE ZONIAN AS CALIBAN

Many of the articles a Zonian read about himself were condescending or critical or both. They were also often inaccurate, written by members of America's gentry, who were reluctant to expose themselves for long to ordinary working people, and who were confident that with a briefing from the embassy and an hour of solitary, analytical thought, they could figure out anything.

In 1904, America's gentry consisted of conservative ladies and gentlemen who looked askance at the socialist "roughnecks" on the Zone. During the next half-century, America's gentry reconstituted itself. By the sixties and seventies, it consisted mainly of liberal professionals and administrators. They are more sympathetic to the idea of socialism and often assume that their social goals are congruent with those of the working class. However, their antipathy to the working-class society on the Zone suggests that this is not so—as do their casual references to "rednecks." But the status liberals did not face up to their class bias. They told themselves that they disliked the Zonians because they were colonialists—and enemies of "progress."

EARLY OBSERVERS: 1904–1948

"Nowhere perhaps in the world are work people so well cared for," wrote an English visitor to the Zone during the construction era.[1] Some American gentry noticed the same thing, and it struck them as, well, inappropriate! William Franklin Sands, an American diplomat assigned to Panama in 1904, was disgusted to observe that the "canal mechanics" traveling to the Zone by ship went first class even as he did, but gambled and drank with the crew.[2] They "pretty well destroyed ship's discipline on all the lines," he complained. Furthermore, their high jinks and inexcusable failure to dress for dinner embarrassed him before the ship's British captain.

Once on the Zone, however, Sands complained that these same high-spirited troublemakers were contemptibly "docile," more "readily robotized," he said, than the Russian "moujik." He went so far as to say that the American workers all looked alike!

The Zone, he declared scathingly, was "a foretaste of those New Jersey and Long Island suburbs of the 1920's where social ratings were according to the number and cost of one's automobiles."

The American diplomat alluded distastefully to the Zonians as "this particular species of American." Among them he met for the first time a type he was to meet later in Moscow—"the typical young Bolshevik commissar"—and still later in Washington—"the typical young draughtsman of New Deal legislation."

This type was epitomized on the Zone by Jackson ("Square Foot") Smith, who was in charge of housing. Sands reported that there was general dissatisfaction with Smith's arbitrary methods of assigning quarters. He did it by the numbers, without any diplomatic adjustments for influential friends or social status: The bigger your salary, the bigger your house, period. Theodore Roosevelt, according to Sands, "undertook to remonstrate" with this unaccommodating young man and opened the conversation by saying that Mr. Jackson Smith was certainly a much criticized official. "So, too, is our worthy President," was Square Foot's cool reply.

Is that the way a Bolshevik commissar talked to Lenin or Stalin? It is not. It is American sass—and Sands, the American gentleman, found it hard to take, much as he liked seeing TR caught off base.

Sands was a member of "a pretty good club"—the United States Foreign Service, which was filled with superior types. However, he lived in a society where money was allocated by the market—an uncontrolled and undiscriminating mechanism. Too often, the "wrong sort" ended up doing quite well—better, even, than their social superiors. Sands would not have been so appalled by the Canal mechanics if they had not been so well paid and uppity.

The kind of man Sands admired was Rufus Lane of Hingham, a man of his own class, who couldn't *do* anything—"He was not an engineer, nor a stenographer, nor a doctor." However, he had arrived on the Zone with a letter from a senator saying he should be given a job. Someone put him in charge of the villages in the jungle, and Lane went from one to the other bringing "patriarchal self-government" to primitive peoples. Sands said Lane was the only man in Panama "who understood how to manage these people." Sands admired managerial gentlemen, and he liked primitive people who needed managing. But he could not abide a prosperous working/middle class that did not respect his credentials nor seek his advice.

Harry Franck, a gentleman who worked on the Zone in 1912 in order to gather material for a book,[3] informed his genteel readers:

> It is doubtful, to be sure, whether one fourth of the "Zoners" of any class ever lived so well before or since. The shovelman's wife who gives five o'clock teas and keeps two servants will find life different when . . . she moves back to the smoky little factory cottage and learns again to do her own washing.

The men Franck worked with were "roughnecks," a breed he assumed his readers knew little about:

> A "rough-neck," it may be essential to explain to those who never ate at the same table with one, is a bull-necked, whole-hearted, hard-headed, cast-iron fellow. . . . created without the insertion of nerves, though he is never lacking in "nerve." He is a fine fellow in his way, but you sometimes wish his way branched off from yours. . . .

Franck complained that his dormitory was distinctly an abode of "rough-necks" because after dinner seven phonographs struck up seven different kinds of ragtime. That was the music of the working class in those days. The Canal was built to the lilt and jangle of rags— and to the barbershop harmonies of ballads like "Juanita." A worker fondly remembered the night two of his loopy pals embraced after a long poker game and "murdered 'Juanita.'" (Roughnecks could embrace while "murdering Juanita,'" but wearing a wristwatch was considered effeminate.)

Franck sneered at the roughnecks who didn't know Spanish *and* at those who were trying to learn. He recorded for his educated readers' amusement the effort of a roughneck to communicate with a Spaniard: "When you know *por la noche* that you're not going to *trabaja por la mañana*, why in———don't you *habla?*" The Zone's commissary managers, according to Franck, were "provincial little fellows" from small towns whose notions of business were "rather those of Podunk, Mass., than of New York."

"Fellows" is a key word. So is "lads." In 1946, a travel agent recalled a Chagres Society banquet at the Tivoli Hotel that took place some years earlier. He wasn't invited, but he peeked in: "The steamshovel lads" were "yelling for more champagne . . . many of them," he asserted knowingly, "had never seen much less tasted the bubbly stuff."[4]

Some of the journalists who visited the Zone in the early days shared the values of the Zone mechanics. Charlie Cushing reported in the *New York Tribune Magazine* in 1924 that there were no white sun helmets, no punka-coolies waving fans, no colonial romanticism of any sort on the Zone. Instead, there was a bourgeois American society complete with Masonic Temple and YMCA. "Perhaps I'm merely thick-witted," he wrote, defensively, "but all this makes me rejoice."[5]

More discriminating Americans who bought Hilton Howell Railey's *Touched With Madness* were shown a different Zone. Railey spent a few months there in the thirties as a government consultant, and it depressed him. Yes, he said, it was "a mechanic's paradise," in the sense that there "manual workers" were "endowed with a standard of living the majority have not experienced in the past and couldn't elsewhere maintain." (For as long as the Zone lasted, intellectuals kept reporting that Canal workers were overpaid and would receive their comeuppance in the States, suggesting that intellectuals do not know much about how much workers are paid.)[6]

Railey also accused the Zonians of being "mentally rutted" and of having "a poverty of initiative." They camped out, he said, in furnished houses they could never own, "content with the collectivist fulfillment of their wants." He concluded, "Those who do not dance, fish, hunt, swim, play golf or the lottery, those who tire of severely restricted motoring . . . and the repetitious pleasures of Panamanian night clubs and beer gardens must fall back on motion pictures in ramshackle clubhouses, for litle else relieves the rigid rectitude of their existence."[7]

Clearly, Railey wants his readers to pity the Zonians, but why? What does "mentally rutted" mean when applied to people from mainly small towns who have adventurously left the United States to make lives for themselves overseas? Although we were never ourselves impressed with the average Zonian's rectitude, what's wrong with rectitude? Why isn't it a good thing?

The nature of Railey's complaint suggests that to him the "mechanic's paradise" he found on the Zone represented a threat. He was not the only intellectual who seemed to feel that way. The new intellectual elite that developed in America during the twentieth century was sympathetic to workers in the abstract, but found the nineteenth-century workers' paradise on the Zone very nervous-making.

In the early forties, Ernie Pyle visited the Zone. He was, in the judgment of the poet and critic Randall Jarrell, the best American journalist of the Second World War. Nobody else, Jarrell said, could make us feel so intensely sorry for the soldiers who were doing the fighting.[8] Pyle did his best to make his readers feel sorry for the Zonians, too—and superior to them. The Zonians, he reported, have "given up personal ambition, natural instinct of competition—all the lovely mystery of life—for the security that gives them a life of calm and vague discontent." Pyle added that the Zonians knew this was wrong. They feel as if they have done something wrong to their souls, he reported. Then he agreed with his own report: they had. A neat trick.[9]

It is hard to know whether to call this snobbery or a failure of the imagination. Perhaps they are the same thing. The rich and talented —men like famous war correspondents—do not need to choose between security and freedom. They can have both. However, unlike the rich, talented, and tenured who enjoy life among the fixed costs, working men and women are classified among the variable costs. It follows that when they have a choice, working people often choose security over "the lovely mystery of life," which becomes so unlovely as one's bank balance diminishes.

Surely there were socialist intellectuals in the States who understood this. But none of them ever wrote about the Zone—the nearest thing to a workers' paradise that Americans have yet produced. They left it to be described by "aristocrats of the spirit"[10] like William Gaddis, who in 1978 recalled his experiences on the Zone thirty years before.[11]

Gaddis had a college friend whose brother owned an English-language newspaper in Panama. So, with a note from "Tony" and another from a classmate whose father had been president of Panama ("It was that kind of college," Gaddis says), he flew south to launch his career as a journalist. His connections treated him like a gentleman, but the New Zealander who ran their newspaper for them did not offer him a job. Gaddis had to look for employment on the Zone. He "caught on," but his co-workers were roughnecks, not gentlemen.

He discovered that the Zone's library was "inexplicably well-stocked," which was evidently a jolt. But he restored his sense of superiority and put the Zonians back in their place by deciding that "there was never any problem of any book of real depth or merit being out on loan." He added, "What writing or reading went on in our compound seemed mainly to be pencil written responses to letters addressed there in pencil from home with a Southern postmark, relieved now and then by a penciled plea from some nearby country opening, 'Why don't you say me?' "

The pencil as a class marker is new to us, but we understand "Southern postmark." That means a person who is uneducated—the sort of person who consorts with foreign girls who write "Why don't you say me?" instead of with the sons of the *Rabiblancos*, who go to "good" schools in the States and speak English grammatically.

Curiously, Sinclair Lewis, once the patron saint of sensitive souls rebelling against the conformity, hypocrisy, and ethnocentrism of small-town, middle-class America, found much to admire about the small-town, ethnocentric, working/middle-class Zonians. Lewis was on the Zone in 1907, looking for a job. He wrote his parents that the Zonians were "a race of strong, self-reliant men, very intelligent all of them as regards their own trades, blacksmithing, plumbing, running steam shovels, or what not." Unlike Gaddis, Lewis failed to "catch on." He missed seven out of twenty-seven on the supply clerk's exam. Then he found there was "nothing doing" in the stenographer's line and, much to his parents' relief, went back for his senior year at Yale.[12]

PRIDE AND PREJUDICE

The intellectual's pride is his ability to make sense of the world. His temptation is to do so without looking at it. His prejudice, at least in America in this century, has been to regard himself as an aristocrat of the spirit who is sickened by the stupid, boring denizens of that "other America," where people live in developments, watch "General Hospital," go to church, save discount coupons, read *The National Enquirer*, worry about being laid off—and, presumably, hate blacks, laugh at ballet, and do not buy books.

Throughout its existence, the Zone exemplified this other America for many visiting literati, newspaper pundits, and American diplomats. Over the years, the gap widened between their perceptions of the Zone and its reality. The last literary man to examine the Zone and the least able to understand it was Paul Theroux, who wrote it up for a chapter in *The Old Patagonian Express.*[13]

Theroux is careful to assert that he was not sponsored by the State Department. But State Department officials ordered up Zone audiences for his lectures, escorted him to the Zone to deliver them, and hovered about him during his conversations with Zonians, interposing veiled, private comments, rather as if they were interpreting for someone not completely familiar with the language.

It was apparently these interpreters who told him that when the jingoistic Zonians become "especially frenzied" they "often burn their Stars and Stripes, and their children cut classes at Balboa High School to trample on its ashes." Theroux says that the diplomatic representative of the United States who accompanied him to Balboa High would not go up on the stage to introduce him. According to Theroux, the diplomat was afraid that if the students learned he was from the embassy, they would riot and overturn his car.

This is alarming testimony: A diplomatic representative of the United States who is afraid to identify himself to the children of United States government employees and United States military personnel! It is even more alarming when you realize that his fears were groundless—mere hallucinations produced by embassy folklore about the mysterious "redneck" Zonians.

It doesn't even make sense to say that super-patriotic American jingoes burn American flags. At the very least, such a paradox calls for an explanation, which it does not get. But then, it never happened. No Zonian ever burned or mutilated an American flag—or a Panamanian one, either, for that matter, though it has become official history in Panama that they once tore a Panamanian flag. No Zone students ever rioted or overturned and burned a car.

Once in the forties some Zone students played a trick with a car. A group of Canal Zone College students, including Demetrio Lakas, the first president of Panama after Torrijos' revolution, carried their favorite English teacher's little English car up to the third floor of the college building and rolled it down the hall past the open door of her classroom—to her astonishment and their great glee.

It seems incredible, but apparently Theroux and his friends from the embassy were confusing the behavior of students on the Zone with the behavior of students in Panama. Panamanian students have, of course, rioted, burned American flags, and overturned cars. Once they burned a car belonging to the United States Embassy! Here is an inability to discriminate that bodes ill for American foreign policy.

Theroux is also confused about history. Upon learning that ships are drawn through the locks by electric-towing locomotives called "mules," he knowingly informs his readers, "Once, the ships were drawn by mules; the engines are still called 'mules.' " Because it seems so right, he does not check. Is he confusing the Panama Canal with the Erie Canal? "I got a mule and her name is Sal . . ." On the other hand, he *saw* the locks. How could he imagine mules scrambling up a 32 degree/29.7 foot smooth concrete incline from one lock chamber to another? Or sliding down, even without a ship in tow? No quadruped ever hauled barges filled with "lumber, coal and hay" or anything else through the Big Ditch.

Theroux makes a habit of pretending to knowledge he does not have. He tells his readers that the Zonians banked at the company bank. There was no company bank. They worship, he says, at company churches. Company churches? And most of the Zonians, he says, were recruited out of New Orleans.

Had he asked, he would have been told that a 1954 survey showed that more of them were from New York than any other single state, as might be expected since the company's home port was New York City for fifty-seven years. It was changed to New Orleans in 1961. In that year, a survey showed that most Zonians came from North Atlantic, Middle Atlantic, or East Central states.[14]

However, by the late sixties, most Zonians were traveling to and from the States by air. By the time Theroux reached the Zone, the Miami airport had long been the "home port" for most Zonians, though supplies continued to be shipped from New Orleans.

Anyone could have told Theroux these things, but he did not ask. He supposed the Zonians were from the South, and since someone had mentioned that the company's home port was New Orleans . . . Thus, he says he heard a Zone train conductor "using his Louisiana drawl on a black." Are we to suppose Theroux can distinguish a Louisiana drawl from, say, a Mississippi drawl?

Theroux also lacks a sense of proportion; the Zonians, he says, are "doomed residents of Panama." Doomed? "The high company officials live like viceroys." But actually the Canal Zone governor's house was a modest mansion, nowhere near as grand as the houses around Ward Parkway in Kansas City or those across State Line in Mission, Kansas. The Zone's lieutenant governor lived in what real estate agents like to call an executive ranch, and no viceroy in British history ever lived in a home as modest as those occupied by bureau chiefs or division heads on the Canal Zone.

Instead of learning about the Zone from the Zonians, Theroux instructed them about what the Zone was really like. It's not really socialism, he told one man. And he offers his readers a neatly packaged account of racism on the Zone:

> About four years ago [he is writing in 1978], the schools on the Zone were reclassified—it meant they didn't have to be integrated. Blacks, who had been brought years ago to work in the Zone, were regarded as Panamanians. So the integration issue was simplified: the Blacks were encouraged to move out of the Zone. They did not move far— they couldn't, they still had jobs in the Zone. The fringes of the Zone are occupied by these rejects, and the far side of the Fourth of July Highway is a slum. They cross the highway to go to work, and in the evening they return to their hovels. And what is interesting is that the Zonian, when particularly worked up about the civilization he has brought to the isthmus, will point to the dividing line and say, "Look at the contrast!" But it was the Zonian who decreed that those people should live there and that all of Panama should stand aside and let him get on with the job.

The West Indians certainly suffered from racial prejudice, as we have pointed out, but that general truth cannot excuse Theroux's inaccurate and misleading summary of their history.

Certainly, his "four" in "about four years ago" is not accurate. The reorganization of the schools took place between 1954 and 1956, over twenty years before Theroux visited the Zone.

A truth that is not quite true is that the West Indians "had been brought" to the Zone. Many of them had been. The company recruited them on their home islands and brought them to Panama, but Theroux's use of the passive voice suggests that the black West Indians were brought involuntarily, which is not so. They came as free men looking for work, and, under the terms of their contracts, were guaranteed free repatriation if they so desired.

Theroux's belief that the slums across the street from the Zone were populated by "rejects" who had jobs with the company is colored by similar misleading connotations and is, furthermore, wrong in its particulars. There are several slums near the Zone border, each with its own character and history. The sardonically named Hollywood is a shantytown with open latrines and pools of foul-smelling water. It was never populated by people with jobs on the Zone. Chorillo, on the other hand, has paved streets and sewers. It was built in 1904 by the Canal Company as worker housing. In the early fifties, many West Indian Canal workers were still living in its overcrowded, dilapidated, two-story wooden barracks, although there were already some West Indians in suburbs like Rio Abajo and Pueblo Nuevo. By the time Theroux reached the Zone, the slums across the street were not occupied by Canal workers.

Only one American reporter visited those slums, Ronald Yates.[15] He went there in 1977 and, to his surprise, found the people outspokenly pro-American and anti-Torrijos. Once the volatility of the loyalties of the very poor have been taken into account, and once the fact that Yates did not talk to a scientific sampling has been duly noted, we are still left with evidence that political opinion in Panama is more complex than its government-controlled press indicates or than American liberal opinion presupposes.

In the early fifties, most of the Canal workers living in Chorillo wanted to live on the Zone. The company had a waiting list of over 2,000 applicants for Zone housing.[16] But although the wooden houses on the Zone were better than what was available to most West Indians in Panama, the Zone's houses were dilapidated, too. In 1951, the company began a $30 million program to build new houses for locally hired workers. Three years later, with only 750 of a projected 4,165 units completed, the company called off the program and decided to restrict still further the number of locally hired workers entitled to live on the Zone. This would relieve it of a grave financial burden and would please the government of Panama, which had long complained that too many relatively affluent Panamanians were permitted to live and shop on the Zone. Theroux never mentions that wages on the Zone were always higher than wages in Panama. Indeed, Mavis and John Biesanz suggest that at least three presidents of Panama complained that the company paid its locally hired workers too much![17] In 1976, the Panamanian labor leader William Sinclair pointed out that a secretary on the Zone would make three to four dollars an hour, while a woman doing similar work in Panama would make eighty to ninety cents an hour.[18]

The new housing policy was implemented on the basis of attrition. It provided financial assistance to employees who wished to purchase medium-priced homes in Panama.[19] Those employees did not move to the slums.

Hollywood, Guachapouli, Chorillo, and Caledonia made a dramatic contrast to the Zone, but we doubt if any Zonian ever stood beside Theroux and said, "Look at the contrast!" Indeed, Theroux does not quite say that ever happened. It is the Zonian in general who says this. It is one of the things "we" know "they" say.

The story of the West Indian Canal workers is not easily told. They faced discrimination both in Panama and on the Zone, but it was patterned differently. In some ways they were better off in Panama; in others, on the Zone. Moreover, their cultural background, which distinguished them from Panama's Spanish-speaking blacks, also distinguished them from American blacks. We could understand if a travel writer skipped them entirely, but since Theroux does mention them, he ought at least to suggest the difficulties of his subject. He is not writing fiction. A man can make things up without leaving home.

Theroux enjoyed another bout of moral revulsion on the Canal Company train as he observed a crass American conductor speaking English to some men whom Theroux described as "blacks who had been reclassified as 'Panamanian.'" However, the native language of those Panamanians was English, just as the native language of many North American Hispanics is Spanish, although they are citizens of the United States.

A few questions would have cleared up Theroux's misconceptions, but he did not ask questions. He hugged his certainties to himself. He revealed nothing and learned little.

A Panamanian he met denied the rumor that the dictator had been put into office by the CIA: "Omar wasn't put there by the gringos," he said, and Theroux bristled. "I found his phraseology objectionable. But the American ambassador was present. I could not say, 'Don't call me a gringo, and I won't call you a spic,' to this swarthy citizen of Panama."

Why not? What's so special about the ambassador? Would *he* sit still for it? Actually, Theroux's secret dream of what he would have said if only the ambassador had not been present was itself based on a misconception, for "gringo" is not a bad word in Panama. A Panamanian can damn the gringos, but he can also use the word without giving offense. It does not carry the same connotation in Panama that we understand it does in Mexico. It is not the equivalent of "spic."

However, when the time came to write his book, Theroux revealed his certainties and his contempt. Of a lecture he gave at the Canal Zone College, he remarks,

> . . . how strange it was to speak of the world and the romance of distance to people who could not conquer their timidity long enough to endure the short drive to Panama City, and who regarded the town of Colón, just up the road, as more savage and dangerous than a whole jungle of Amazonian head-hunters.

Some of the students who listened to him that day lived in Panama City and Colón. They were Panamanians, but Theroux did not ask. The people in front of him were Canal Zone College students. He assumed that meant they were Zonians, and he knew all about *them*. His friends from the embassy had filled him in.

Some of the Zonians in that room had, at least at that point in Theroux's journey, traveled more widely in South America than he had. He did not ask. Moreover, later, when he himself visited Colón, he was unwilling to spend the night there.

> If I were to stay in Colón, I would have to choose between the chaos and violence of the native quarter or the colonial antisepsis of the Zone. I took the easy way out, bought a ticket back to Panama City. . . .

Colón is a largely black town. That is where he gets "native quarter." But it is not a quarter. It is Panama's second largest city. At least a third of its labor force is unemployed. Many of the Latin Panamanian managers and accountants who work there go back to Panama City each night, just as Theroux did. The *Guardia* remain. They carry rifles and stand in pairs on street corners, as if they belonged to an invading army. The man who told Theroux, "This is not a safe place," was right. However, it ill-behooves a man who won't spend a night in Colón to condescend to those who, he erroneously imagines, cannot conquer their timidity long enough to go there.

The college students Theroux addressed were respectful. The high-school students were not. One philistine came right out with, "How much money do you make?" And a girl asked, "Why bother to take a train all that way? I mean, if it takes so wicked long?"

An excellent question, we thought. Paul Fussell answered it a few years later when he pointed out, instancing Theroux's book, that the traditional travel book had become the stunt travel book, and its emphasis had shifted from the character of the places visited to the anomaly of the means used to get there.[20] But Theroux did not take the question seriously. Proudly, he records his snide reply to the teenager: "Because you can take a six pack of beer in your compartment and guzzle it, and by the time you've sobered up, you've arrived."

Theroux says, "Much of the Canal hysteria in the States was whipped up by the news that the Zonians were living the life of Riley, with servants and princely salaries and subsidized pleasures."

That explains a good deal. Obviously it was not those who opposed the treaties who were subject to this hysteria. (They were sometimes hysterical but for other reasons.) It was the members of Theroux's own class, the aristocrats of the spirit, who were "hysterical" at the thought of *workers* living "the life of Riley." Theroux reassures them. There is no need to be jealous. The Zonian is but a simple "fellow."

> His restrictions and rules have killed his imagination and deafened him to any of the subtleties of political speech; he is a Christian [Baptists predominate, says Theroux]; he is proud of the canal and has a dim unphrased distrust of the Company; his salary is about the same as that of his counterpart in the United States—after all, the fellow is a mechanic or a welder: why shouldn't he get sixteen dollars an hour?

A woman on the Zone told Theroux, "Goodness, we're ordinary people!" and he, with a wink at his reader, replied, "That I can vouch for." Rarely does an aristocrat of the spirit draw the line so plainly.

17
Diplomats and Workingmen

IDENTIFYING THE ENEMY

As far as the State Department was concerned, the Panama Canal Commission was the enemy from the day it was established. Its chairman reported to the secretary of war—later to the secretary of the army—not to the secretary of state. Worst of all, the importance of the Canal Commission to the Republic of Panama quite overshadowed that of the United States Embassy, an intolerable state of affairs for the diplomats.

The institutional conflicts between the embassy and the company often had the effect of allying the embassy and the Panamanians against the Americans on the Zone. In 1934, a government consultant remarked, "At times the State Department appears to have been better informed concerning Panama's side of the question than it has concerning the Canal Zone's."[1] He recommended that the governor of the Zone also serve as the American ambassador to Panama. That recommendation was not well received by the diplomats. A few years later, another consultant reported that nothing had changed: "The State Department plays one game, the Canal another. They rarely see eye-to-eye. Panama . . . grins impudently—and muscles in."[2]

The debate over the 1978 Canal treaties was in part a principled debate about American foreign policy, but it was also, to an undeterminable extent, a struggle for bureaucratic turf, which was exacerbated by differences of class and style between the diplomats and the Canal workers.

Can any serious person believe that 3,500 Canal workers and their families could have prevented the governments of Panama and the United States from doing anything they wanted? However, the fantasy that the Canal workers' amazing political adroitness accounted for the lack of harmony between the United States and Panama had important diplomatic advantages. The State Department and Panama did not need to blame each other for anything. They could remain friends while blaming the Zonians. After the 1964 riots, these friends in pursuit of their separate goals found themselves cooperating to engineer a melodrama that would rally support for a new treaty between the United States and Panama. That archimperialist Teddy Roosevelt and his "redneck" henchmen the Zonians were cast as the villains. Panama was the victim. The heroes would be the morally sensitive citizens of the United States—the aristocrats of the spirit—who would free the oppressed Panamanians from the shackles of Roosevelt's 1904 treaty and apologize for the behavior of their inferior fellow citizens on the Zone.

The American ambassador agreed with the Panamanians that they had been exploited and oppressed by the United States. He called their version of history "logical" and "all true." But he urged them to moderate their demands. Otherwise, Congress and the American people would balk at giving the Canal to Panama.[3]

Panamanian newspapers took the lead. They branded the Zonians as "intransigent egotists, retrograde Americans who will kill in order to preserve prerogatives to which they have no right."[4] A less outwardly hysterical Panamanian businessman told an American reporter that the Zonians were "descendants of the Canal builders" who had "lost touch completely with their own country and the changing world. They have become accustomed to privileged and unrealistic social conditions that they will not easily surrender."[5]

(This myth was repeated so often that it came to be widely believed. Actually, in 1964, only 15.5 percent of the American Zonians were descendants of Zonians. A much smaller percentage were descendants of Canal builders.)[6]

Panamanian officials like Octavio Fabrega declared that the Zonians had the mentality of *colons*: "A mentality which is even something foreign to the U.S. citizens who come [to the Canal Zone] from the U.S." He compared the Zonians to the French in Vietnam.[7] Ambassador Nander Pitty Velasquez told the Organization of American States that "Zonian elements are the bitterest enemies of an understanding between Panama and the United States." They spend, he asserted, "part of their juicy salaries to wage political campaigns against the governments of Panama and the United States." He raised the possibility that they might "implant a new Rhodesia or new South Africa in our territory," and proclaimed that they had shown "an infinite capacity for evil."[8] At the United Nations, Ambassador Aquilino Boyd circulated a letter accusing the Zonians of being "determined to foil negotiations" between Panama and the United States.[9]

American diplomats did not often respond to verbal attacks on their countrymen. When some sort of denial was absolutely necessary, they made it as mild as possible, and they worked behind the scenes to persuade American journalists and public figures to speak out against the retrograde Zonians. Some journalists were undiplomatic enough to attribute remarks about the "imperialist mentality" of the Zonians to unidentified State Department officials.[10] Others passed such conclusions off as their own.

By the 1970s a growing number of journalists were predisposed to see the situation in Panama from the State Department's point of view. A few years earlier, most journalists came from working/middle-class families and made working-class salaries. During the 1960s, however, more and more journalists obtained graduate degrees and began making relatively high salaries.[11] They became "thinking Americans."

As such, they were more influenced than the rest of the population by the ideas of the turn-of-the-century progressive reformers whose ideas had become part of the general climate of informed opinion, the ideas of Henry Demarest Lloyd, for instance, who believed that men in close association *had* to love one another, and of the economist Richard T. Ely, who preached "fraternalism" and regarded the state as "an educational and ethical agency."[12]

Robert Bartley of the *Wall Street Journal* called the young reporters "an idealistic elite."[13] They were morally ambitious to make Americans better, but at the same time, as David Broder observed to the National Press Club in 1979, the press had grown isolated from the public it claimed to serve.[14] This had long been true of some politicians. During his brief visit to the Isthmus in 1960, Adlai Stevenson consulted with the embassy and then announced that "the greatest problem we have in Panama is the exclusive community of American citizens that has grown up in the Zone and has little contact with the friendly country around them."[15]

That the Zonians had little contact with the Panamanians was not true, but it was the cardinal article of the diplomats' faith. They briefed reporters like Bernard Collier, whose subsequent insight enabled him to disclose in 1964: "The trouble is that the Zonians know in their hearts that they are relics from the age of Teddy Roosevelt, living just on the other side of a cyclone fence from a rabidly nationalistic people they can barely tolerate."[16] That same year, Trevor Armbrister of the *Saturday Evening Post* noticed that same "eight-foot mesh fence that shuts Panamanians out of the Zone" and behind which live "frequently arrogant" United States citizens in their "tidy homes" with their "shiny cars."[17]

Collier and Armbrister were not the only ones to "see" that fence. It got to be famous. But it wasn't there! (Arnulfo Arias threatened to put one up once, but nothing came of the idea. He wanted to keep the Panamanians and the Americans *apart!*)[18]

There *was* a fence around an American army base that shared a block of border with Panama, and another around a grade-school playground that abutted the border, which at that point was a busy street —but there was no fence shutting Panamanians out of the Zone. In 1976, the British writer Jan Morris was impressed by the fact that the Zone was not physically insulated: "There are no barriers, check points, or wire fences, not even a *cordon sanitaire.* . . ."[19]

But Morris is an outsider. Of course she couldn't see that fence. Only true believers could see it, men who "knew" how ethnocentric and bigoted working-class Americans really are. And if true believers can see a tangible, eight-foot thing that isn't there, how much easier for them to see the intangible things that people "know in their hearts."

(It is worth noting, we think, that ten years before Collier, Armbrister, and others began seeing that fence, some American tourists on the Zone were expressing a determination to see it. In 1953, a bemused Zonian commented in the company newspaper that some tourists expected border barriers between the Canal Zone and Panama and dismissed as "ignorance or subtle intrigue" the fact that even long-time residents of the Zone did not know exactly where one jurisdiction stopped and the other began.)[20]

A fence *had* to be there. Disagreements existed between the United States and Panama. How else could a person account for these disagreements except by attributing them to a lack of friendly down-home get-togethers? Accordingly, when the Canal Company newspaper printed an article saying that Zonians danced Panamanian folk dances, ate Panamanian food, shopped in Panamanian stores, went to Panama for social functions, entertainment, country fairs, and fiestas—and that some Zonians owned homes in Panama, some had retired there, and that some were married to Panamanians—a journalist like Armbrister had to deny it. "This, of course, is mostly nonsense," he wrote.[21] It *had* to be, because if there was contact between the two groups, there would be love; and if there was love, there would be no problems about the Panama Canal.

As "proof" of the lack of contact between the Zonians and the Panamanians, Armbrister cited the fact that Spanish was not taught on the Zone until 1956. But this is a fact like his fence is a fence. In 1955, the Spanish-as-a-second-language program, which had been introduced in grades four through six in 1952, was expanded to include grades one through three. That must have been what someone told him about. On the secondary level, an outstanding Spanish program had been offered since 1908, and the Zone's junior college offered a Spanish program comparable to those at four-year colleges in the United States.

Armbrister and the journalists like him whose values were shaped by the American progressives were a new sort of clergy. Their mission was to convert, or at least damn, the heathen, as defined by progressive Social Gospel preachers like Walter Rauschenbusch. According to Rauschenbusch, Original Sin "really" symbolized man's inability to overcome racial, cultural, religious, and sexual prejudices without divine help.[22] The Unwashed were people still ensnared in personal, selfish concerns and mired in local cultural values, people who had not yet "risen" toward universal brotherhood, sharing, and cooperation —people like the damned Zonians.

After the 1964 riots, Evans and Novak revealed, "The only way to insure U.S. control over the Panama Canal without future violence is to strike at the real source of U.S.-Panamanian friction: The Panama Canal Zone and its inhabitants."[23]

Garry Wills, arriving fourteen years late, was still glibly striking at them in 1978. "The main thing about the 1964 event was its drama-tization of the Zone residents' hatred for the Panamanians," he revealed.[24]

Some writers were more subtle. In 1960, Harold Martin tried to pin the badge of discrimination on the Canal workers. Writing in the *Saturday Evening Post*, he explained that they were "mechanics and artisans by trade" and that thus "their roles in life did not bring them in contact with the educated, highly cultured, white Panamanians of Spanish descent." He said, "The Panamanians they did meet looked to them exactly like the colored folk they had left back home, and they were quick to raise barriers that would keep the two races sepa-rate. . . ."[25]

Barriers there were, but to attribute them solely or mainly to the "mechanics and artisans" is obviously a class ploy, as a glance at the number of "colored folk" on the staff of the *Post* in 1960 would show.

Eighteen years later, Joan Peters, writing in *Harper's*, used yet another class ploy to discredit the Canal workers. She passed on the news that the Zone was described by Panama City residents and the United States Embassy alike as a remnant of "the day of the Raj," but added on her own that it was "a colony, complete with Baptist, gothic-style churches. . . ."[26]

The Union Church, an alliance of some but not all Protestant denominations, was built in a barn-gothic style, but there was no gothic-style Baptist church on the Zone. There were, however, Baptist churches. The Baptists were not members of the Union. What is curious is why it takes Baptist churches to "complete" a colony.

It is no accident, as they say, that the Zone's Baptist churches were so often singled out. There were many denominations on the Zone, and the two largest church buildings were not Baptist. Yet no one ever described the Zone as a colony, complete with a Catholic Church or with a Union Church.

One reason that Baptist churches were so often mentioned by critics of the Zone goes back to the reform movement that reshaped America's goals and values at the turn of the century. The progressive reformers consisted of secular liberals and liberal Christians. The latter called themselves Social Gospel Christians and counted several Baptists among their leaders. But by and large Baptist churches rejected the Social Gospel revelation. To this day most Baptists believe that the locus of salvation is in the heart of the individual, not in the organization of society. This shows that the Baptists have not yet made "the transition from an unsocial to the social mind."

And all along, of course, the failure of many Baptists to compromise their belief in Creationism in order to accommodate Darwinism really put them beyond the pale as far as the enlightened, Christian or secular, were concerned. Thus, to say that a community is a colony, complete with Baptist churches, is a way of associating colonies (bad) with that other America (bad) where "they" live.

The Social Gospel Christians who run the National Council of Churches of Christ sent a delegation to Panama in 1976 to denounce the Zonians. This was in accord with their policy of bearing Christian witness through progressive social action. Their delegation declared that the Zonians were exercising "excessive" influence on American public opinion. The delegation did not explain how the clever Zonians were doing this but wanted them to stop. It also condemned the

Zonians for failing to rise above "personal concerns" and "to take into account the most important interests of justice"—in this case, "justice for the Panamanian people."[27]

KEEPING THE FAITH

A woman who once worked at the United States Embassy said that everyone there saw the Zonians as "rednecks" and tried to have as little to do with them as possible. John Jackley, an intern who worked in the embassy's Political Section, admitted that the diplomats had no background material on the Zonians, no files on their living conditions or attitudes, and in his report on the Zonians, he wrote, "I found little accurate knowledge of life in the Canal Zone or of the Canal Zone resident within the U.S. Embassy in Panama City. . . . The image of the stereotyped Zonian—spoiled, pampered, and racially biased—prevails in State and DoD circles."[28]

Once in a blue moon a diplomat would show up at a Zone party. After a few drinks, one such adventurer began lamenting the Zonians' inability to get along with the Panamanians. His hostess challenged him. She spoke Spanish. She got around in Panama. "You're the exception," he explained. She marched him around, introducing him to Zonians with houses in the interior or business or cultural connections in Panama. Exceptions, all exceptions—which was why he'd felt free to bad-mouth the Zonians in the first place. The only real Zonians were the ones he'd never met.

THE GENTEEL TRADITION

It is hard to talk about social class in America because of our tradition that it is a subjective phenomenon: "You are what you think you are." That was an idea that became popular in the first half of the nineteenth century. Status was a matter of self-reliance. But as the nineteenth century waned, social status came to be measured almost entirely by how much money a person had. That, too, was partly a matter of self-reliance, of course, but was not at all what Finney,

Emerson, and the other early nineteenth-century reformers had in mind when they proclaimed the new and liberating idea that every American was responsible for his own salvation.

Then, during the twentieth century, a new class of experts appeared. These experts and their degreed fellow travelers claimed upper-class status not on the basis of their wealth but on the basis of their superior qualifications—their academic credentials and their enlightened compassion. They were superior because they had the right ideas and because they were going to make society better. Thus, whenever a political debate took place, it became necessary to assert that all the really smart people were on the same side. The workers, it was assumed, would ally themselves with the smart people who had their —indeed, everyone's—best interests in mind—not "at heart." So the Liberal-Conservative debate became the Intellectual-Yahoo debate, and then degenerated still further into the Sensitive-Insensitive debate. As Suzannah Lessard remarked in her essay "Taste, Class, and Mary Tyler Moore," "the old question, are you a lady or a gentleman? has been replaced by the query, are you an aristocrat of the spirit?"[29] Most workers are not.

Most diplomats are. How does one qualify? It is not entirely a matter of money. A middle-aged poor person would find it hard to qualify, but so would some rich businessmen. Nor is it entirely a matter of degrees and credentials. It has to do with having the right style, which is the sum of your clothes, your manners, your alertness to fashion, the people you sneer at, how you decorate your house, where you go, who you know, and what you read.

We have always thought we were invited to an AID party in Panama because the hostess discovered we read the *New York Times*, an expensive habit in Panama. The party was at a sumptuous apartment in La Cresta, one of Panama's best districts. Everyone but us was AID or embassy. There were no Panamanians present except the servants.

A man from the embassy introduced us to a friend as faculty members of Florida State University. We protested. He argued with us. "Florida State runs the college program for the army."

"Yes, but . . ." And we explained. "You mean the Canal Company has a college?" he said.

"Just a junior college except for medical technology. We . . ."

"It's too bad, isn't it, that they won't go to the University of Panama. They've got some excellent people there."

We murmured that we didn't think it was so bad, but our interrogator was off on a new tack. He wanted to know how long we had been on the Zone. Nine years. Had we met any Panamanians?

Trying to convey irony, we mentioned that about a third of the students at the college were Panamanian citizens. He smiled knowingly, in disbelief, and got rid of us, passing us on to a woman who was the center of attention because she and her husband were being transferred to Washington. She asked us about the "ugly Americans" on the Zone. She wanted to understand them, forgetting that in the famous book the ugly American is the good guy, while the beautiful people at AID and State—the ones who keep committing "Social Incest in the Golden Ghetto"—were the bad ones.

Lessard observed in her essay that "the chief damage done by the excessive preoccupation with and fear of philistinism is that it cramps growth and exchange of ideas."[30] This was brought home to us in 1977 when a Zone labor leader who occasionally wrote a column on labor matters for an English-language Panamanian newspaper told us that whenever he wanted to get the embassy to pay attention to what he was saying, he had his column translated and published in a Spanish-language newspaper. "It's a trick I learned from a secretary at the embassy. She told me how they do over there. They say, 'Hey this guy's tryin' to reach the Panamanians,' and quick they translate it back into English. Heck, the Panamanians don't give a hoot what *I* say. I'm tryin' to reach the U.S. Embassy."

In 1979, one of the American diplomats in Panama came to see us. He characterized himself, provocatively, we thought, as a Mexican rather than as an American, or even as a Mexican-American. He wanted us to lecture—in English—to Panamanian English teachers at the University of Panama. He explained that now that the treaties were ratified, the embassy had decided it was time to start bringing the Zonians and the Panamanians together. It didn't occur to us to mention that the head of the English department at the University of Panama had worked for a while at the Canal Zone College. The embassy people were visibly irked when they discovered that they didn't need to introduce us. They never did discover that our audience was sprinkled with Panamanians who had taken a course or two at the Canal Zone College.

AID and embassy people were not the only aristocrats of the spirit on the Isthmus. There were a few on the Zone, too—some schoolteachers, for instance, who spoke openly of students who accepted apprenticeships or chose technical schools instead of liberal arts colleges as belonging to the lower orders. But on the Zone this sort of snobbery was futile. There weren't enough people who shared that opinion to form a clique. Come Friday night, the "aristocrats" were out dancing to Lucho's music and drinking Ron Cortez with everyone else.

DIFFERENT PERSPECTIVES

In his report to the embassy, Jackley wrote that few Zonians had any bias against Panamanians—this was in 1976—but that they distrusted the government of Panama.[31] He said that the State Department's and the media's belief that the Zonians were adamantly opposed to a new treaty was much exaggerated. After interviewing seventy Zonians and talking informally or in groups to several hundred more, he said that 85 percent of the people he talked to agreed that some sort of new arrangement with Panama was necessary. Ten percent opposed any change. Five percent had no opinion. Jackley quoted a Zonian who was active in what passed for local politics as saying, "These people can still be sold on a treaty."[32]

But to do that, as a Los Rios resident remarked, the State Department would have to stop "looking down on us and treating us like children."[33]

That proved too difficult for the State Department to do. Jackley reported that the Zonians' concern was economic not political. They were worried about their jobs. So a man from the State Department pointed out to a group of them that a company in the States could lay off 50,000 people, and that those people would have no redress or compensation.[34] His point was that the spoiled Zonians were going to have to realize they were variable costs—quite unlike the fixed-cost specialists at the State Department.

Then, in 1975, John Blacken, the embassy's political counselor, made a speech to the Zonians in the Balboa High School auditorium. The idea that life in Panama for a diplomat or an influential foreign businessman might differ from life there for a manual worker had obviously never crossed his mind. After listening to Blacken say that he lived in Panama and that everything over there was just fine, an electrician's apprentice remarked, "Hell, if I had the money to live in La Cresta and diplomatic immunity, I wouldn't care how they ran the country, either."

Briefed by his associates at the embassy, Blacken evidently assumed that Zonians knew little about Panama. He explained that in Panama "grass-roots participation" in the government was fostered by "a different legislative structure from our own." At that, all the usual audience rustlings stopped. A few people snickered. Then there was general laughter and whoops. As Jackley put it, "in the minds of the Canal Zone residents, the credibility of the State Department went from very little to absolutely nothing," for as every Zonian knew, Panama was a dictatorship.[35]

Liberal American journalists referred to the Panamanian dictator as a "genial" or "moderate" despot. Sometimes they said he was a "strongman" instead of a "dictator." They often called his regime "authoritarian" instead of "dictatorial." (Later, when United Nations ambassador Jeane Kirkpatrick applied that distinction to right-wing regimes, liberal commentators accused her of making excuses for tyrants.) Naturally, the American workers who were going to have to live under the strongman's genial authoritarianism without the benefit of diplomatic immunity had a rather more jaundiced view of him.

A Panamanian exile group in Miami told a *Miami Herald* reporter that the Torrijos government had exiled 1,300 Panamanians and tortured and killed 500. Trying to give balance to the story, the reporter checked with unidentified sources who conceded that there was repression in Panama, but said it was far less brutal than that of some other governments and less extensive than the exiles claimed. The Zonians suspected that those unidentified sources who quantified Torrijos' repression and absolved him, relatively speaking, were members of the United States Department of State. However, as Joyce Canel wrote in the Canal Zone College newspaper, "One person tortured and killed is one too many in my book. Instances of repression don't lend themselves to comparison, and I don't like reporters implying that they do."[36]

18

American Ideals
and a Pensioned Press

ONLY THE NEWS THAT'S FIT TO PRINT

The social engineers who presided over the Zone believed it was essential for them to control the news in order to keep the workers tranquil and to prevent international misunderstandings. They succeeded only in hiding from themselves their failure to do either.

They thought the way to keep people tranquil was to pretend that nothing bad ever happened. A newcomer to the Zone was astonished to learn that crime existed there. "What? I never read about it in the newspapers."[1]

That was because there were no news-gathering organizations on the Isthmus. The company's newspaper, *The Spillway*; the military newspapers, *The Southern Command News* and *The Banner*; and the military radio and television stations were all, as a matter of policy, merely bulletin boards for the authorities. The local news on the American military television station consisted of film clips of official ceremonies: General X saying good-bye or hello to General Y, for example, or General Z sliding his eyes back and forth as he delivered his three-line Christmas message to the troops. Occasionally, a soldier would read aloud the dinner menus of the officers' clubs.

Although several Panamanian newspapers published English editions—the number varied over the years—they were no better sources of local news than the bulletin boards on the Zone. The Panamanian papers were not, of course, controlled by the Zone authorities, but as the Panamanian journalist sees it, his job is not to assemble or discover facts but to impose his opinions.

Crime was not the only thing a person did not read about. Suicides, divorces, most accidents, worker discontent, racism, sexism, bureaucratic arrogance, mismanagement, waste: it was as if they did not exist. A community problem was mentioned only when the authorities could announce that they had solved it. The Civic Councils distributed their own newsletter for a while because there was so little about community issues in *The Spillway*.

A ship that went through the Canal with an extra-large cargo was news. A ship that was sent through with a deeper draft than the rules allowed was not. If a ship went down in the Canal, *The Spillway* would run a story about it. That was not something that could be overlooked, but the story would omit all the interesting details. And when *The Spillway* was obliged to run a story with political implications—something it did with the greatest reluctance—the story was so carefully camouflaged that a hasty reader might think it was about something else—truck maintenance, for example.

However, *The Spillway*'s civilian journalists were positively reckless about what they would print compared to the military journalists who wrote *The Southern Command News*. After the Zone was abolished, the company hospital was given to the military. The army took charge. Naturally, when two patients were raped and the military police were unable to apprehend the rapist, military journalists ignored the story. However, *The Spillway* managed to slip a confusing allusion to what had happened into a story about the Civilian Advisory Councils— enough, at least, to alert readers to a possible danger. *The Spillway* journalists were civilians who felt a responsibility to their community as well as to their bosses—and women who felt a responsibility to their sex. The military journalists were responsible only to their bosses.

The Canal Company's sensitivity went back to the construction era when some reporters wrote dramatic and alarmist stories about conditions on the Isthmus. Energy that should have been spent making the dirt fly was spent washing the dirt off the reputation of the Canal Commission. From then on, the authorities warned the Canal workers not to disclose any information to the press that would be contrary to the best interests of the Canal Commission, which later became the Canal Company.

However, even if all the rumors we heard of kickbacks and diversions of company material for private use were true, the total would not amount to much. In the 1930s, a consultant said, "It is doubtful whether any enterprise anywhere surpasses the record of faithful, unblemished stewardship recorded by the officials and employees of the Isthmian enterprises."[2] We believe that record remained unsurpassed as long as the company existed.

However, the company's secrecy made its employees uneasy. Behind-the-scenes things were always being decided or investigated, and while there were no secrets on the Zone, at the same time nobody knew exactly what was going on. This produced an atmosphere of simmering resentment, confusion, and paranoia that all the reassurances of the authorities could not dispel.

During the construction period, the authorities were determined to prevent corruption. They remembered—and knew that the American people remembered—how greed and chicanery had destroyed the French canal project in the 1880s. That was not going to happen to the American project. A Zone policeman remarked that in those days the chief engineer received information from his own "private gum-shoe," from Chinese agents, from soldiers in civilian clothes, "and probably a lot of other underground sources . . . neither you nor I shall ever hear of."[3]

"Secret Service men were everywhere," recalled William Sands, the American diplomat. And they checked on everybody—including, to his surprise, him. "One might have expected that the diplomatic representative of the United States would be exempt from this surveillance," he huffed.[4]

The company's vigilance seemed to diminish once the Canal was completed, but who could be sure? During our years on the Zone, we met what seemed to us an extraordinary number of people who were sure their phones were tapped—which tells something about the atmosphere of the place.

GENTEEL JOURNALISM

The company's social engineers justified their control of the news by citing the need to avoid misunderstandings with Panama. They thought they were accomplishing this goal by ignoring whatever Panamanian politicians or journalists said about America or the Zone. Actually, of course, such a policy avoids only argument. Misunderstanding flourishes.

However once in a great while, the company could not resist at least mumbling back at its tormentors. Take the great garbage-truck imbroglio. The story goes back to 1953. Up to that year, the company had been collecting the garbage in Panama's two largest cities. In 1953, however, it turned that responsibility over to the government of Panama, along with the garbage trucks that had been doing the job and the Panamanian crews that had been manning them. Panamanian officials praised the company for the job it had done and thanked it for the equipment. Twenty-three years later, the Panamanian press began admonishing the Panamanian treaty negotiators not to accept any unserviceable equipment from the Americans when they gave the Canal to Panama, citing, as an example of what Panama could expect from the devious gringos, the garbage trucks it had received from them back in 1953. Those trucks, the Panamanian press reminded its readers, had broken down as soon as they were received. Didn't everyone remember that?

This infuriated the Canal managers. They prided themselves on the way they maintained the Canal and all the company's equipment. So *The Spillway* talked back! It published a story about maintenance in general.[5] Halfway through, the writer worked the story around to evidence that those garbage trucks had been in first-class condition in 1953. And the reader who persevered to the end learned that the reason the garbage-collection system—not the trucks—had broken down when Panama took over was that the Panamanian government had cut the wages of the men who did the collecting.

The military and the embassy were far too sensitive about embarrassing the Panamanians ever to write anything like that. When there was a revolution, a riot, or a violent demonstration in Panama, the American military radio station on the Zone would squeamishly pass along reports of "traffic congestion." The American Military Information Office even rewrote an obituary of the Panamanian dictator because the original copy mentioned that he "took power," implying that he was indeed a dictator. The soldiers were not about to risk that —not in a story about Ham Jordan's drinking buddy and President Carter's friend.

But when the United States military and the United States Embassy got together, their sensitivity reached quivering heights. For example, in 1977, a Canal worker walked into *Importadora Selecta* in Panama and found 32,000 yards of material in the design of United States, Confederate, and bicentennial flags for sale at three yards for a dollar. A salesman said the material was for washing cars. The Zonians were angry, and the next day the proprietor quit selling the material. The Zone's governor complained to the American embassy, which presumably carried his complaint to the government of Panama. That was it. Case closed.

Five days later, the embassy and the military, over the objections of the company, reopened the incident with a news release superciliously aimed at "putting to rest any doubts or uneasiness" on the Zone. The embassy was afraid that the Zonians had got the idea that the fabric was flag material and that it was being sold for use in anti-American demonstrations. There had been an article saying as much in the *Miami Herald*. The embassy was responding to what it thought the Zonians thought of what the *Miami Herald* said. Of course, the embassy might have checked with the Zonians to see what they thought, but no one at the embassy knew any Zonians.

In order to absolve the Panamanians and soothe the Zonians, the embassy and the military referred to the material as "American flag bunting," which revived memories of the incident but this time focused the Zonians' resentment on the embassy.

An embassy spokesman told a reporter from the Canal Zone College newspaper that the embassy had issued its statement because "people were very upset." Asked why the embassy called the material "bunt-ing" instead of flag material, he replied, "I don't know why they said that," and admitted, "Certainly, I saw it myself and it was very clearly the American flag."

Next the student interviewed the officers at the Southern Command Information Office. A pedantic bully told her that he had looked up "bunting" in a dictionary and "according to the dictionary," the material was bunting. Told that Public Law 829 clearly states the difference between flag material and bunting, he decided he did not want to quibble over definitions. "We looked at it, and it looked like bunting," he barked. A colonel interposed soothingly that the word "bunting" was not meant to be misleading and that the whole purpose of the statement was to "clarify rumor with fact."[6]

What it clarified for the Zonians was the fact that the United States Army and the United States Embassy in Panama, working together, were unable to tell an American flag when they saw one.

THE STRUGGLE FOR TRUTH

What the Zone needed was an independent newspaper, staffed by journalists who were trained to present the news as objectively as possible in this imperfect world *and* who lived among the people they wrote about. By prohibiting an independent newspaper on the Zone, the Zone's managers deprived themselves of a considered public re-sponse to their ideas. Trying to keep things simple, they made them unnecessarily mysterious. And they encouraged extremism. A person had to build up a head of steam to make himself heard on the Zone.

It may be objected that the Zone was hardly off limits to journalists from independent news organizations in the States. But that merely underlines our point. A free press is not enough. What is needed is a *local*, free press.

It would have given company officials headaches, of course. Sometimes it would have infuriated the government of Panama and made life difficult for the embassy. But an independent newspaper could have moderated the class prejudice that poisoned relationships between the Zonians and the diplomats. It could have destroyed the stereotype of the jingo-gringo Zonian, contemptuous of all things Panamanian. And it could have pressured visiting journalists to concern themselves with conflicting national interests instead of filing so many stories about the appearance of the Zone and the "insensitivity" of the Zonians.

A local American newspaper could have provided a forum for different opinions. There was a variety of opinion about everything on the Zone, especially about the treaties that turned it over to Panama—but without a free press those opinions were expressed only in private conversations.

Independent local reporters could have dispelled the atmosphere of helplessness and uncertainty that was caused by a lack of trustworthy information. In 1950, Governor F. K. Newcomer said that the circulation of rumors on the Zone was a practice he could not too strongly condemn. Rumors, he said, were a serious impediment to the Canal administration and served only to "stampede many into hasty action which they otherwise might not take."[7]

To stop the rumors, he established "shirtsleeve conferences"—himself and his top aides on one side of a table and the leaders of various employee organizations on the other. He also started the *Panama Canal Review*. However, he remained firmly in charge of how much information his employees received. The *Review* emphasized that it would not give general coverage to local news, and in its first issue, the governor, after inviting comments, warned, "Mere criticisms of course can serve no useful purpose. . . ."[8] Not surprisingly, he failed to stop the rumors.

More specifically, a local and independent American newspaper might have altered the nature and sequence of events leading up to the Flag Riots of 1964. It could have urged the president to stop "managing the problem" and to begin "leading the people" by making the purpose and the limits of his dual-flag policy clear. A newspaper could have provided the governor with more accurate information about the feelings of the American students. And it might have forced him to have stopped procrastinating—to have either removed the one flagpole or to have put up a second one and settled the matter one way or another before he lost control of the situation. The events leading up to the Flag Riots could hardly have been made worse by the existence of an American newspaper on the Zone—and might have been made much better.

Local reporters might also have curbed the willingness of United States news organizations to make matters worse by rushing to print with inflammatory and unverified reports, for instance, the incorrect wire-service story that President Chiari had asked that American troops be sent into Panama to restore order; the incorrect report on NBC that two Americans had been lynched in David;[9] and the incorrect story in the *Times* that the Canal Company had laid off 5,000 of its Panamanian employees[10] when the actual number was zero.

Moreover, local reporters would have been the appropriate people to have investigated Assistant Secretary of the Army Victor Veysey's alleged remark that the Zonians were "gutless sheep," which contributed to the wildcat strike in 1976. Most importantly, a local free press would have reminded everyone, Americans and Panamanians, managers, diplomats, and workers, that at the core of the democratic ethic is the struggle for truth.

Would it have been possible to have had an editorially independent newspaper on the Zone, where everything was run by the government? We cannot say for sure, but if not, there is no way to accommodate traditional American ideals to a paternalistic Bellamyite society.

If a government-pensioned press were editorially independent, its journalists would never have to make any real decisions, only professional ones. Their economic independence would free them from that complex obligation to their readers that a healthy relationship between the press and the community requires. On the other hand, if a pensioned press is not editorially independent, it is a mere bulletin board for the authorities. But we are not ready to say there is no way to create a government-sponsored press that is both free and rooted in the community, because for a brief period in the seventies, Zonians caught a glimpse of what might have been.

The nearest thing to an independent newspaper on the Zone was published by the students of the Canal Zone College while Joyce Canel taught journalism there. Like the newspapers in Bellamy's utopia, it was printed at the government printing plant, carried no ads, and was written by unproductive "social parasites," supported in this case by their parents or spouses. Bellamy saw no real need for newspapers in his perfect society. Since it was perfect, it follows that there was no news there. He tolerated journalists, apparently out of sentiment, since he was one himself—but he expected them to write only philosophic essays and lyric poetry.

The student journalists at the college were saved from that, a common fate of student journalists, by their teacher. Canel had worked on newspapers in the United States and Venezuela but could not practice her trade on the Zone because of the laws against nepotism. Her husband ran the company's Information Office. So she taught journalism part-time at the college.

She was not the kind of teacher the Zone's social engineers were used to dealing with. Once the governor's office told the civil affairs director to tell the Schools Division to tell the college to tell its newspaper that it had made a mistake and had to publish a correction. That was the way things were done on the Zone. The newspaper ran the correction, but it also ran an editorial defending the accuracy of the original story, citing sources, and denouncing the correction as based upon third-hand information. The editorial said that in the future if the governor wanted to clarify or correct a story, he should call the newspaper directly.[11]

To the amazement of some observers, the sky did not fall, and the students continued to publish stories that appeared nowhere else on the Isthmus. To some extent their paper was protected by the redefinition and expansion of student rights during the sixties, but its main protection was Canel's idealism and professionalism. She imposed a rigorous standard of accuracy on her students' work. They, for their part, ensured that the paper was rooted in the community.

However, their newspaper was not big enough nor did it appear often enough to supply the community with all the news it needed. In order to keep up, Zonians continued to listen to their police-band radios and to exchange information on golf courses, at parties, churches, union meetings, exercise classes, the Elks Club bar, the American Legion restaurant, and the commissary. When a Zonian walked into the commissary and saw people standing in threes with empty grocery carts beside them, he knew something had happened.

Bellamy imagined that the citizens of his utopia would live less intimately with each other than Americans did in the capitalist turmoil of the 1880s. Free of drudgery and insecurity, they would mainly concern themselves with the universal, philosophical aspects of existence. That was not the way it worked on the Zone. Deprived of the background and texture of community events that could have been provided by a local news-gathering organization, people felt vaguely incomplete and set out to gather news on their own. That was a quest that brought all of us together.

19
The Campaign
to Ratify the Treaties

A COLONY?

Proponents of the treaties declared that the Zone was a colony. This served two purposes: It showed that the speaker did not approve of the Zone and allowed him to believe he knew all about it. However, lumping the Zone with India, Algeria, and the Congo obscures more than it reveals—about the Zone.

There has been a good deal of loose talk over the past twenty years based on just this sort of analogy. The United States, it is said, is an imperialist power, no different *really* from England or France. Those countries called what they did "imperialism"; we called what we did "manifest destiny," but it was the same thing, *really*.

It is true that nineteenth-century Americans believed in something called manifest destiny. However, nobody knew exactly what that meant. Indeed, the American "destiny" was so uncertain that, as Daniel Boorstin has remarked, it was necessary to call it "manifest."[1]

Manifest destiny involved the idea of a national mission, an idea partly derived from the Puritans, whose mission it was to establish a holy commonwealth in America as an example and a refuge, but also partly from Tom Paine, the international revolutionary, who saw the American war for independence as the first step in the worldwide struggle of the common man against warrior aristocracies.

Manifest destiny also involved the idea of free land and of a divinely inspired westward migration across the continent. However, the equalitarian and democratic ideas the Americans took with them into the lands taken from Mexico and ceded by Great Britain were very different from those the British carried to India or the Spanish to Latin America and the Philippines.

Whatever manifest destiny meant exactly, it had more to do with society than with the state, and it was not a synonym for imperialism. The latter has to do with the state and its prerogatives: a strong central government, a large army and navy, and state-controlled trade with once-independent territories.

In 1898, the United States launched itself as a world power by fighting what was popularly considered a humanitarian and anti-materialist crusade. Senator George F. Hoar, that four-square anti-imperialist, said it was "the most honorable single war in all history." Even the American Socialists supported it.[2]

Spain was fighting an antiguerrilla war in Cuba. American sympathy was wholly with the *insurrectos*. Only big business opposed America's entry into the war on the side of the Cubans—at least that is what people thought, and that perception served to ally idealistic Eastern conservatives like Theodore Roosevelt with their erstwhile enemies, the radical Populists of the West, against "the craven fear and brutal selfishness of the mere money makers," who were blocking the war for humanity.[3]

Ironically, largely because of that war, America became an imperial power itself. It had already annexed Hawaii in 1897. After the Spanish-American war, it took Puerto Rico, the Philippines, and Guam from Spain. The following year, it partitioned Samoa in a deal with Britain and Germany.

Initially, the business and religious communities were pleased, as were the anglophiles, who wanted the United States to be more like glorious Great Britain. However, the historian Ernest R. May points out that less than a year later "scarcely a Congressman or newspaper editor raised his voice in favor of further colonial extension."[4] Imperialism? The American people "concluded to forget it," wrote contemporary journalist and historian Mark Sullivan.[5] The anti-colonialist consensus of the 1880s reasserted itself as strongly as ever.

Most nations have images of themselves that they try to live up to, not always successfully. Americans rejected imperialism because it conflicted with their basic image of themselves as antiaristocrats, because it required a large standing army, and because it is a system that directly or indirectly enables the state to monopolize trade. Americans believe in private enterprise, not state monopolies.

Then, in 1904, the United States acquired yet another overseas territory—the Panama Canal Zone. That, however, was a special case. Both Panama and the United States had been distant, misunderstood provinces. Americans could see themselves helping Panama liberate itself from Colombia. It would have been a different story if the majority of Americans had seen their government as trying to acquire a new colony in Central America. Moreover, private enterprise, paradoxically, was what the state-run Panama Canal would promote.

Without American help, Panama would not have remained an independent nation for more than a couple of weeks, but at the same time, Theodore Roosevelt's personality—his desire to appear as the director of events—has made it easy to overestimate the role of the United States in Panama's revolution. "I took the Isthmus," Roosevelt boasted, but privately he is supposed to have said, "I took Panama because Bunau-Varilla brought it to me on a silver platter,"[6] which is better but still not accurate.

Nobody "took" Panama, and in his less bombastic moments, Roosevelt made clear that he did not regard Panama or the Zone as a colony. In 1906, he wrote to Taft, saying: "We have not the slightest intention of establishing an independent colony in the middle of the State of Panama, or of exercising any greater governmental functions than are necessary to enable us conveniently and safely to construct, maintain and operate the canal, under the rights given us by the treaty."[7]

Of course, those rights were very broad. They included the right to appropriate any additional land that was "necessary and convenient" for the construction, operation, sanitation, or defense of the Canal. Quite legally, then, the United States could have appropriated all of Panama, thus precluding arguments about the status of the Zone. Panama would have been a sovereign but nonexistent nation, a legal curiosity. However, by 1906, the reassertion of America's anti-colonialist consensus had made that impossible.

Certainly, the Zone never became a colony of settlement. With the previously mentioned exception of the Atlantic-side Masons, no Americans owned property on the Zone, and with a few exceptions, no Americans retired there. A few retired widows lived with their children and grandchildren, and a couple of elderly bachelors roomed at the YMCA.

Nor was the Zone ever a colony of exploitation, although many Panamanians disagree. They argue that the Canal is a "natural resource." (A Panamanian with no sympathy for that idea told us, "The schoolchildren grow up thinking God made it [the Canal] with three sets of locks, and the Americans came and took it away from us.") The Panamanians claim they were exploited, because the Canal was not run primarily for their benefit. It is risible, however, to think that the United States would undertake to build and operate a Canal on the Isthmus for the primary benefit of the Panamanians. America built the Canal for the benefit of the United States Navy, United States and world commerce, and Panama, in that order, which does not seem unreasonable.

Panama's argument also ignores the extent to which America has contributed to Panama's development by granting it more foreign aid per capita than any other nation, by backing its currency at par with the dollar, by encouraging private investment, by training its workers, by funneling money from the Canal Company into its economy, and by providing the example of the Zone, where working men and women enjoyed both prosperity and respect.

Of course, Panama wanted more. "We need a treaty that brings a strong infusion of American money," announced the director of Panama's Chamber of Commerce.[8] The amount of money Panama deserves or can use effectively is debatable, but Panama's argument that it was exploited because the Canal was not built and operated primarily for its benefit belongs in one of those surreal Latin American novels where mere reality is subordinated to a higher truth.

The argument that Panama was the "victim of a colonial situation" is equally without merit. It is worth remembering that the United States did not force Panama to add Article 136 to its constitution. Panama's founding fathers, for reasons of their own, were responsible for Article 136, the article that gave the United States the right to intervene "to re-establish public peace and constitutional order."[9]

At various times, Panamanian leaders of both liberal and conservative persuasions pleaded with the United States to do just that—sometimes successfully.[10] However, the United States was never eager to intervene. Elihu Root, the representative of the "predatory imperialists," tried to convince one group of Panamanian liberals that such requests were compromising their nation's sovereignty, but he was not persuasive. As late as 1927, President Belisario Porras, perhaps the most revered figure in Panamanian history, went to Washington to ask the Americans to intervene and to supervise the next Panamanian election. Their refusal was beyond his comprehension.[11]

The United States encouraged democracy in Panama. It did not install its agents as Panama's rulers, nor guarantee any government's tenure. Nor did it impose its rule over unwilling Panamanians on the Zone. No one was forced to live there. Nevertheless, Panama chose to make its case for control of the Canal and the Zone on the grounds that it had been exploited and oppressed. It was a way of repudiating its psychological debt to the United States. Privately, many Panamanians freely admit that they owe a great deal to the United States —more than to any other country. They say they are *really* grateful but resent having to appear grateful. As a Panamanian woman told the Biesanzes, "I don't want to feel obliged to show my gratitude like an orphan in an asylum."[12]

But at least during the years we lived on the Zone, the United States did not oblige Panama to show its gratitude. On the contrary, it displayed endless patience and understanding—a rather condescending understanding, it might be argued—with regard to Panama's need to cast its primary benefactor in the role of an oppressor. Certainly the Carter administration's sensitivity in this regard cannot be faulted.

Panama was plainly not a colony like Algeria or India, nor a satellite nation like Poland or the Ukraine. Is it possible to imagine any imperial power in history meekly allowing a nation under its suzerainty to defame it in international forums the way Panama regularly defamed the United States during the sixties and seventies?

The Canal Zone had in common with all colonies that it was a foreign territory administered from a distant capital. But very dissimilar things often have certain features in common. In our view, recognizing the differences between the Zone and Afghanistan or Hong Kong is essential in order to understand what the Zone was really like. Over the years, those critical differences were ignored or disparaged by many American journalists, academics, and government officials, who distinguish themselves from their fathers and grandfathers by habitually looking at the world in terms of similarities rather than of differences.

A MILITARY RESERVATION?

In 1913, the secretary of the Isthmian Canal Commission referred to the Zone as a military reservation.[13] But that's not quite right, either. The Zone's governor reported to the secretary of the army, but the Canal Zone Code, not the Uniform Code of Military Justice, applied on the Zone. The Zonians were emphatically civilians, not semi-civilians working for the army.

Congress called the Zone a zone, and that is what was—not a territory, colony, or military reservation—a zone.

THE CASE FOR THE TREATIES

When the American Canal workers arrived in Panama, the Panamanians did what they could to help. Their officials cooperated with the American engineers and doctors who rid the Canal area of yellow fever. Facundo Mutís Durán, who had twice served as governor of Panama while it was a province of Colombia, served as the first chief justice of the Canal Zone Supreme Court. (He was also a justice on the Supreme Court of the Republic.) However, generally speaking, Panama's population was scanty, undernourished, and uneducated.

Even its educated elite knew little of technology, and nothing in their experience had prepared them for the uncultured but highly skilled and highly paid American mechanics. The new Panamanian government did not have the capability to police or to provide for the needs of the brawny, polyglot army of West Indian and European laborers from more than forty countries that was soon to descend upon the Isthmus. There was no local tradition of political cooperation, civic improvement, or long-range planning.

By 1978, largely as a result of Panama's special relationship to the United States, its population was one of the fastest growing, healthiest, most prosperous, educated, and bilingual in Latin America.[14] Its middle class was perhaps larger proportionately than that of any Latin American country. It was clearly time for Panama to take a larger and more responsible role in the operation of the Canal and a larger share of the Canal revenues.

New treaties were necessary—but as a result of the good the United States had done in Panama, not as a result of what the United States had failed to do or of what it had done wrong. The behavior of the United States was not perfect, but if perfection is our standard, our nation is not going to succeed anywhere and might as well stop trying. New treaties between Panama and the United States were the logical next step in a long, historically friendly, mutually beneficial relationship of which every American can in general be proud.

The thing in particular that we cannot be proud of about that relationship is that after encouraging democracy in Panama for sixty-four years, we negotiated the treaties that turned the Zone and the Canal over to Panama with that country's first dictator and in the process signaled to the world that the way to secure concessions from the United States is to mount a strident hate-America campaign.

By failing to defend America's record in Panama, Carter put his negotiators at a disadvantage from the start. They had to negotiate in the shadow of America's "understood" guilt and its need to make reparations. The Panamanian politicians, of course, were delighted by Carter's attitude. By adopting the posture of the oppressed, they hoped to gain stature in the world.

RAPED FOR SEVENTY-THREE YEARS

On election day in 1968, the red, yellow, and purple banners of the Arnulfistas were everywhere. Thinking Panamanians were appalled. They consoled themselves with the proverb, "He who counts, elects." As the challenger, Arnulfo Arias would not do much of the counting.

He won anyway, which means his plurality must have been overwhelming, and for the third time the xenophobic, anti-gringo Arias was president of Panama. Eleven days later, he fled to the Canal Zone where the gringos would protect him from a disgruntled general who was slated to be replaced. The general's coup set off a power struggle within the *Guardia* from which Omar Torrijos emerged victorious.

Arias went into exile in Miami, where he was ignored by the American press. The contrast between its silence about his overthrow and its protracted lamentation about the overthrow of Salvador Allende five years later is instructive. Allende had received only 36 percent of the vote to begin with. He had remained in office long enough to lead Chile into spectacular financial chaos. That had not increased his popularity, but he was a progressive, a man of the Left. Thus, his overthrow was a matter of lasting concern to a segment of the American press. The immediate overthrow of the newly elected, everpopular Arias by a soldier who immediately adopted a vaguely leftish stance did not seem to bother anyone in the States.

Indeed, it may have been welcomed, both by those who approve only of governments that are "progressive" and by those who approve only of governments that are friendly to the United States. Arias does not fit the simple categories of our public debate. He is anti-Communist, antigringo, and antiestablishment. A fervent racist who has said that the concepts of private property and individual freedom are outmoded, he is also a great moralist who often scolds his admirers. Even his closest friends cannot predict what his position will be on particular issues. He is directed by mystical "forces." Though he has little use for democracy, he *is* electable.

Torrijos was not electable and thus had even less use for democracy than Arias. He banned political parties, took charge of the media, and banished, imprisoned, or killed his most dangerous opponents. In 1972, the American ambassador, Robert Sayre, helped the dictator see to it that his disreputable brother, Moises, eluded United States agents who had a warrant for his arrest on heroin-smuggling charges.[15] Once things settled down, Torrijos became the Carter administration's favorite dictator. Liberal magazines and newspapers called him a populist and a prankster. Eulogizing Torrijos in 1981, Robert Pastor, Carter's National Security Council staff member for Latin America, assured liberals that "To his friends, Omar was the nearest thing Latin America had to a leprechaun."[16]

It was Torrijos who engineered the Panamanian campaign for a new Canal treaty—a campaign based on two assumptions: one, that Americans could be made to feel ashamed of their nation's behavior in Panama; and two, that at the same time they could be made to fear a Panamanian "Vietnam." The Americans would turn over the Canal to Panama to calm their fears, but would tell themselves they were doing it to salve their conscience.

"When the American people realize the real situation [in Panama] they will feel deeply ashamed," predicted the dictator, adding magnanimously, "I admire the American people very much for their technology and their great sense of shame." However, in the same speech, he mentioned ominously, "We have set 1977 as a goal. Patience has its limits."[17] In Mexico, in 1975, with President Luis Echeverria beaming at his side, he told the press that "when all peaceful ways are closed to the people, they have to resort to the liberation struggle, just as Ho Chi Minh did."[18]

Panamanian newsmen and diplomats echoed their leader: Panama's ambassador to the United Nations declared that the inalienable rights of the Panamanian people had been trampled underfoot for seventy-three years.[19] In Atlanta, in 1976, a Panamanian spokesman told an assembly of United States experts on South America how glad he was to observe "the increasing awareness in the American public opinion that Panama is the victim of a colonial situation. . . ."[20]

Panama's dictator cabled President Ford in 1976 that "the 63 [sic] years of colonialism in the Canal Zone fill the 200 years of North American independence with shame. . . ."[21] But Torrijos was increasingly irritated by the failure of the average American to realize this and complained, "Sometimes I don't know what there is about North American politics to put up with so much infantality,"[22] meaning, apparently, that North American politicians should not put up with the infantile opinions of the masses—the lower ranks. With equal chutzpa, Panamanian journalists reported in their state-controlled press that the media and money play too big a role in American elections.

When Carter took office, Torrijos was jubilant. He announced on January 23, 1977, long before most Americans realized it, that the Carter administration had "a higher concept of shame" than its predecessors.[23]

Panamanian officials and journalists repeated their story of Panama's oppression and exploitation like gamblers chanting "Red, red, red . . ." before a spinning wheel. It was a form of self-assertion, a way of attempting to dominate reality with language—to cast a spell. "We have been raped for 73 years," groaned the Panamanian consul general in New York.[24]

AMERICANS DIVIDED

President Carter claimed that the Canal treaties were not a partisan issue, which was true only in the sense that they did not divide Americans along traditional party lines.

The protreaty activists were drawn mainly from three overlapping groups. There were the purists led by President Carter. These were the people who had learned the lesson of Vietnam—which was that the United States was an immoral imperialist bully. Carter was careful not to say this explicitly, but he implied it clearly and repeatedly, for instance when he pointed out with his customary dolefulness that "our country was almost universally condemned by the rest of the world for our investment of military effort in Vietnam,"[25] as if the popularity of a policy determined its morality.

To Carter, America's Panama adventure was also a moral failure, although, again, he never quite said so. He simply reported Panama's charges without refuting them, alluded to the "alleged American colonialism"[26] in Panama without denying it, and slyly protested, "I don't condemn my predecessors for having signed it [the 1903 treaty with Panama]."[27] But no one had accused him of doing so. He denied what he had never been accused of doing, thereby suggesting that he, too, thought their behavior was a disgrace, even if, in his official capacity, he could not plainly say so.

Now, at last, according to the purists, there was a generation of Americans wise enough, mature enough, *good* enough to finally begin setting the world right—really right, unlike their interventionist grandfathers who had gone about setting it right the wrong way.

A second group of treaty supporters consisted of the members of the new class of experts, America's natural aristocracy. They had logical, prudential reasons for wanting a new treaty, and since they, the expert class, had reached a consensus on the matter, they expected "the people" to fall in line. Unfortunately, the people were not yet mature enough to take the word of the experts. That being the case, the experts were willing to go along with the purists' "guilt trip," if that was what it took to get the treaties ratified.

The third group supporting the treaties consisted of the members of the American financial community. When Torrijos took over Panama, the country owed foreign lenders less than $200 million. After nine years of his "maximum leadership," it owed $1.8 billion to American lenders alone and its economy was in a shambles.[28] Between 1958 and 1972, Panama had the highest rate of economic growth in the Western Hemisphere, 8 percent annually, but in 1973, its growth rate began to drop. By 1975 it was down to 1.7 percent.[29] The Panamanians denied that this was in any way their fault, and it was certainly not the fault of the Maximum Leader. But there it was, and something had to be done about it. If Torrijos defaulted on the loans coming due in 1977, American banks would lose $323.6 million right away and much more on down the line.[30] Thus, it was important to the banks that their client acquire enough revenue from some source to meet his obligations to them. There was only one source for the money—the American taxpayer.

Not surprisingly, Carter appointed an American with close ties to the banking community, Sol Linowitz, as codirector of the American negotiating team. Carter's passion to avoid even the appearance of colonialism in Latin America was not matched by an equal passion to avoid even the appearance of impropriety. He could imagine people doubting the motives of the United States, but who could doubt his?

The financial stake of the banks in the new treaties was largely ignored by liberal newspapers and magazines. To have discussed it in detail would have jeopardized ratification of the treaties—the greater good. And, naturally, "responsible" conservatives, the natural allies of the banks, did not press the matter on the public's attention.

Later, in 1982, some alarmed liberals discovered the influence of the banks. "The bankers are now conducting the West's foreign policy in Poland," complained a writer in *The New Republic*.[31] The occasion of this revelation was President Reagan's order to the Department of Agriculture to pay almost $400 million of Poland's debt to banks in the United States, without first requiring those banks to declare Poland in default, as would have been the normal procedure. Had the banks been required to do this, they would have had to write off their loans to Poland, and that, they claimed, would have forced some of them out of business. Accordingly, to protect the solvency of the so-called capitalist bankers of the West, the government of the United States paid the debt of the repressive Communist government of Poland!

Since then the imprudent loans of American banks to Communist and Third World countries have been widely reported, but as a crisis, not a scandal. Responsible politicians of both parties have argued that the United States has to go on lending money to those same nations, so that they can go on making their interest payments to private American banks, so that those banks can continue to show a profit. Otherwise, it is said, "the system" will collapse.

The opposition to the treaties consisted of union liberals—workers, like the Zonians—and rank-and-file conservatives—small businessmen who, if they cannot pay their debts, are declared in default and bankrupt—unlike Poland.

Presuming that what Americans feared most was another Vietnam, the social engineers in the State Department did not discourage or reply to Torrijos' bellicose pronouncements of what he would do to the United States if the treaties were not ratified.

Ex-President Ford had already warned that Panama could become "another Vietnam."[32] On July 2, 1976, Senator Dick Clark released a report—the joint effort of experts from the State Department and the Defense Department—that estimated it would take 100,000 men with the support of naval and air forces to protect the Canal against a "Cuban-backed Panamanian attack." President Carter rushed forward to assure Americans that even though it would be a terrible, bloody task, he would defend the Canal: "I will defend it, and our country will be able to defend the Canal."[33] (The man had a genius for raising doubts about things that ordinary Americans took for granted.)

However, according to Carter, 100,000 men might not be enough to do the job. He declared that even if the 9,000 men of Panama's *Guardia Nacional* stayed out of it, even if all he had to cope with was an attack by "non-governmental forces," he might still require 200,000 men to defend the Canal! "But it can be done, and it will be done," Carter cried—adding thoughtfully that he really preferred "not to face this prospect."[34]

The Canal is forty-three miles long. Two hundred thousand men— that would be 4,651 men per mile! Would the Russians require so many? The Israelis? If it takes 200,000 men to defend the Canal, is it still possible to contemplate defending Western Europe?

The State Department, however, had already begun backtracking. Steve May, undersecretary of the United States Embassy in Panama, diplomatically told reporters, "As far as the threat of violence here in Panama is concerned, I'd have to say yes . . . and no." When reminded that Ambassador Ellsworth Bunker had warned of the threat of guerrilla warfare in Panama, May primly set the record straight: "Ambassador Bunker did not say 'guerrilla warfare.' He said 'conflict.' "[35]

Apparently because it was not working, the campaign to frighten Americans into surrendering the Canal was de-emphasized, but the campaign to shame them into surrendering the Canal rolled right along. Yet, it, too, failed to produce the expected result. The best and the brightest were puzzled by the widespread resistance to their redeeming vision of a penitential America. By 1976, everyone *they* knew had been completely purged of chauvinism, by which they meant pride in anything American. Beverly Sills could not even say, "I take pride in what the arts are accomplishing in America," in an Atlantic-Richfield ad, without cautiously prefacing that provocative remark with an apologetic "I hate to sound chauvinistic, but . . ."[36]

Angry protreaty forces attributed the mulishness of their fellow Americans to the fact that America's schoolbooks had failed to tell students the truth about the perfidies of their great-grandfathers. "We stole it [the Canal] and removed the incriminating evidence from our history books," shrilled the ever-penitent *New York Times*, revealing yet another "cover-up."[37]

There are several problems here. The Canal did not exist until we built it. Can one steal what does not exist? We did not steal the Zone or Panama, either, but if we had, the owner to whom we should have returned them is Colombia. Not even the *Times* was in favor of *that* much justice. What the *Times* was in favor of was asserting the difference between the party of "reason," to which it belonged, and the rest of the nation, which is composed of dangerous, emotional, romantic materialists: "We [meaning 'they'] have romanticized our courage in the theft and the military value of it. Our people sit in colonial luxury in the Canal Zone, defending this history and mythology more than the Canal and driving politicians to demagogic fury against any change in the arrangement."

There they were again, those 3,500 electricians, machinists, pilots, and bureaucrats lolling in "colonial luxury" and calling the tune America's politicians danced to. A person who can believe that can believe anything.

It never occurred to the protreaty crowd that the case for America's wickedness was simply unconvincing in the face of Panama's prosperity and independence, or that their tone of scorn and contempt was itself enough to arouse ire in the provinces.

Many politicians worked to defeat the Carter-Torrijos treaties, but no political figure defended America's record in Panama. The antitreaty politicians could not, because the logic of that record of assistance and progress led inexorably to the conclusion that Panama deserved a greater role in the operation of the Canal. The most vocal protreaty people were committed to the proposition that America's record on the Isthmus was indefensible. They declared that the real question was "Is America big enough to do the right thing?"—meaning, to make restitution to Panama. Curiously, they sometimes answered that question by saying that America was so rich that it would not even notice giving away the Canal. *Business Week* went so far as to dismiss it as a white elephant.

A *New Yorker* cartoon showed a man in a bar saying to his companion, "What's wrong with me? For years I never gave a thought to the Panama Canal. Now, I can't live without it." But it was not the Canal that he could not live without. It was a vision of America as a nation with a destiny—a mission. That's what the protreaty forces were asking him to live without. Having discovered in Vietnam that America was not perfect, the purists concluded that it was not different, either. The tidy-minded social engineers and bankers concurred. They had always found the idea of a national mission inconvenient. Indeed, to thinking Americans, it was a joke; no one could even define it satisfactorily. And in their zeal to destroy what they could not neatly define, and to affirm thereby their own superiority, the protreaty forces distorted their nation's record in Panama, then turned around and accused the antitreaty forces of oversimplifying.

The protreaty people were asking the man in the bar to disinherit himself of his past and to repudiate his forefathers' American dream, on the grounds that it had been humbug from the beginning. They were asking him to "grow up" and be like them. If he refused, it would be because he was not yet "mature" enough to "lose face" again so soon after Vietnam—or intelligent enough to acknowledge the superiority of the protreaty forces' "illusionless" point of view.

No wonder he was drinking.

But the political experts who said the Canal would not be a decisive issue in the 1978 and 1980 elections were right—even though Ronald Reagan, who had opposed them, won the presidency in 1980 from Jimmy Carter, who advertised them as one of his greatest achievements. The experts were right, however, in that the two treaties providing for the gradual transfer of the Canal to Panama and guaranteeing the Canal's neutrality soon faded as a public issue.

But the campaign to ratify those treaties had brought into question the authority and competence of the radical-purists and status liberals to interpret what the United States had meant and could mean to the world. The widespread dissatisfaction with their vision of our nation's past as wicked and its future as penitential endured and helped send a new president and twenty new senators to Washington.

The people's resistance to their "teachers'" vision of American history was not based on a militant patriotism that would admit no American faults. Rather, it was based on a mature awareness of the perils of good intentions, of the existence of national differences, of the complexity of all relationships, and on a faith in the virtues of democracy. It was also in many cases based on personal experience in American projects abroad.

When you came right down to it, many Zonians were hoping that the treaties would be ratified. They were not happy about them. They did not think the treaties adequately took into account their situation as the only civilian American work force living permanently overseas. They also had misgivings about the gradual transfer of Canal operations to Panama between 1979 and 1999. They suspected that the United States would discover that it had retained responsibility for a project that it did not have adequate authority to control or direct. But under the circumstances, many Zonians were ready to accept what was on the table as preferable to no treaties at all. However, their disgust with Carter and the purists in the Senate and in the media was every bit as great as that of their neighbors who hoped the treaties would be voted down.

AMERICAN JOURNALISTS

Briefed by the embassy, they came to the Zone looking for "rednecks" and drama. Even the *Miami Herald*, the most responsible of the lot, ran a three-column headline over a story about a "mysterious" Zone Liberation Organization—the ZLO. With a little more digging, the mystery and hence the story would have evaporated, since the ZLO was the fantasy of a single teenage malcontent whose well-known grumblings had long been ignored by his classmates.[38]

However, by and large, the news stories in the daily press were accurate within their limits. Those formulaic limits were too narrow to let the whole truth about the situation on the Isthmus emerge, but they provided a discipline for those stories that was often lacking in more interpretative magazine articles, radio and television reports, and editorials.

A *Washington Post* editorial in 1976 was particularly notable for its freewheeling contempt for the Zonians.[39] Because the Canal workers were on a wildcat strike, the *Post* called them irresponsible, although it did not pretend to know what the strike was about. It said that the workers "seem to have been protesting, among other things . . ." and went on to get the issues all wrong. The writer's purpose was clearly not to present a reasoned argument. It was to rail against "the 15,000 privileged Americans who profit[ed] personally from maintenance of the status quo" on the Zone, which meant that they got paid for doing their jobs. Although "15,000" was roughly correct for the total number of Canal employees, only 3,500 of those employees were Americans. The *Post* described the Zone as "this little pocket of social backwardness" and as "the well-air-conditioned Zone." It charged the Zonians with propagandizing "to the effect that Panamanians are a lesser breed" but offered no examples. It sneered at Ronald Reagan for taking advantage of "older and conservative Americans" by exploiting the "emotional grip" that the Canal had on them; sneered at the Corps of Engineers for running the Canal in a unbusinesslike way; and sneered at the Zonians for resisting a "modern treaty." It had praise only for Panama's dictator—whom it referred to delicately as Panama's "leader."

The writer's attitude toward the Zonians was plain; it was an attitude many journalists shared. There was, for instance, the condescending television journalist from CBS who asked the Zone aborigines who had consented to be interviewed if they knew who Walter Cronkite was. He followed that stunner by demanding, "What right do you have to be here?"[40] That they were there working for the government of the United States—*his* government—had apparently never crossed his mind.

Journalists asked to meet Zonians who disliked Panamanians or who had never visited Panama. They wanted inflammatory quotations and contrasts. They wanted to see "the fence." The first thing a National Public Radio reporter asked us was for examples of police brutality—the brutality of the Zone police toward the Panamanians. When we pointed out that the Zone police had never caused an international incident and had done a great deal to promote understanding by serving as a liaison between the Zone and the *Guardia*, the reporter went on to other questions. The *Guardia*, on the other hand, had a well-deserved reputation for brutality, and . . . But he did not want to hear about that. American brutality was news; Panamanian brutality was not.

The NPR man assumed he could be frank with us because he had read an article we wrote for the *Wall Street Journal*, urging the Senate to ratify the treaties.[41] He confided that he had talked the Canal issue over with his Latin friends in Texas before leaving the States, and they had decided that "ratification was the only way to go." We mentioned that at this point in the situation a lot of Zonians agreed. He was surprised and tried to get us to say that the Zonians who favored ratification were rising above their self-interest. The idea that, considering the way things had developed, many Zonians might perceive ratification as being *in* their self-interest was difficult for him. So was the idea that while most Zonians thought some sort of new treaty was necessary, they suspected that the Carter-Torrijos treaties would merely allow Panama to use the Canal Company to provide *botellas* (sinecures) for Panamanians while saddling the United States with the bills.

That was too complex to fit the reporter's idea of news. He wanted the world divided between the bad guys, with narrow, selfish interests, and the good guys, with broad, unselfish interests. We began to see reporters as divided between those with simple, idealistic interests— who often affected a pose of cynical knowingness—and the few who were interested in the messy complexity of the real world.

We used to defend the media to our students. Most journalists tried to be objective, we said. They had professional standards. Nobody could be expected to say everything in one story, and the whole point of a free press is that it provides a variety of points of view. Bad stories are the result of incompetence or a hunger for inches or air time, not bias, at least not usually. Besides, there is no alternative to a free press that isn't ten thousand times worse.

We still feel that way, but after *Playboy* published its interview with Geraldo Rivera, we stopped defending the media in our classes.[42] That interview gave our students too many quotations to use against us.

"Objectivity, I'm certain, was invented by journalism schools," observed Rivera, breezily, and dismissed it as having little to do with "real life." He claimed, however, to have reported the Canal story "just as a recorder and a communicator." Then, contradicting himself, he admitted that he was "clearly in favor of the treaty." This, however, just showed his ability to rise above his personal sympathies and see what was best for everyone, because his personal sympathies were with the Panamanian radicals. He felt an "identity" with "the Panamanian left" and its desire for a treaty that was more favorable to Panama. (By "the left," he did not mean the orthodox Communists; they supported Torrijos.) But Rivera was sure that the treaty, "weak as it was," was the best deal Panama could get. So he coached the Panamanians who appeared before his cameras on how best to behave in order to influence American opinion. He liked "the idea of being an educator." He was afraid, he said, that the rejection of the treaty would lead to violence.

Not realizing how he felt, Torrijos' none-too-discriminating police arrested him. Rivera's wife told a journalist from the college newspaper that her husband was handcuffed and "brutally mistreated." She said, "At the headquarters, he was struck in the face with such force that his eye glasses flew to the floor, he landed on his arms, and at this point felt that he had better calm down before he was brutalized further."[43]

However, from his ideological position above the battle, Rivera pitied the poor policemen. In his *Playboy* interview, he said, ". . . they were so unsophisticated. They thought that was the way to prevent bad publicity, and it was really the way to *generate* bad publicity. I could have made the whole country pay for the stupidity of twelve secret policemen."

When he was released, he had dinner with some people from the *New York Times* and *Washington Post*. They decided that although his arrest was "a great story," they had a responsibility to downplay it. "I had to be very careful about what I said," Rivera recalled, "because I could defeat the very thing I wanted to achieve." Indeed, the treaty vote was so imminent that according to Rivera, he and his friends "*stopped hoping for violence* [our italics] and started hoping for passivity," even though their stories would not be "as dramatic or vivid." They were afraid any more violence would cause the Senate to reject the treaties.

Rivera thinks he is the equivalent of an elected official: "I definitely think of it [the government] as the executive, the legislative, the judicial, and then the media." He believes that he has been "elected in an indirect way" because people opt to watch either him or someone else: "I think it is a pure democracy in that sense, a democracy that works on an almost nightly basis. It is pure choice." He also sees himself as a reformer: "I'm in the business of change," he said.

Rivera's confusion about the meaning of democracy, the nature of his job, and the value of reform reflects the continuing influence of the ideas of the turn-of-the-century progressives among contemporary liberals and radicals. The progressives were a largely professional, consciously altruistic group who saw themselves as "the self-appointed arbiters of man's destiny."[44] Equating righteousness with reform, they believed truth was "not discovered but manufactured."[45] They assumed that truth, like man and society, was malleable and that men had to free themselves from the "truths" of the past in order to create a brave new world. However, since ordinary people—the helpless products of their environments—could not do this, it was up to the progressive elite—enlightened journalists, engineers, teachers, civil servants, lawyers, and doctors—to reshape the environment and direct the creation of new Adams. In the early 1900s, progressive physicians saw themselves as the "moral directors" of their patients.[46] Rivera seems to feel the same way toward his viewers.

THE UNQUIET ENGLISHMAN

Just as the curtain was coming down on the Canal drama, who should walk onstage but Graham Greene. He was enjoying what he perceived to be an American defeat and tooting the horn for Torrijos and his authoritarian brand of "democracy." Between puffs, Greene preached his weary European-style jeremiad to his favorite audience, the Americans he despises.

Greene accompanied the Panamanian delegation to the extravaganza Carter organized to celebrate the end of the treaty negotiations. According to Greene, Carter looked "miserably unhappy" and made a "banal little speech that was almost inaudible." The glorious Torrijos, on the other hand, "spoke in a voice with a cutting edge very unlike Carter's."[47] Greene was proud to be "a temporary Panamanian of General Torrijos," who was such an extraordinary man: "Sometimes a touch of poetry appears unexpectedly and unnoticed by himself when he speaks. 'Intellectuals are like fine glass, crystal glass, which can be cracked by a sound. Panama is rock and earth.' "[48]

Greene confided to his readers that the Maximum Leader was much possessed by death: ". . . he dreams a good deal of death and his dreams are reflected in his eyes."[49]

There is a bit more along these lines in Greene's Panama essays. He reveals, for example, that Torrijos looked forward to "the simple solution of violence which has often been in his mind, with desire and apprehension balanced as in a sexual encounter."[50] Obviously, Greene saw the general as a late version of the romantic hero, a Latin American Heathcliff, yearning to challenge the horde of gum-chewing Yankee bourgeois barbarians.

Greene denied reports of his hero's habitual drunkenness but ignored more damaging reports of "a relationship" with the CIA. To even admit suspicions that such a relationship existed would tarnish the image of the hero, but certainly Torrijos was much beloved by the American establishment. One report says that during the first eight years of Torrijos' rule, Panama received more United States money than during the previous sixty-five years.[51]

In 1969, Torrijos went to Mexico. A coup in Panama left him temporarily deposed and stranded. According to historian Walter LaFeber, Anastasio Somoza of Nicaragua provided the plane that flew him home.[52] If true, Somoza must have wished he had left him in Mexico when Torrijos later aided the Sandinistas. Why would Somoza be so obliging? Possibly in response to a request from the United States which could not very well send Torrijos home in one of its own planes! It also cannot be overlooked that Arias, the man Torrijos replaced, was a popular leader who had in the past proved unpredictable—unmanageable?—in his relations with the United States.

DECONSTRUCTING DEMOCRACY

The American ambassador, William J. Jorden, in his book on the Canal treaty negotiations, makes the astonishing assertion that in Panama visiting American senators could see "grass-roots democracy in action." Most of them, he suggests, were unfamiliar with this phenomenon.[53] Graham Greene agrees that the Torrijos' dictatorship was a "grass-roots democracy." He declares that the dictator was "popular in the countryside (especially with the children)."[54] However, Torrijos never tested his grass-roots popularity against anyone in an election.

Robert Pastor, Carter's expert on Latin America, dubbed Torrijos a "populist" and remarked complacently that he had a "low regard for the political party system . . . viewing it as corrupt and serving the interests of the wealthy in Panama City."[55] Both Greene and Pastor give the impression that Torrijos swept into power on a wave of public discontent with democratic corruption, instead, as was actually the case, of winning power in an intramural struggle among the *Guardia*, after they alone, with no public support, had deposed the legally elected Arnulfo Arias.

Greene sneers at Arias as an "old man" who "hardly counts"[56] and without any apparent qualms rewrites Panama's history so that it conforms to fashionable expectations. He invents an "Arias oligarchy" that he says had ruled Panama since 1903. Thus, Torrijos, the man of the people, can be seen as liberating Panama from the oppressive Arias oligarchy, which was allied to the United States.

However, the unpredictable Arias, who has never been allowed to finish a single term in office, was never a favorite of the oligarchy or the United States. Born in a thatched hut in the province of Coclé, he has long been a charismatic figure in Panamanian politics, beloved by many. One might even call him a man of the people.

"Panama does not have a democratic government like our own," admitted President Carter,[57] leaving the way open for his audience to infer that it had a democratic government of some other kind. Carter went on to lavish praise on the dictator for giving the Panamanian people "a right . . . to vote in an open and free referendum or plebiscite" to approve or disapprove the treaties. Carter called this "an unprecedented expression of democratic principles."

The idea that rights are bestowed upon the people by their leaders is an intriguing one for an American president to have, especially when we remember that this "unprecedented expression of democratic principles" was unprecedented in Panama only since Torrijos took power, and it was actually a sham anyhow, since the result was never in doubt.

It is one thing to deal with dictators. It is something else to pretend they are democrats.

Greene maintained that the English—so far ahead of us in so many ways—were coming around to where they could "recognize other forms of democracy, even under a military chief of state, than the Parliamentary, which worked satisfactorily for about a hundred years in the special circumstances of those hundred years."[58] Greene seems to yearn for a hierarchical society in which everyone accepts the tragic limitations of mankind, as defined for them by their proper rulers. In such a society, the Quality does what is possible in this vale of tears for the Folk, who gratefully accept whatever is done for them because they know their administrators (masters) care. In their different ways, the members of both groups suffer—that's important—but during festivals and when their backs are to the wall, they leap forth vibrant with life and defiance.

Greene accompanied Torrijos to Chorillo, a black slum in Panama City. He watched the royal Torrijos fidget and suffer while the petty bureaucrats made their speeches, but when "the people" spoke, the meeting "sprang to life." "The General no longer twisted his cigar." "A colored girl . . . shrieked like a Voodoo dancer. . . ." "A Negro speaker talked with great dignity and confidence and fire." "A girl spoke up with anger, a woman had hysterics, the drums beat." Greene reassures his readers: "The faces might appear fierce and fanatical and angry, but they were friendly."[59]

Greene knows, because he is an expert at "knowing the people." He also knows who "the people's" enemies are—the Americans and their democracy.

After the meeting in Chorillo, which was organized by the dictator's henchmen, Greene went to a meeting on the Zone, which was organized by labor leaders and Civic Council representatives. There were no drums. No hysteria. As if that weren't bad enough, one of the speakers had thin legs. Greene compared him to a grasshopper. The Americans, Greene said, looked "very lost and lonely in the vast stadium." (He is talking about a high-school athletic field, not the equivalent of Yankee Stadium or the Astrodome.) He affected to pity the Americans: "God and country would probably let them down just as Jerry [Ford] and Henry [Kissinger] had." He is struck by the way the Americans use their leaders' Christian names and belittles the practice. It offends his sense of decorum.[60] He listened as a young woman asked the audience to send "letters and 'clippings' to congressmen," and reported, "She wasn't as impressive as the Negro in Chorillo."

However, because of her country's democratic traditions, she was a good deal more effective in shaping her own destiny, as we will explain shortly. That seems to be what Greene cannot abide—the effrontery, the presumptuous effectiveness of ordinary people who are not content to let God and country and Jerry and Henry let them down but insist on taking a shot at influencing events themselves— people who will not stay in their place.

Greene's and Rivera's ideas about democracy are more important in some ways than those of more discriminating thinkers. As popular communicators, they reflect as well as influence considerable bodies of opinion. They reflect, for instance, Bellamy's insistence that his authoritarian brand of socialism was *real* democracy, and John Dewey's insistence that Bellamy had grasped the "*human* meaning of democracy."

They both seem to think that *real* or *human* democracy refers to a government of the Good Guys, not to a procedure for reaching decisions. But there are important differences in their ideas, too.

Rivera is an American optimist. He sees opportunities for reform everywhere, and he prefers to be free of the shackles of office in order to pursue those opportunities more effectively. "Even if I were electable," he said, "I still think I could be more effective and influential outside Government. It's not *really* [our italics] outside. It's only outside Washington. It's not outside the hearts and minds of the people."

Greene, on the other hand, is a pessimist. He dislikes democracy and the party system because it is corrupt and optimistic. He seems to think that optimism is irrational and appears to be convinced that no just society can be very prosperous or happy. He may be right, since absolute justice would seem to require absolute stasis in order not to upset its perfect balance. The only good society may be a dead society! If so, the relatively prosperous, messy, and forever "dealing" democratic society in the United States is obviously a bad place.

However, both Greene and Rivera are enchanted by the possibility that a person can acquire *noblesse* by assuming obligations to those who are less fortunate—poorer, less sophisticated, less influential. Greene lauds Torrijos for bestowing national pride on Panama and also for intending to bestow free school meals and milk on all Panamanian children, new houses on the slum dwellers of Colón, and "pleasure parks" on the poor. Rivera praises himself for "making a difference" and hopes to continue to bestow correct views upon Americans through broadcast journalism.

However, like so many members of the so-called helping professions, Greene and Rivera seem to require a certain degree of helplessness in their "clients," the recipients of their largesse. The poor, the sick, left-wing rebels, outcasts of various sorts: these are all suitable candidates, but not the members of the middle class. We are reminded of Jane Austen's Emma, who remarked: "The yeomanry are precisely the order of people with whom I feel I can have nothing to do. A degree or two lower, and . . . I might hope to be useful to their families in some way or another."

However, the complexity of people's needs are too great ever to be satisfied by those who would do *for* them from above. Benevolent dictators; progressive, reform-minded intellectuals; and some idealistic schoolteachers (who often combine within themselves a little of both of the other two) soon burn out and drift from their initial optimism and enthusiasm to something like Greene's pessimism. They call it maturity. When they are mature, the ex-enthusiasts either console themselves with apocalyptic visions of a reform to end all reforms or go about muttering of a "national malaise," comforting themselves with the glamor of decline and complexity.

THE GLAMOR OF DECLINE AND COMPLEXITY

It never caught on among ordinary Americans but was popular among the status liberals during the seventies. They flaunted their disillusion during the bicentennial celebrations by wearing T-shirts that read, "Happy Birthday, America—Faded Glory." And in 1978, Joel Grey sang "A Yankee Doodle Boy" on the "Today" show just for them.

He didn't sing it the way George M. Cohan did when he introduced it back in 1904. That was the year the first Yankee mechanics arrived in Panama. Cohan strutted onstage announcing, "I'm a Yankee Doodle Dandy—a Yankee Doodle do or die." Grey did not strut. He sang as if he were having an identity crisis: "I am? I am? [a what?] A Yankee Doodle Dandy [wistfully]."

Grey was reflecting the mood of the status liberals. America had disappointed them. Vietnam and Watergate are often cited as the reasons, but we suspect a more fundamental reason was the fact that the country was no longer looking to them for leadership. After all, things had reached the point where the electorate preferred Richard Nixon to both the liberal Hubert Humphrey and to the radical-purist George McGovern. We suspect, too, that some status liberals found the idea of their nation's decline and wickedness rather attractive. It assuaged their lingering sense of colonial inferiority.

In 1898, many conservative Americans were enthusiastic imperialists. They wanted America to be more like England. They envied the English their white man's burden, their imperial glory, their dons and lords. Seventy-five years later, some status liberals were envying the English for quite different reasons: for their decolonialization and decline, for their oh-so-civilized drabness, for their socialism and national health insurance, which America had inexplicably failed to copy. To them, the English seemed so much more mature and complex than Americans. After McGovern's bid for the presidency failed in 1972, he said he was "very, very tempted" to settle in England.[61]

Also, the clichéd contrast between the complex, corrupt Old World sophisticate and the simple, honest New World innocent had come to irritate many thinking Americans. Simple, honest, and innocent added up to provincial and stupid, which they were not. They were as sophisticated, complex, and corrupt (not personally corrupt, of course, but as Americans)—and as intelligent as anybody. Maybe more so! So they welcomed any opportunity to claim a complex, corrupt past for America.

Of course, America is complex, dauntingly so, but its real complexity was not what interested the status liberals. It was the *idea* of complexity that they liked. During their heyday, they had argued that America was too complex to be run by amateurs. Only credentialed, independent, nonpolitical experts could understand and manage America. But after they had overcommitted America's military in Vietnam, overcommitted America's revenues to human-services programs, and sent the economy into an inflationary spiral, they began arguing that the nation's problems were too complex for *anyone* to understand or to do anything about. Thinking Americans could be smart by doing nothing, for only the simpleminded and those lacking in compassion would even try to do anything different.

THE NUCLEAR ENGINEER

On April 18, 1978, the treaties were ratified by one vote, and things began happening fast on the Zone, with appearance and reality doing their usual waltz. Carter congratulated the protreaty senators for "doing what was right." Torrijos announced the end of colonialism and, in a boozy television interview, bragged of what he would have done to the gringos if they had not ratified his treaties. He would have, he said, attacked the Canal with his helicopters—helicopters the United States had given to him.

In June, Carter flew to Panama to formally give away the Canal. At the airport, he talked vaguely about colonial empires disappearing without ever quite saying that he thought the Zone was a colony and the United States an imperial nation.

In town, he made a speech to 200,000 Panamanians who had been corralled for the occasion. Government workers had to appear and sign in or face dismissal. *Campesinos* were bussed in and given signs to wave. On the speakers' stand, the dictator in a white and gold uniform directed the cheering, palms up for more noise, palms down for *pianissimo*. A pep club near the speakers' stand chanted, "Give it to the gringos! Hit them hard!"

Carter's speech was about human rights. He ended with a big smile and a hearty, *"VIVA PANAMA!"* Much cheering. Then silence. Torrijos did not respond with *"Viva los Estados Unidos."* Carter kept smiling.

On the Zone, Carter made a speech directed to the Canal workers, and anyone reading accounts of that speech today would assume it had been given to an audience of Canal workers. However, Carter went to a good deal of trouble not to actually confront very many workers. Instead of giving his speech at the high-school stadium on the Pacific side, which is only a couple of hundred yards from the train station, Carter chose to give it at a stadium on an army post—a site apparently chosen to make it as inconvenient as possible for any Canal workers to attend. The military attended in civilian clothes. Their presence, according to Colonel Antonio Lopez, was "voluntary, sort of."[62] But Carter spoke to the crowd as if it were composed of workers. It was a triumph of social engineering—sort of.

What was his purpose? To avoid boos? Or signs reminding him that when seeking election he had said he would never give up control of the Canal? Or that he had said giving up the Canal would not cost the American taxpayer a cent? Or that he had said he would never lie to the American people? Or were his advisors at the embassy actually afraid of "redneck" violence? We wouldn't be surprised. The diplomats had a very strange view of the generally middle-aged government employees on the Zone.

Carter bluntly told "the workers" that he was relying on them to make the transition as smooth as possible. "That is your duty, your responsibility, and the people of both nations expect nothing less."[63]

Our duty. Not our patriotic duty. Something we owed both nations. Our duty. When a managerial thinker like President Carter begins appealing to duty, he is desperate. Duty is the ghost in the social machine. Duty is what we owe our community. It has to do with leadership and patriotism. It is not something that can be owed to both nations. And when leadership has become impersonal, rational, and managerial, people do not respond to appeals to duty.

Then Carter tried to be conciliatory. He tried to soothe us, as if our expressions of concern for the reputation and future of our country had merely been childish ways of asking for attention. "In the millions of words spoken and written about the treaties," he said, "our appreciation and concern have not been clearly expressed. The American people and I care what happens to you."[64]

The Canal workers did not believe him. Probably the majority of them had voted for him, but none of them believed anything he said anymore.

Then Senators Frank Church and Paul Sarbanes, who had accompanied Carter to Panama, held a totally unnecessary press conference. Sarbanes, with cheerful innocence, brought the news that Torrijos intended to assign police to the Zone who were fully bilingual and would do his best to "sensitize" his people. Church sanctimoniously reminded the Zonians that the Panamanians were resentful, too, and referred to the "constant friction" between Panamanians and Zone police.[65]

That was the sort of thing that drove the Zonians wild—the simplicity of their leaders. Sarbanes and Church dashed down to the Isthmus, listened credulously to the dictator, brushed aside the misgivings of their fellow citizens, some of whom had lived on the Isthmus for decades, and proceeded to lecture those same fellow citizens about the good intentions and rightful resentment of the Panamanians. Quickly, the senators flew off to Washington, having refreshed themselves by condescending to the Great Unwashed.

Not all senators were like that. Byrd wasn't, and he retained the Zonians' respect in spite of leading the fight for ratification.

Carter, too, flew off to Washington. He told the Americans back home that his trip had been a symbol of a new relationship.

"We're trying to put it in a broader context than just Panama," said one of his advisors. "It's a new era of partnership with Latin America."[66] Among themselves, the president's aides concluded that his smooth and friendly visit had indeed inaugurated that new relationship. One of them said he bet that if the Panamanians held the

treaty plebiscite again, it would pass by an even wider margin.⁶⁷ He
was unquestionably right. The alliance of Panamanians who wanted
a treaty more favorable to Panama and those who didn't want to see
a nonelected dictator sign the historic treaty would be at least three
votes shy of their previous total. The three Panamanian students that
Torrijos' secret police had sprayed with a Uzi submachine gun during
an antitreaty demonstration just two days before Carter arrived would
not be able to vote against it again, ever.

MAKING A DIFFERENCE

So the Zone was Panama's? Not quite. The treaty would not go into
effect until October 1, 1979. In the meantime, the House had to
pass enabling legislation to finance the transition. That legislation was
the fine print that would actually determine the Zonians' fates. We
had come to believe that we had been suckered into staying on the job
for the president's convenience and that after we smoothly transferred
our jobs to Panamanians, we would be dumped at the president's convenience. As a group, we had never been 100 percent opposed to the
treaties, but we were 100 percent for our jobs—and almost all of us
were deeply suspicious of our government's promises to take care of
us. So we went to work to save ourselves. It was a business both sad
and inspiring.

Sad, because we were a group of American patriots—often accused
of being too patriotic—who had been transformed into a group of
one-dimensional "economic men and women." That was what Bellamy,
Marx, and assorted reductionist liberals had assumed all along—that
money was what everything was *really* all about. Anything else was
mere appearance.

We had heard America maligned while our leaders smiled sheep-
ishly and said it wasn't *really* important. We had heard ourselves
maligned while our leaders sat mute. That wasn't *really* important,
either. And we knew, no matter how earnestly Carter insisted that the
transition, as he narrowly defined it, would not cost the American

taxpayers a cent, that in reality it was going to cost all of us a bundle. A lot of that money would end up in the pockets of Panamanian politicians. Our leaders knew that, too, but this time they said nothing because *that was* important! And on the sly, they voted themselves ever more generous salaries and retirement benefits. *That* was important, too.

It looked to us as if it were every man for himself. It had come to this: If we were no more than "economic men and women," if money was the name of the game, then we were determined to do as well as we could. And from another angle what followed was inspiring. Graham Greene might sneer at the woman who urged her fellow citizens to send clippings and letters to congressmen, but she, far better than he, understood how the democracy business works.

Zonians collected money to send union leaders and Civic Council representatives to Washington for a few days at a time to testify and lobby for favorable enabling legislation. The men and women who went were not trying to shape national policy. They were negotiating a labor settlement. They were not experts, just "ordinary people"— but they were not ineffective for all their ordinariness. They explained; they kidded around; they lined up votes. There was no Central Committee masterminding things. People representing the AFGE, the AFT, the Metal Trades Council, the pilots, the tugboat operators, the Civic Councils, and dozens of individuals acting on their own talked to each other but went their own ways—American style.

Zonians wrote letters to Congress and urged their friends and relatives to write. One group of twelve women collected the names of 2,000 friends and relatives of Zonians in the States, then, working from eight model letters, they wrote a letter for each person, addressed to the appropriate congressman. They made sure no congressman got more than one letter of each kind. If there were more than eight persons in the same district, they wrote variations. They even made sure each congressman got a mix of letters typed on manual and electric machines.

The finished letter, accompanied by a stamped, addressed envelope, went to the contact on the Zone who sent it on to the friend or relative in the States. All that person had to do was sign it and drop it in the mail. Many people in the States sent the replies they received back to the Zone. We were amused to discover that some congressmen were using the same answering service—sending out identical, slightly off the subject, machine-signed letters that were written on a word processor. That gave someone the idea of sneaking into an army office at night and running off a few letters to Congress on its Wang. Wang to Wang. It was all very American—half Tom Sawyer and half civics text.

Four things made the Canal worker's job easier than it might have been. First was Carter's personality. People understood when the Zonians said they couldn't trust him. Second was the resentment in the House and Senate left by Carter's successful but inept campaign to ratify the treaties. Third was the unanimity of the Zone community. Unanimity was no more common on the Zone than it is in any other American community, but the widely understood need to obtain favorable enabling legislation produced a folk movement.

After the manner of bureaucratic folklore in America, much of the Zone's folklore was written down and passed from hand to hand: a parody of the Lord's Prayer that read in part, "Give us this day our enabling legislation, / And forgive us our manicured lawns, / As we forgive those who take them from us. / Lead us not into the *Carcelo Modelo*. / And deliver us from the *Guardia*. . . ." There were parodies of songs. One, to the tune of "Jingle Bells," was called "Treaty Time." It included the lines, "When asked what wine he'd like to have, / Torrijos cried, 'Your port.' " There was a list of redefined terms: "Chief of State—Richest man in Panama," "Stalwart Panamanian Patriot—Man who does not ask questions," "Demonstrations—Panamanians throwing rocks while the United States hands out onions," and so on. There were also folkloric acronyms and parodic memos to explain them, "R.A.P.E.," for instance (Retire All Personnel Early).

The fourth thing that made the Zonians' job easier was the shadow of the Great Sickout—a wildcat strike that had taken place two years earlier, in 1976. It had closed the Canal for six days and caused the biggest backlog in Canal history—175 ships. They were strung out for ten miles at either end of the Canal. Shipowners lost millions. Some people, at least, remembered that the workers had closed the Canal once and could conceivably close it again, although nobody so much as whispered of such a thing.

The sickout was a social engineers' nightmare—a spontaneous protest from below. The *Miami Herald* reported that the Canal administration found the sickout difficult to deal with because of its spontaneous nature and the lack of any apparent leadership.[68]

What had happened was that Assistant Secretary of the Army Victor Veysey had decided to freeze the wages of four low-paid grades composed mainly of Panamanian workers and to eliminate the 15 percent tropical differential in the future for all locally hired United States citizens. Those cutbacks were apparently what the strike was about.

Really, they were just an excuse. Nor was the strike a protest against the ongoing treaty negotiations, a point the *Miami Herald* accurately emphasized. It was a protest against uncertainty. People wanted to know what kinds of options they had. They wanted to decide whether to leave or stay. The diplomats who were working on the new treaties with Panama had assumed that labor matters could be postponed until the last minute, along with other unimportant details. The workers wanted some assurance that they, the people directly affected, would have some say in those matters when they finally came up. In the meantime, the workers did not intend to sit by and watch their salaries and benefits whittled away by clever chaps like Veysey.

The law provided for "consultation" with the employees about changes in wages, so Governor Harold Parfitt announced that the changes would not go into effect until April. Employees were told to put their objections in writing and that they would then be considered. That was what passed for "consultation" on the Zone. Everyone knew the so-called proposals were really decisions. In 1974, a labor expert had warned the Canal administration that it would not be able to get away with such high-handedness much longer.[69]

And, according to rumor, when the governor had expressed reservations about the wage freeze, Veysey had told him there would be no problem because the Canal workers were "gutless sheep."

At a workers' rally in the high-school stadium, all the union leaders except the leader of the Policemen's Union urged caution. A collection was taken to send one union leader to Washington. The chiefs of the pilots' and tugboat operators' unions said they would go, too, at their own expense. When they returned, there was a second, larger rally.

The union leaders brought promises of help and a letter from Veysey denying that the words "gutless sheep" were in his vocabulary. "I am not in the habit of referring to people in terms like that," he wrote, with a touch of hauteur. When his letter was read, the crowd groaned.

The president of the Central Labor Council said George Meany wouldn't sanction a strike. The crowd was silent. The pilots' chief said, "That's right, he won't." The tugboat chief said, "Work safely," which was a call for a slowdown, strikes being illegal. The president of the Policemen's Union said the whole thing made him sick, which was a call for a sickout. Finally, the president of the AFGE said, "Do what your conscience tells you." He said it several times.

There was scattered applause, but most people sat quietly, thinking. This was too serious to get excited about.

On Sunday, the admeasurers and pilots on the Atlantic side were sick. As the news spread, tugboat operators, lock workers, electricians, and machinists began calling in sick. On Monday, a few teachers were sick. Monday afternoon, people began holding meetings and voting. On Tuesday, the schools were closed; the Canal was closed. "Get sick" was spray-painted on buildings. "Baa-baa" appeared on the sides of cars. People said that a wit at the hospital had written a parody of a medical paper, announcing an outbreak of anthrax on the Zone, but we never saw it.

No one was free of symptoms, but not everyone came down with the disease. Some people kept reporting to work. There was remarkably little bitterness toward them. People recognized that not everyone's conscience worked the same way. Friends stayed friends. It was complicated.

Then some high-level social engineers in the States collected a group of military pilots whom they proposed to send to the Isthmus to break the strike. This was highly gratifying to the liberal newspapers in the States. It should have been, since it was a charade put on for their benefit. At least, it's hard to believe that anyone who knew anything about the Canal ever seriously contemplated replacing the Canal pilots. *That* would have torn it.

The shipowners would have had to decide if they dared send a ship through under the command of a pilot unfamiliar with the Canal who would be working with untrained or hostile lockmasters, tugboat operators, muledrivers, and so on. The insurance companies would have screamed. There would very likely have been sympathy strikes by pilots and tugboat operators in the States. Congress would have wanted to investigate. To forestall all that, the governor announced that he would recommend and support changes in the controversial wage proposals and that he would form a labor-management committee to study collective bargaining for the Zone. Everyone was relieved, except for a few militants who claimed the settlement made them "sick." And, in a sense, the strikers had a victory—although they couldn't boast of it because there had never *really* been a strike, any more than there had been a settlement about what was *really* bothering the Zonians.

Not until three years later, in 1979, when the enabling legislation sponsored by Carter and the "liberals" was defeated and a bill more acceptable to the workers, a bill sponsored by "conservatives"—Democrat and Republican—was passed and signed, could people take stock and begin making plans. The "liberal" bill left the workers' futures almost entirely in the hands of benevolent bureaucrats who would assuredly do everything possible to help them. The "conservative" bill gave more decision-making power to each individual worker. A key element in the bill was a provision for voluntary early retirement with a reduced annuity after eighteen years of service at age forty-eight. It was designed to keep younger workers who were scheduled to be replaced in a few years from seeking new jobs and to keep older workers on the job for a few more years by giving them the option of leaving if in their judgment the situation got too bad.

The workers in Bellamy's utopia are able to retire at forty-five. The Zonians were not quite able to match that, but then the Zone was never exactly like Bellamy's utopia, either—just close.

OCTOBER 1, 1979

We have been anticipating this day for so long. It's nine in the morning. We're waiting for the ceremony at ten, which we'll watch on TV. They expect 200,000 Panamanians to march through the Zone. Anything can happen with a crowd that big.

Of course, they may not get 200,000. The Panamanian schoolteachers are boycotting it. They have been on strike for two months. (If the students aren't on strike, the teachers are.) They want more money, of course, but they are also complaining about the new national curriculum that's been imposed on them. They claim it's Communist and designed to stop social mobility. The doctors joined them for a while, as did the bus drivers. The profesores collect money for their strike fund on street corners. But the teachers may not be missed. Government employees are being bussed in from everywhere. It looks like a bright, sunny day in spite of our prayers for rain.

Last night we went to the final flag-lowering ceremony. We were prepared to be moved. Once again we were disappointed. They had erected a dais and draped it with bunting on the stairs in front of the Building. Fred Cotton introduced the Zone officials. Governor Parfitt looked worn out and spoke as if he were on automatic.

It was a time for inspirational speeches, a time to praise the Zonians for preserving a distinct American identity while at the same time being friendly to the outsiders surrounding them. (That a community has to have outsiders is something we've learned down here. An "open community" that imposes no standards and accepts anyone is about as viable as the so-called open marriage that the fashionable enemies of intimacy were touting a few years back.)

Our leaders might also have mentioned that just as the United States realized that the Zone could not be a sanitary enclave surrounded by an unsanitary Panama, it realized that the Zone should not remain an enclave of well-paid technicians surrounded by a nation of poor, technologically illiterate peasants. Just as the United States sanitized Panama, so it made major contributions to Panama's technological and economic progress and to the development of its still fragile, democratic tradition. But none of our leaders mentions these things.

Our government really has lost sight of the Panama Canal and of America's record in Panama as achievements—as specific applications of the general American mission to bring the nations of the world together. Panamanian realists scorn such vaporings, of course, as do American liberals these days. The Panamanian realists say the Canal was never anything more than a project to give the U.S. military and commercial advantages and that the U.S. policy of keeping the tolls low was really just a way of subsidizing the American consumer at Panama's expense. Thus when the Panamanians jack up the tolls and run the Canal for their local advantage they will not "really" be acting any differently from the Americans. The new brand of liberal cynic agrees. No fuzzy-minded idealism for him. He even argues that Panama deserved to run the Canal as a business from the beginning and that America exploited Panama by not letting it do so —or rather by not running the Canal mainly for Panama's benefit, since Panama couldn't have done the job.

The old-fashioned liberal ideal of bringing the nations together has been reduced to the idea that all the nations are alike—"really"—and that America is no different, especially no better, than the rest— "really."

It won't wash. The Americans—immigrants and the children of immigrants from dozens of countries—who got together to build the Canal and who ran it for seventy-five years had something more than profit and power in mind. They had a vision of a better world.

The prayers at the flag lowering were horrible. Not even the preachers can say the right things these days. The music was barely audible, since they put the band behind the dais. Were other people as disappointed as we were?

But when the band played "God Bless America," the American flag did its thing. A breeze happened to catch it—and it alone. The Panamanian flag hung limply while Old Glory flapped and fluttered and rippled for the TV cameras. A Panamanian woman in front of us leaned to her companion and said, "Ay, what does it mean?"

The Governor ordered the flags lowered. First the Panamanian flag. The band played the Panamanian national anthem. Then "The Star-Spangled Banner." As the Stars and Stripes came down, the crowd began to sing softly, joining the band to help it out. A few of the dignitaries on the speakers' stand joined in.

Last night we were awakened at midnight by bangs and the rattle of firecrackers. It lasted fifteen or twenty minutes. A few cars drove through the neighborhood, honking.

This morning we watched the raising of the Panamanian flag on Ancon Hill on TV. Mondale was there and made a speech. He was ostentatiously ignored by our new partners in Latin America, by the dignitaries from other countries as well as those from Panama. The American ambassador to Panama was there, too. He and Mondale can make it to the Panamanian ceremony but not to the American one! Where were they yesterday afternoon?

What is it with our government? Doesn't it know whose side it's on? Does it think the Panamanians are going to guard its frontiers, rewire its broken switches, dig its canals? Vote in its elections? Is it ashamed of us, its own employees? Or is it ashamed of America's Canal adventure? Or has it risen above mere nationalism?

Took the dog out. A man we do not know waved to us as he drove by. Then two G.I.'s went by. They waved, too, like we were old friends. We waved back like we'd known them all our lives. Maybe the ex-Zonians will be drawn closer together than ever by all this. No need to check the mail. Our P.O. closed last night. A mob was up at the corner mailing letters with "Last Day of Operation" cancellations. We'll just have to wait and see.

20
Saying Good-bye to the Zone

When the treaties went into effect in 1979, the Canal Company was reorganized as a commission and divested of most functions not directly connected to putting ships through the Canal. Temporarily, it continued to act as landlord for some of its employees and to operate a court system and police force, though with much reduced jurisdictions. Its policemen were to conduct joint patrols with the *Guardia* during a transition period that would last until April 1, 1982.

Three months after that we would be able to retire early under the provisions of the enabling legislation.

The company's hospitals, commissaries, and schools were transferred to the Department of Defense, and those of us employed in those institutions set about learning the DOD system. It was not much different from the Army-Navy system that paralyzed work on the Canal back in 1904. Both were characterized by unwieldy methods of procurement and bizarre quantities of paper work.

"You're just going from a small bureaucracy to a large one," an NPR reporter explained to us and went on to ask if we were seeing more Panamanians on the Zone. We started to tell him that we couldn't tell Panamanians from Americans by their looks but said, "Oh, sure," instead. That was what he wanted to hear, and it was all he had time for.

A friend who was retiring showed us the forms he had to fill out. He said that C.P.O. (Civilian Personnel Office) had told him to have twenty copies made before he went to Transportation. There were even more forms, he said, if you wanted to ship a P.O.V. (Privately Owned Vehicle, sometimes known as a c-a-r.)

Peevishly, the army radio station announced that it was not going to play "Take This Job and Shove It" anymore, no matter how many times people requested it.

We learned there was a DOD rule against keeping defective equipment for more than six months but that it took longer than that to get replacement parts. The unofficial DOD solution was to order everything new every two years.

We also learned that at the end of the new bureaucracy's twisty maze, we might unexpectedly come upon—ourselves! A general on the board of trustees of the Panama Canal College (formerly the Canal Zone College) offered to sign a letter to another general requesting something that the college thought it needed. Mary and the dean drafted a letter. General Y signed it and sent it to General Z, who gave it to a member of his staff and told him to draft a reply. The staff man gave it to the D.O.D.D.S. (Department of Defense Dependent Schools) office on the Isthmus, which passed it on to the college. Whereupon, Mary and the dean sat down and wrote themselves a letter, which General Z duly signed and sent to General Y, who passed it on to the college, where it was received with appropriate expressions of appreciation.

While we were adjusting to the DOD system, the Panamanians were reshaping the Zone. They put up flags and signs. "Bolera-Pepsi," said the new neon letters on top of the bowling alley. (For us, that, more than anything, spelled the end of Bellamy's noncommercial utopia.) Lottery vendors set up their folding tables in front of the post office.

Soon potholes began dimpling the streets. Long grass began combing the moist air. Dennis McAuliffe, the newly appointed administrator of the newly formed Canal Commission, conceded to an American reporter, "Some of what has been turned over to Panama has not been kept up."[1]

At the commissary—still functioning temporarily—we met our

friend Josie Olsen, who came to the Zone as a newlywed in 1920. "It'll be the mosquitoes next. Oh, boy. Yellow fever again. Just you wait," she warned us. We asked her when she was leaving. "Leaving? Oh, honey, I'm not leaving! I've got to see what happens!"

We felt as if we had seen enough. No students recited the Pledge of Allegiance anymore, nor did they study *Robert's Rules of Order*. The only rule left was no bare feet. The reforms in the curriculum and the school's policies about dress and behavior had carried all of us past reform and into formlessness. Reforms had shattered not just the authority of traditional grammar, history, and math, and of teachers and principals, but the authority of principles and values—of education itself. We had to get out of teaching and out of Panama.

In 1980, Carter and Mondale ran for reelection. They dragged about the country delivering European-style jeremiads, omitting the traditional American ending, the news that God's punishments were meant as correctives and that tomorrow would be better. Instead, they declared that there were no quick and easy solutions—no solutions at all, in fact. They urged us to accept the inevitable and despair in a composed, mature, European way.

They lost.

On July 31, 1981, Torrijos was killed in a plane crash. An accident, the newspapers said, but every Panamanian we knew said, "They got him." Just who "they" were varied from speaker to speaker. The estimates of the dictator's immense popularity by Carter's experts and by Graham Greene were not borne out by the small crowd that met his cortege at Cathedral Plaza.[2]

President Royo, Torrijos' puppet president, was soon forced from office by his own party. The new president, Ricardo de la Espriella, announced with a smile that his predecessor had health problems— "throat trouble."

But, in the midst of change, some things remained the same. While newly elected President Reagan was cutting the nation's budget, the newly appointed dean of the Panama Canal College, a veteran DOD bureaucrat, was urging us to spend. "He who spends the most, gets the most," he advised sagely.

And our American friend who identifies with Latin American "liberation" parties continued to complain bitterly about the "privileged" position of the Americans in the former Zone. "The envy problem is still there," she declared, as if revealing yet another instance of American insensitivity. (The only good American, apparently, is the unenviable American.)

The time came for the ex-Zone police to disband. On February 6, 1982, they held a farewell ball. The souvenir book compiled for the occasion contains ads from businesses in Panama that wish the police well and congratulate them for a job well done. This suggests that the "constant friction" that Senator Church discovered between the Zone police and the Panamanians did not exist between the police and *all* Panamanians and may, in fact, have been more in the nature of an ideological convenience than a reality.

On March 31, 1982, the American community gathered once again before the steps of The Building, this time to tell its policemen good-bye. The new administrator made everyone wait for him to arrive. The policemen waited in the sun at attention. The crowd milled about. It was smaller than it would have been two years earlier.

The next day, April 1, Administrator Dennis McAuliffe and American Ambassador Ambler Moss attended the Panamanian ceremony marking Panama's assumption of full control over the former Zone. Dignitaries sat on a wooden platform that had been erected in front of the old Zone police station. Bunting was draped everywhere. Sets of four loudspeakers were mounted on nearby lamp posts.

Next to McAuliffe, the Panamanians sat Lester Leon Greaves, a rapist who had served sixteen years in the Canal Zone penitentiary before being pardoned in 1962. He was a guest of honor, a symbol of American oppression and injustice. Behind him, the Panamanians sat Ambassador Moss. Moss and McAuliffe did what bureaucratic administrators do best—stayed put.

The newspapers gave the pictures a big play. *"Contraste,"* blared *Crítica,* under a picture of Greaves and McAuliffe, and mentioned the tremendous injustices committed by North Americans against Panamanians. *"No Más Injusticias,"* bannered *Matutino.* "Greaves with VIP's" said the *Republic*, which also declared, "Panama Will Never Again Shed Tears Over Hostile Foreign Police Presence." The stories referred to America's "hideous discrimination" against Panamanian labor, commerce, and industry; to American "atrocities and injustices," and to the "decrepit and anachronistic" American system of justice.[3]

The words of the Panamanians should not be dismissed as mere rhetoric, which we, as the more responsible people, are obliged to ignore. Ignoring Latin fits of tremendousness may be the worst thing we can do for them—and for ourselves. Latins overestimate the power of rhetoric and are preoccupied with the master-servant relationship. Hence, their rhetoric proceeds easily from an expression of pride to a denial of reality and into a spiral of absolutism, violence, and destructive heroism.

We Americans, on the other hand, underestimate rhetoric's magic. Claiming to be pragmatists, we dismiss rhetoric as something that gets in the way as we are getting dinner. "Sticks and stones," we say, but we are wrong. Words *can* harm us. They can affect us for the better, too. Without the words of our preachers, songwriters, and presidents, we would be a different people because we would imagine ourselves differently.

Panamanians have every right to revile us if they wish, but what reason do our representatives have for cooperating? No Panamanian official would have stayed put had the situation been reversed—whether the charges were true or not. However, if the charges *had* been true, most Americans would have expected their representatives to stay and "take their medicine." That was what made Moss and McAuliffe's behavior so reprehensible. They were symbolically saying that the United States understood and accepted its guilt, which was exactly what the Panamanians who set them up intended for them "to say." They were also symbolically expressing solidarity with the Panamanians and, through that association, contempt for the Canal Company and its police.

Of course, Moss and McAuliffe were doing their duty by attending this ceremony. Had they refused to attend—and surely their liaison men knew what had been planned—we have no doubt that they would have been severely criticized by their superiors in Washington for "making waves." The word on the Zone was that nothing should be done during the transition to embarrass the Panamanians.

But there is an imbalance at work here that is gradually undermining respect for the United States abroad and respect for the American foreign policy establishment at home. Foreign elites often find it expedient to make the United States the scapegoat for whatever is wrong with their country, knowing that our Department of State will diplomatically ignore their assertions. The American foreign policy establishment masks its moral confusion with reiterated assertions of its professionalism and its effectiveness behind the scenes. However, its apparent preference for tranquility to truth and its apparent indifference to the way the United States is portrayed by foreign leaders are undermining the willingness of ordinary Americans to accept on faith the diplomats' claims for their quiet efficiency behind the scenes, and in a democracy, a foreign policy establishment cannot function effectively in the long run without the trust of the electorate.

While bitter comments about the behavior of Moss and McAuliffe circulated among the remaining Americans, we began sorting our stuff, deciding what to leave and what to take. We had already decided where to go.

Some of our friends were going to Florida, where there were lots of ex-Zonians. Others were going to Texas, where there were lots of jobs. We had decided on New England—where there were town meetings and four seasons—sometimes more.

21

Looking Backward and Forward

COMING HOME

Our families were backtrailers. Our grandfathers and grandmothers moved from frontier farms to small towns. Our parents moved to Kansas City. We dreamed of Chicago and New York—of getting still closer to The Center. We envied the sophisticates at The Center. Their lives, we supposed, were Works of Art.

We thought we were giving up that dream when we went to the Canal Zone. How much farther from The Center can you get? But there we found ourselves in a different version of the same dream, only on the Zone it was society that was the Work of Art, not the individual.

In the America we have come home to, there is no Center—no cultural capital or strong social norm—no accepted idea of education, respectability, or national direction. It is as if a limit had been reached and a new and different sense of national identity and direction is in the making.

Sophisticates are moving from the big city to Zenith and Gopher Prairie. They are searching for a better quality of life. Some liberal magazines have published articles endorsing at least a limited amount of patriotism and protesting that the disillusioned view of America has often become as automatic as the uncritical faith in America's goodness that characterized an earlier era. Some educators are suggesting that it is more important to teach good citizenship than critical thinking. However, good citizenship does not translate into an uncritical respect for authority. Everyone is more suspicious of the authorities—the wise few—than they were when we left. The un-critical respect for the doctor or loyalty to the company or the union that characterized our fathers' generation is a curiosity these days.

On the other hand, people are increasingly aware of the need for community—of the fact that doing one's own thing has its limits. No one was talking about limits when we left the States in 1963. John Kenneth Galbraith was telling us that America had solved the problem of production: We lived in an affluent society; all that was left to do was to solve the Bellamyite problem of resource allocation between public and private use. President Kennedy was telling us that America would "pay any price, bear any burden." A few years later, many Americans were celebrating their emancipation from all traditional restraints on public dress and behavior, and Congress was spending money faster than the Federal Reserve could print it.

In the America we have come home to, everyone is talking about limits—the limits imposed by career choices; the limits of the SAT tests; the limits of natural resources; the limits of government regula-tion, of social security, of welfare and medical costs, of defense spend-ing; the limits of accommodation for the sake of peace—the limits of reason itself.

Public education is no longer anybody's Great Panacea. Indeed, Great Panaceas and permanent solutions seem to have had their day. And who still believes the United Nations is the harbinger of world federalism?

"Success" is being redefined. So is "national mission." Eventually there will be a new appreciation of America's distinctive qualities—of its peculiar equalitarianism, of its role as a model and proponent of democratic government, and of its openness, within a democratic framework, to political and social experiment. Given the particular conditions and choices of our times, that may mean a special apprecia-tion of America's inadvertent experiment in collectivism on the banks of the Panama Canal.

LEARNING FROM THE PAST

In time, the Zone may be regarded as an anomaly—a nineteenth-century American "utopian" community that survived in an out-of-the-way place for three-quarters of the twentieth century. On the other hand, many Americans still hope that someday America will become a full-fledged welfare state, where they will be able to live in perfect security, tranquility, and brotherhood, under the direction of "the most perfect aristocracy." Should that come to pass, the version of Bellamy's utopian dream that developed on the banks of the Panama Canal will go into the history books as a precursor of the future. It just may be possible, however, that the inadvertent experiment on the Zone can teach us something about how we need to balance tranquility, security, efficiency, and brotherhood with opportunity, risk, competition, the pain of failure, and the waste that attends all innovation. Possibly, too, the history of the way Americans have perceived the Zone and the Zonians can make us more conscious of the way a passion for dramatic moral simplicities and a scorn for the values and concerns of ordinary working people can create an unhealthy divisiveness in our society at a time in our history when Americans particularly need each other.

We are not sorry we went to the Zone. We had time there to watch our kids grow, to enjoy each other, to reflect, to study, and to perfect our professional skills. During a period when the United States was beset by gurus with visions of musical-mystical-pastoral-chemical utopias dancing in their heads, we lived quietly in an old-fashioned "rational" utopian dream come almost true.

However, we could not have stayed on the Zone if we hadn't been able to get away to Panama regularly and to the States every year or two. All Zonians understood when somebody who loved the Zone said, "I've *got* to get out of here!"

The Zone's system was designed to provide the greatest good for the greatest number. It provided everyone with work, comfort, leisure, and a clear conscience, except with regard to racism, but that was not a flaw in the system. The system was not dependent in any way on racism, which had diminished considerably by the seventies. But the system had its limits. It provided only a small number of narrow avenues to predestined kinds of success, diminished the value of the individual, and it brought change and history almost to a halt.

Moreover, the Zone's American-style socialism was only provisionally nicer than forms of socialism found elsewhere. Its propensity toward arbitrary authoritarianism was checked only by its ties to the democratic United States and by the fact that the Zonians—administrators and workers alike—having lived free in the States, could never completely abandon their democratic expectations.

What was left of those expectations, however, was not much. Zonians knew that they were expected to adjust themselves to the demands of the Zone's peaceful, coherent, rational, nondemocratic system.

We have come home to a society where people expect the system to adjust itself to them—and to their ever-changing ideals. As a result, their "system" is incoherent—an intellectual scandal, an offense to the wise few at home and abroad. Nevertheless, for all its irrational contradictions, it is preferable to the tranquil, rational, almost unchanging, and more nearly "perfect" system we left behind.

In fact, it is the contradictory nature of the democratic American system that we especially learned to value while we were on the Zone. Americans believe quite irrationally in free *and* equal, to each according to his needs *and* to each according to his abilities, religious faith *and* religious freedom, free speech *and* public decorum, science *and* sentiment, the heart *and* the head, compassion *and* competition, conscience *and* country, a loyalty to the old country *and* to the new, a loyalty to America *and* a concern for the world. "A foolish consistency," as Emerson says, "is the hobgoblin of little minds, adored by little statesmen and philosophers and divines." Or, as the greatest American poet puts it, "Do I contradict myself? / Very well, then I contradict myself, / (I am large, I contain multitudes.)."

No society can provide opportunities for everyone to shine at the same time. Different talents require different circumstances, goals, and values. Once Americans periodically redefined their goals and values during nationwide Protestant revivals called Awakenings. Today, though America has become a more pluralistic and secular nation, Americans have not lost the habit of Awakening—of periodically reviving their commitment to the contradictory, inherently destabilizing American dream of liberty and justice for all. Now, as always, Americans are searching for a New Light, though the Old Light never quite dies, and the process is never finished.

Notes

Newspapers, news magazines, and publications of the Panama Canal Company are cited in full. Complete information on abbreviated citations will be found in Sources. Unpublished and privately published material is available at the Canal Commission Library in Panama, the Panama Canal College Library, or the Library of Congress.

PART ONE

Chapter 1

1. Pepperman, p. 134.
2. Abbot, *Panama and the Canal*, p. 144.
3. George Washington Goethals, "Address, July 4, 1911," reprint, *Panama Canal Review* (Spring 1976), p. 6.
4. Society of the Chagres, *Yearbook, 1912*, p. 51.
5. Abbot, *Panama and the Canal*, p. 328.
6. Franck, p. 216.
7. Heald, p. 120.
8. Bowman, *The Year 2000*, p. 120; see also Bowman and others, *Edward Bellamy Abroad*; Franklin; and Sadler.
9. Weeks, p. 278.
10. Tarbell, p. 137.
11. Richard Hudson, "Storm Over the Canal," *New York Times Magazine*, May 16, 1976, p. 22.
12. See "Canal Treaty Fails to Materialize as a Campaign Issue," *Miami Herald*, September 17, 1978, p. 13-AW. The story says only that the treaty was not a key issue. See also Christian.

Chapter 2

1. Cameron, p. 262. For the corruption that undermined the French, see Simon.
2. Pepperman, p. 315.
3. DuVal, *Cadiz to Cathay*, p. 405; LaFeber, pp. 39–40.
4. Pepperman, pp. 132–33.
5. Abbot, *Panama and the Canal*, p. 120.
6. Mack, p. 350.
7. Bunau-Varilla, *From Panama to Verdun*, pp. 217–25.
8. Bunau-Varilla, *The Great Adventure*, pp. 17–19, 35–36, 51, 60.
9. Mack, p. 472.

10. McCullough, p. 277.
11. Sands, p. 51.
12. Society of the Chagres, *Yearbook, 1914*, pp. 142–43.
13. Abbot, *Panama and the Canal*, pp. 287–88.
14. Ibid., p. 412.
15. DuVal, *And the Mountains Will Move*, p. 212.
16. Bennett and others, p. 408.
17. Seeley, p. 68; Society of the Chagres, *Yearbook, 1914*, p. 194.
18. Sands, p. 37.
19. Gibson, p. 193.
20. Pennell, p. 9.
21. See the brief biographies, Society of the Chagres, *Yearbooks, 1911* and *1912*.
22. Van Hardeveld, p. 116.
23. Ibid., p. 139.
24. Our contrast of Stevens and Goethals owes much to the ideas of David Riesman. We also benefited from Nicholas Lemann's "Success in America."
25. For Stevens' life we relied on his addresses and recollections; on books by Pepperman, DuVal, Haskins, Kennan, and McCullough; on articles by McCullough and Webster; and on the *Annual Report of the Isthmian Canal Commission, 1905*.
26. Minter, p. 345.
27. Ibid., p. 346.
28. Wood, p. 190.
29. For Goethals' life we relied on books by Joseph Bishop, Farnham Bishop, Bennett and others, DuVal, Edwards, Marie Gorgas, and McCullough; and on an article by Baker.
30. Stevens, *An Engineer's Recollections*, p. 14.
31. Baker, p. 23.
32. Boorstin, *The Democratic Experience*, pp. 259–60.
33. "Publick Occurrences," *Saturday Evening Post*, October 27, 1900, in Brosseau, p. 230.
34. Charles R. Flint, "How Business Success Will Be Won in the Twentieth Century," *Saturday Evening Post*, November 17, 1900, in Brosseau, p. 55.

Chapter 3

1. Longfellow, "The Two Rivers."
2. Perry Miller, *The Life of the Mind in America*, p. 33.
3. Edwards, p. 578.
4. Abbot, *Panama and the Canal*, p. 326.
5. Sharpe, p. 395.
6. McLoughlin, p. 167.
7. Cavallo, p. 519.
8. McLoughlin, p. 166.
9. Heald, p. 43.

Chapter 4

1. McLoughlin, p. 164.
2. See Davis and the responses to his article.

3. Perry Miller, *The New England Mind,* p. 462.
4. Bercovitch, p. 6.
5. Ibid., p. xi.

Chapter 5

1. Vinton, p. 8.
2. Ibid., pp. 100, 102, 217–18.
3. *Panama Canal Review,* November 2, 1956.
4. Arthur S. Davis, "Jamaican," *Tropical Collegian* (1967), p. 35; Albert V. McGeachy, "Zonelore," in Rolofson, p. 30.

Chapter 6

1. Dubois gives the fullest account of the riots: eyewitness reports, interviews, and transcripts of press conferences. For the sequence of events, see pp. 223–26 and 243–44.
2. See also [Murphy], "Transcription," p. 7.
3. Dubois, p. 251; and "Gaddis Wall Denies Police Fired on Rioters," *Panama American,* January 15, 1964, p. 8.
4. Dubois, p. 250.
5. "Inside Story of Panama Riots," *U.S. News and World Report,* March 30, 1964, p. 48.
6. *Panama Canal Spillway,* January 20, 1964.
7. Dubois, pp. 285ff.
8. Ibid., p. 308.
9. Ibid., p. 307.
10. See also Dubois, pp. 276, 280.
11. LaFeber, p. 142.
12. [Murphy], "Transcription," p. 6.
13. Dubois, pp. 209–12, 221.
14. Ibid., p. 227.
15. Ibid., p. 238. See p. 210 for Eisenhower's intention.
16. Ibid., p. 226.
17. [Murphy], "Transcription," p. 5.
18. Dubois, pp. 286–87, 289.
19. Investigating Committee Appointed by the International Commission of Jurists, Geneva, Switzerland, *Report on the Events in Panama, January 9–12, 1964.*
20. Dubois, pp. 240, 357.
21. Armbrister, p. 77.
22. *Panama Canal Spillway,* January 20, 1964.
23. [Murphy], "Transcription," p. 11.
24. Ibid., p. 10.

Chapter 7

1. Kenneth Darg, *Panama American,* January 15, 1964, p. 1.
2. The phrase is Lafcadio Hearn's.
3. See also Sylvia Thomas, who has given birth to girls in both Mexico and Panama. She found the cult of the male far more dominant in Panama: "Nurses, doctors,

attendants, nurses aides, and even janitors—all seem to be alike in their response: 'Varon?' . . . 'No, niña.' . . . Then silence. Instead of even saying, as in Mexico, that well, she's cute anyway—the word 'niña' evokes silence. . . . You'd think having a girl was a time for mourning around this hospital." "The Distaff Beat," *Star and Herald* (Panama), December 19, 1976.

4. Quoted by Reid, p. 80.

5. Moynihan, p. 24.

6. Mrs. Olsen's speech is drawn from an interview by Sherry Elliott in *Isthmian Folklore*, edited by Jackie Gregory. She covered the same information in conversation with us but not in such concentrated form.

Chapter 8

1. See the similar ideas of George Kennan. He would like to restrict nominations to the Senate to a pool of outstanding people selected by "some detached and austere authority." He says, "I have nothing against people making their own decisions, but I do strongly object to the fact that our political parties confront the electorate time after time with a choice of deplorable mediocrities." Urban, p. 21.

2. Bellamy's ideological heirs do not agree. "Surely one should be content with a modest station in life if one has modest capabilities," George Kennan declares, with a utopian's nonchalance about his ability to ascertain other people's capabilities. The Society of Jesus and the Marine Corps are examples, he says, of the kind of meritocracy he has in mind. See Urban, p. 23.

3. Willie K. Friar, "Brawn and Brains Built the Canal," *Panama Canal Review* (Spring 1976), p. 19.

4. Downen, p. 70. During the treaty negotiations, the State Department advised the Masons to trust the dictator. Only when Senator Robert Dole threatened to amend the treaty did the diplomats obtain a guarantee of the Masons' title.

5. Vicki M. Boatwright, "Watercraft Fleet Keeps Canal Afloat," *Panama Canal Review* (Summer 1978), p. 12.

6. Abbot was proud to have written a definition of fascism that pleased Mussolini. According to Abbot, "fascism" was really "liberty." It stood for "emancipation from the rule of politicians 'nutured in a creed outworn,' for freedom from the tyranny of the lawless, for exemption from the demands, often unreasonable and extortionate, of trades unions, for liberation from the bonds of official and traditional red tape, and for emancipation from the bondage of moldy tradition and worn out theories." See *Watching the World Go By*, pp. 340–42. Abbot was not the only American progressive to admire the Duce (see Diggins) or to think that democracy should be replaced by scientific management (see Minogue).

7. Hollander, "Intellectuals, Estrangement, and Wish Fulfillment," p. 17.

8. Hollander, *Political Pilgrims*, pp. 232–46.

9. Halberstam quoted in Stephen J. Morris, p. 47.

10. Fitzgerald, p. 211.

11. Bishop and Bishop, p. 249.

12. Stevens, "The Panama Canal," p. 949.

13. Abbot, *Watching the World Go By*, pp. 299–300.

14. Bishop and Bishop, p. 453.

15. Society of the Chagres, *Yearbook, 1916–17*, pp. 134, 342.

16. Bishop and Bishop, p. 449.
17. V. I. Lenin, *Collected Works* (5th Russian edition). Vol. 41, p. 383. Quoted in Kirkpatrick, p. 10.
18. For the development of the Canal Zone Code, see Bray; Padelford; and Ealy, *Yanqui Politics*, chap. 9.
19. Hibbard, p. 7.
20. Dubois, pp. 358, 386.
21. Heald, pp. 41, 43.
22. Diana Sanford, "Coping with Big Brother: Civic Councils Fight Red Tape," *Saltwater Papaya* (Spring 1976), p. 6.
23. Franck, p. 206; Heald, p. 22.
24. George Miller, p. 231.
25. Martin, p. 116.
26. Tim Connor, "Cheville Refutes CZ Stereotype," *Deviled Ham,* April 26, 1976, p. 7.
27. Jackley, pp. 5–6.
28. Joseph Bishop, *Panama Gateway,* p. 283.
29. Pestillo.
30. "Life in the Great Outdoors Awaits Retired Deputy Executive Secretary Bob Jeffrey," *Panama Canal Spillway,* May 11, 1979, p. 1.
31. Bennett and others, pp. 221–22.
32. Ibid., p. 254.
33. Abbot, *Panama and the Canal,* pp. 160, 169, 329.
34. Bennett and others, p. 159.
35. Dimock, pp. 212–13.

Chapter 9

1. Rolofson, see subtitle.
2. Vicki M. Boatwright, "Administration Building Unites Past, Present, and Future," *Panama Canal Review* (October 1, 1979), p. 9.
3. *Panama Canal Review,* May 5, 1950.

Chapter 10

1. Showalter, p. 205.
2. Paul, Society of the Chagres, *Yearbook, 1914,* p. 278.
3. Our description of work on the Canal is drawn from the *Panama Canal Review* of December 7, 1951, and January 4, 1952; Marlise Simons, "Panama Canal Is Still an American Operation," *Guardian Weekly,* September 18, 1977, p. 15; and Vicki M. Boatwright, "Maintaining the Waterway," *Panama Canal Review* (Winter 1978).

Chapter 11

1. Atkin, *Western Breezes,* p. 6.
2. Hall, p. 45.
3. Percy MacKaye, "The Canal Builder," reprint in *Panama Canal Review,* April 2, 1954, p. 1.
4. Glen Ward Dresbach, Society of the Chagres, *Yearbook, 1914,* p. 3.

5. Gilbert, passim.
6. Goldstein, pp. 37, 54–56.
7. Dorothy Moody, frequently published on the Isthmus but in unindexed publications.
8. Dunning, p. 44.
9. Arthur Payne, "The Mail Box," *The Panama American*, January 9, 1964.
10. L. M. Scull, *The Panama Canal Society of the United States Souvenir Yearbook,* 1947.
11. *Panama Canal Review*, November 7, 1952; January 7, 1955; May 3, 1957.
12. Bowen, p. 25.
13. Farson, p. 100.
14. Jan Morris, p. 49.
15. Peter Bland, "L.A. Suburban," *The Times Literary Supplement*, November 19, 1982, p. 1282.
16. *Panama Canal Review*, October 7, 1955.
17. Gregory, ed., *Isthmian Folklore.*
18. Society of the Chagres, *Yearbook, 1914,* p. 127.
19. Barth, pp. 187–88.
20. Heim, p. 18.
21. Phi Delta Kappa, pp. 72–73.
22. *Panama Canal Review*, September 7, 1956; July 4, 1958.

Chapter 12

1. Theroux, p. 203.
2. Sally Quinn, "A Psychiatrist Analyzes the Zone of Stress," *Washington Post,* March 7, 1978, p. C-1.
3. McCullough, pp. 460, 472–73, 504.
4. Hodges, p. 169.
5. Van Hardeveld, p. 101.
6. Verrill, p. 103; see also Scott on "elastic class distinction," p. 210.
7. Augelli, p. 7.
8. Tocqueville, "What Sort of Despotism Democratic Nations Have to Fear," p. 308.
9. Tocqueville, "Of the Use Which Americans Make of Public Associations in Civil Life," p. 200.
10. Dimock, p. 181.
11. Verrill, p. 104.
12. Hall, p. 27.
13. Biesanz, "Inter-American Marriages," p. 161.
14. Biesanz and Biesanz, p. 312.
15. Ibid.
16. U.S. Department of Commerce Bureau of Census, *General Population Characteristics, Canal Zone 1970 Census of Population.*
17. Joseph Bishop, *Panama Gateway*, p. 317.
18. Society of the Chagres, *Yearbook, 1913,* pp. 199–200.
19. Tocqueville, "That the Sentiments of Democratic Nations Accord with Their Opinions in Leading Them to Concentrate Political Power," p. 295.

20. Tocqueville, "What Sort of Despotism Democratic Nations Have to Fear," pp. 302–04.

PART TWO

Chapter 13

1. Liberals who would never use a derogatory term for a racial, ethnic, or sexual type freely refer to "rednecks." For examples, see Jay Parini, "Thailand Diarist," *New Republic*, August 15 and 22, 1983, p. 43; and Horace Freeland Judson, "Thumbprints in Our Clay," *New Republic*, September 19 and 26, 1983, p. 16, and Robert M. Kaus, "Getting Tough on Trade," *Washington Monthly* (November 1978), p. 26. For an example of the irrelevant use of "amateur" to belittle, see Morton Kondracke, "Q: Is He Running? A: Why Not?" *New Republic*, September 12, 1983, p. 19.
2. Thomas, p. 37.
3. Bowman, *The Year 2000*, p. 214.
4. In 1960, the College Board decided to tell students their SAT scores. The board's president announced: "There was great fear that students would have their values warped by learning their own scores," but when he learned that they were dismissing as "jerks" the students who scored 420 while regarding those who scored 700 with "awe," he was relieved (Boorstin, *The Democratic Experience*, p. 226). His great fear apparently was that students would sneer at the "egghead" instead of the "jerk." Three years later the scores began their twenty-year decline, a rejection, at least in part, of the values the scores represented, the values of the organization man, the status seekers, the power elite, the social engineers.
5. Pritchett, p. 111.
6. Taylor, p. 52.
7. Lasch notes the growing fear of anti-intellectualism during the fifties and sixties—the vision of a civilization threatened from below. See "The Life of Kennedy's Death."

Chapter 14

1. Noble, pp. 204–07.
2. Haskin, p. 186.
3. Bennett and others, p. 169.
4. Abbot, *Panama and the Canal*, p. 144.
5. Mrs. Bruce Sanders, *Isthmian Historical Society Scrapbook*, Vol. 3.
6. Society of the Chagres, *Yearbook, 1914*, p. 177.
7. George Natanson for the *Washington Post*, reprint, Niemeier, p. 211.
8. Norman Cousins, "What Have We Learned from Panama?" *Saturday Review*, February 1, 1964, reprint, Niemeier, pp. 219–20.
9. Jan Morris, p. 66.
10. Biesanz and Biesanz, pp. 155–56.
11. Alan Riding, "A Panamanian Who Casts a Spell," *New York Times*, June 13, 1978, p. 2.

12. DuVal, *And The Mountains Will Move*, p. 306.
13. Hall, p. 19.
14. Franck, p. 220.
15. Biesanz and Biesanz, pp. 111–13; Alan Riding, "Panama: Troubled Passage for a U.S. Ally," *New York Times Magazine*, November 22, 1981, p. 126.
16. *Miami Herald*, December 9, 1980, p. 3-AW: To obtain Colombia's support for a new Canal treaty, Torrijos secretly promised that its warships could transit the Canal free in perpetuity. Panama's legislature balked at ratifying this agreement, having previously called the perpetuity clause in the 1904 treaty with the United States an unbearable insult. When troops surrounded the Legislative Palace, the legislators decided Panama could bear the unbearable.
17. Juan de Onís, "Panama's Strongman Hopeful for U.S. Pact," *New York Times*, January 14, 1977, p. A-1.
18. Fenton, pp. 18–19.
19. Diamond, p. 25.
20. Revel, p. 50.
21. Paz, pp. 139, 148; Richard Rodriguez makes a similar point in *The New Republic*, November 7, 1983, pp. 37–38.
22. Martin, p. 116; Biesanz and Biesanz, pp. 83–84.
23. William Gorgas, pp. 287–92.
24. Atkin, *Western Breezes*, p. 23.
25. *Isthmian Historical Society Scrapbook*, Vol. 2; DuVal, p. 248.
26. Biesanz and Biesanz, p. 214; Sands, p. 21.
27. Core, p. 94; Van Hardeveld, p. 41.
28. Grier, p. 76.
29. McCullough, p. 477.
30. Van Hardeveld, p. 23.
31. McCullough, p. 477.
32. Wood, p. 199.
33. McCullough, p. 579.
34. Bishop and Bishop, pp. 3–4.
35. Franck, pp. 11, 29–30.
36. Phi Delta Kappa, pp. 112, 120; Biesanz and Biesanz, p. 267.
37. Grier, p. 77; Van Hardeveld, pp. 114–15.
38. Westerman, p. 9.
39. Alfonso Chardy, "Zone Panamanians Lose Under Treaties," *Miami Herald*, December 16, 1979, p. 3-AW.
40. West, p. 66.
41. Meeker and Meeker, pp. 151–52.
42. Hibbard, p. 8.
43. Barbara Gleb, "A Touch of the Tragic," *New York Times Magazine*, December 11, 1977, pp. 43–44.
44. Biesanz and Biesanz, p. 230.
45. Wood, p. 198.
46. Biesanz and Biesanz, p. 224.
47. LaFeber, p. 84.
48. Alan Riding, "A Panamanian Who Casts a Spell," *New York Times*, June 13, 1978, p. 2.

49. John Dorschner, "The People Caught in No–Man's–Land," *Tropic Magazine* (*Miami Herald*), December 12, 1976, pp. 24, 33–34.
50. Biesanz and Biesanz, pp. 341–51; Phi Delta Kappa, pp. 125–27.
51. Melinda Hoppe, "Council Voices Fears at Hearings," *Deviled Ham*, April 18, 1977, p. 10.
52. Augelli, p. 12.
53. Ibid., p. 11.
54. Ibid., p. 12.
55. John Dorschner, "The People Caught in No–Man's–Land," *Tropic Magazine* (*Miami Herald*), December 12, 1976, p. 26.

Chapter 15

1. Linderman, pp. 120–22.
2. Gause and Carr, pp. 240, 255.
3. Van Hardeveld, pp. 32–33.
4. Gause and Carr, p. 251.
5. Haskin, pp. 180–81, 188.
6. Phi Delta Kappa, p. 29.
7. This instruction appeared in numerous places. Our copy is from *La Estrella*, 7 de Marzo de 1972.
8. Martin, p. 116.
9. Abbot, *Panama and the Canal*, p. 290.
10. *Panama Canal Review*, March 7, 1958; see also May 6, 1955.
11. Mr. Malsbury, *Isthmian Historical Society Scrapbook*, Vol. 3.
12. Shalett, p. 49.
13. Lawrenson, p. 198.
14. Van Hardeveld, pp. 32–33.
15. Rolofson, p. 36.
16. Biesanz and Biesanz, p. 235.
17. Bowen, pp. 1–3.
18. LaFeber, p. 137.
19. Biesanz and Biesanz, p. 187.
20. Fraser, p. 102.
21. McCormack, *U.S. Lady* (April 1964), pp. 40ff.
22. Dubois, pp. 292–93.
23. Dimock, p. 8.
24. Biesanz and Biesanz, pp. 83–84, 187.
25. Armbrister, p. 77.
26. Jackley, p. 10.
27. Jan Morris, p. 66.
28. Augelli, pp. 7–8.
29. *Panama Canal Spillway*, July 16, 1976.
30. Ted Wilber, "A Few Personal Recollections," *Star and Herald*, April 14, 1982, p. A-4.
31. Fernando Manfredo, "Speech at Annual YMCA Awards Presentation,"April 15, 1982.
32. David L. White, "Demetrio Lakas, Class of '46," *Saltwater Papaya* (Fall 1973), back cover.

33. Demetrio Lakas, "Graduation Address," Panama Canal College, Forty–Fifth Commencement Exercises, June 1, 1979.

Chapter 16

1. Bryce, pp. 27–28.
2. Sands, pp. 13–14, 25–31, 36.
3. Franck, pp. 86, 154, 217, 220.
4. Chamberlin, p. 29.
5. Charles Phelps Cushing, "Yankee Notions in the Canal Zone." *New York Tribune Magazine*, March 30, 1924, p. 1.
6. The compensation study done by the management consultant firm of Booz, Allen, and Hamilton in 1953 says (pp. 52, 56) that ten of eleven private firms paid a larger overseas differential than the Canal Company and that 48 percent of the Canal workers who left the Zone the previous year found higher-paying jobs in the United States. Twenty-nine percent found jobs paying the same. Twenty-three percent (mostly teachers, we suspect) had to take lower-paying jobs.
7. Railey, pp. 339–40.
8. Jarrell, p. 116.
9. Biesanz and Biesanz, p. 70.
10. The phrase is Lessard's, p. 51.
11. William Gaddis, "In the Zone," *New York Times*, March 13, 1978, p. A-21.
12. Schorer, pp. 123–24.
13. All quotations from Theroux are from chapter 12 of *The Old Patagonian Express*.
14. *Panama Canal Review*, December 3, 1954; March 3, 1961.
15. Ronald Yates, "Panama's Dictator Tells U.S. To Get Out, Poor Beg Us To Stay," *Chicago Tribune*, March 27, 1977, p. 1.
16. Biesanz and Biesanz, p. 267; Phi Delta Kappa, p. 112.
17. Biesanz and Biesanz, pp. 81–82 (Boyd, de la Guardia, and Harmodio Arias).
18. John Dorschner, "The People Caught in No–Man's–Land," *Tropic Magazine* (*Miami Herald*), December 12, 1976, p. 36.
19. Phi Delta Kappa, p. 127; *Panama Canal Review*, May 4, 1962.
20. Fussell, p. 1227.

Chapter 17

1. Dimock, p. 224.
2. Railey, p. 343.
3. Jorden, p. 3. Carter staged a similar drama in trade negotiations. His "responsible people" told their counterparts overseas, "Give us freer access to your markets or we won't be able to control 'them'—the protectionist 'rednecks.' " No effort was made to arouse popular support for free trade and for the idea that American businessmen overseas deserve to be treated the same way foreign businessmen are treated here, for fear that the revelation of how American exports are unfairly blocked would play into the hands of the "rednecks" at the AFL–CIO. See Kaus, p. 26.
4. In "U.S. Latin Image Imperiled by Crisis," *Sunday Capital-Journal* (Topeka), January 19, 1964, p. 1.
5. Ibid., pp. 1–2.
6. *Panama Canal Spillway*, January 20, 1964, p. 3.

7. Dubois, p. 323.
8. "Panama Envoy Flays Zonians," *Star and Herald* (Panama), March 24, 1976, p. 1.
9. "Zone Imperils Peace, Panama Warns U.N.," *Star and Herald* (Panama), March 30, 1976, p. 1.
10. *Wall Street Journal*, January 13, 1964, p. 4.
11. See Kraft; and Rothman and Lichter, who employed interviews, TAT tests, and factor analysis to determine the attitudes of the media elite. They concluded that it has a more liberal outlook than either business leaders or the general public. Within the media, journalists at *The New York Times* and *Washington Post* are more liberal than those at other papers; television journalists are more liberal still, and public-television journalists led every group in "economic liberalism, alienation, and support for the 'new morality,'" pp. 118–19.
12. Noble, p. 206; McLoughlin, pp. 169–70.
13. Kraft, p. 38.
14. David S. Broder, "The Press is Guilty of Consumer Fraud," *Washington Post*, June 3, 1979, p. D-1.
15. Martin, p. 116.
16. Collier, for the *Herald Tribune*, reprint, Niemeier, p. 216.
17. Armbrister, p. 76.
18. Shalett, p. 48.
19. Jan Morris, p. 66.
20. *Panama Canal Review*, January 2, 1953.
21. Armbrister, p. 77.
22. McLoughlin, p. 177.
23. Evans and Novak, *Tampa Tribune*, February 15, 1964.
24. Garry Wills, "Torrijos Trying Hard to Keep the Lid On," *Miami Herald*, April 10, 1978, p. 7-A.
25. Martin, p. 116.
26. Peters, p. 62.
27. "Churchmen Rap Zone Residents on Treaty," *Star and Herald* (Panama), April 29, 1976, p. 1.
28. Jackley, "Background" and p. 14; see also James J. O'Donnell's *AFGE Local 14 Newsletter*, June [1978].
29. Lessard, p. 51.
30. Ibid., p. 53.
31. Jackley, see "Background" and pp. 9–10; Juan de Onís, "U.S. Nationalists in Panama Canal Zone Resist Turnover of Control," *New York Times*, January 19, 1977, p. 2.
32. Jackley, see "Preface" and pp. 13–14.
33. Ibid., p. 13.
34. Ibid., see "Background" and p. 9.
35. Ibid., p. 16.
36. Joyce Canel, "Editorial," *Deviled Ham*, February 22, 1977, pp. 3–5.

Chapter 18

1. Marilu Rios, "The Zone—A Dream or a Nightmare?" *Saltwater Papaya* (Spring 1978), p. 3.

2. Dimock, p. 213.
3. Franck, pp. 205–6.
4. Sands, pp. 33–35.
5. "Meticulous Maintenance Is Watchword of Waterway," *Panama Canal Spillway*, August 13, 1976, p. 1.
6. Vicki M. Boatwright, "Old Glory and Old Bunting," *Deviled Ham*, March 21, 1977, pp. 1, 3, 5.
7. *Panama Canal Review*, November 3, 1950.
8. *Panama Canal Review*, May 5, 1950.
9. Dubois, pp. 376–77.
10. "Panama Weighing Economic Charge," *New York Times*, January 22, 1964, p. 2.
11. *Deviled Ham*, October 27, 1976, p. 3.

Chapter 19

1. Boorstin, *The National Experience*, p. 274.
2. Linderman, pp. 6–7; see also Goethals' "Address, July 4, 1911," reprint, *Panama Canal Review* (Spring 1976), p. 6.
3. Linderman, p. 7.
4. Bell, p. 252. See Bell's whole discussion of imperialism.
5. Sullivan, pp. 55–56.
6. Bunau-Varilla, *The Great Adventure*, p. 34.
7. Roosevelt, p. 986.
8. Jonathan Kandell, "For Panama, Talks with the U.S. Come at a Time of Discontent," *New York Times*, February 17, 1977, p. 2.
9. Mellander, pp. 52–54, 192.
10. Ibid., pp. 185–86, 192–94; Ealy, *The Republic of Panama in World Affairs*, pp. 20–22.
11. Biesanz and Biesanz, pp. 149–50, 170; Mellander, pp. 87–89.
12. Biesanz and Biesanz, p. 188.
13. Joseph Bishop, *The Panama Gateway*, pp. 415ff.
14. Prewett, p. 29.
15. Through a spokesman, Sayre denied that he "warned" Torrijos, but admitted that he "told him" that the United States agents were aware of Moises' travel plans. Sayre acted on instructions from his superiors who wished to avoid a "diplomatic incident." *Washington Post*, February 25, 1978, p. A-16; and April 28, 1978, p. C-9.
16. Pastor, p. 8.
17. "Treaty by '77 Is Panama's Goal," *Star and Herald* (Panama), April 10, 1976, p. 1.
18. Lucier, p. 990.
19. "Panama Abstains In UN Council Voting on Raid," *Star and Herald* (Panama), July 16, 1976, p. 1.
20. Dr. Carlos A. Lopez Guevara, "A Challenge to Peacemakers: The Panama Canal Negotiations," *Star and Herald* (Panama), April 18, 1976, p. 1.
21. "Torrijos Sends Cable to Ford," *Star and Herald* (Panama), July 4, 1976, p. 1.
22. Charles Green, "Leftists Like Reagan," *Star and Herald* (Panama), April 5, 1976, p. 1.

23. "Torrijos Scores Optimism On Treaty," *Star and Herald* (Panama), January 23, 1977, p. 1.
24. Juan Antonio Stagg, "Letter," *New York Times*, October 30, 1976.
25. Carter, "Question and Answer Session in Denver," p. 723.
26. Carter, "Address to the Nation."
27. Carter, "Question and Answer Session in Denver," p. 722.
28. Rasen, p. 204.
29. "RP Business Urged To Help In Recovery," *Star and Herald* (Panama), May 31, 1976, p. 1.
30. Rasen, p. 204.
31. Quirk, p. 17.
32. George Gedda, "AP Survey Seeks Answers to Issues Raised on Canal," *Star and Herald* (Panama), May 7, 1976, p. 1.
33. Carter, "Question and Answer Session in Denver," p. 721.
34. Ibid.
35. Diamond, p. 31.
36. *Commentary* (June 1976), p. 28.
37. "Looking South With Sympathy," *New York Times*, February 14, 1977, p. 26-C.
38. "Canal Zone Residents Urged to Hinder Takeover in Fall," *Miami Herald*, April 12, 1979, p. 3-AW.
39. "Editorial," *Washington Post*, March 25, 1976.
40. Pam Whitlaw, "Every Word Counts in TV Interviews," *Deviled Ham* [n.d., pages in possession of authors].
41. Herbert and Mary Knapp, "A View From The Canal Zone," *Wall Street Journal*, February 1, 1978, p. 22.
42. Siegelman, pp. 79ff.
43. Cindy Kincaid, "Press Harassed by Guardia," *Deviled Ham*, September 12, 1977.
44. Burnham, p. 458.
45. Noble, p. 205.
46. See Burnham, pp. 462, 465. He notes that progressive psychiatry was uniquely American. European psychiatrists did not share the American passion for social control.
47. Greene, "The Great Spectacular," p. 9.
48. Greene, "The Country With Five Frontiers," p. 10.
49. Greene, "The Great Spectacular," p. 9.
50. Ibid.
51. Diamond, p. 34.
52. LaFeber, p. 162.
53. Jorden, p. 484.
54. Greene, "The Great Spectacular," p. 9.
55. Pastor, p. 8.
56. Greene, "The Country With Five Frontiers," p. 13.
57. Carter, "Question and Answer Session in Denver," p. 721.
58. Greene, "The Country With Five Frontiers," p. 10.
59. Ibid., p. 12.
60. Greene's hero in *The Quiet American* (chap. 2, part 3) displays a similar attitude: " 'It's me—Fowler.' (Even then I couldn't bring myself to use my Christian name to him)."

61. Joe McGinnis, "Second Thoughts of George McGovern," *New York Times Magazine*, May 6, 1973.
62. Alan Riding, "Cold Shoulder Awaiting Carter in Canal Zone," *New York Times*, June 15, 1978, p. 46.
63. Don Bohning, "Carter to Yanks in Zone: Cool It," *Miami Herald*, June 18, 1978, p. 1.
64. Martin Tolchin, "President Cautions Panama to Respect Rights of Americans," *New York Times*, June 18, 1978, p. 15.
65. Ibid.
66. David Butler, with Ron Moreau and Eleanor Clift, "A Leap Into History," *Newsweek*, June 26, 1978, p. 35.
67. Ibid.
68. Don Bohning, " 'Sickout' Almost Shuts Panama Canal," *Miami Herald*, March 17, 1976, p. 1; and "Sickout Was Desperate Attempt to Be Heard," *Miami Herald*, March 22, 1976, p. 3-AW.
69. Pestillo.

Chapter 20

1. Joseph Benham, "Why U.S. Keeps a Wary Eye on Panama," *U.S. News and World Report*, November 16, 1981, p. 47.
2. William R. Long, "Torrijos' Cortege Makes Stop in Former U.S. Canal Zone," *Miami Herald*, August 5, 1981, p. 4-A.
3. *Crítica*, 2 de abril de 1982; *Matutino*, 2 de abril de 1982; *The Republic* (Panama), April 5, 1982. For background on Greaves' crime, see Ted Wilber, "Believe Me," *Star and Herald* (Panama), April 7, 1982.

Sources

Student publications, reports, addresses, manuscripts, privately printed sources, and government publications are grouped separately at the end of this section.

Abbot, Willis J. *Panama and the Canal in Picture and Prose*. New York: Syndicate Publishing Co., 1913.
———. *Watching the World Go By*. Boston: Little, Brown & Co., 1934.
Armbrister, Trevor. "Why They Hate Us." *Saturday Evening Post*, March 7, 1964.
Atkin, Randolph Henry. *The Spell of the Tropics*. London: T. Fisher Unwin, 1920.
———. *Western Breezes; or, Ballads of a Gringo*. N.p., 1914.
Augelli, John P. "The Panama Canal Area in Transition, Part 1: The Treaties and the Zonian." *American Universities Field Staff Reports, 1981, No. 3, North America*.
Baker, Ray Stannard. "Goethals: The Man and How He Works." *American Magazine* (October 1913).
Barth, Gunther. *City People: The Rise of Modern City Culture in Nineteenth Century America*. New York: Oxford University Press, 1980.
Bell, Daniel. *The Winding Passage: Essays and Sociological Journeys*. Cambridge: Abt Books, 1980.
Bennett, Ira E., and others. *History of the Panama Canal: Its Construction and Builders*. Washington, D.C.: Historical Publishing Co., 1915.
Bercovitch, Sacvan. *The American Jeremiad*. Madison: University of Wisconsin Press, 1978.
Biesanz, John. "Inter-American Marriages on the Isthmus of Panama." *Social Forces* (December 1950).
———, and Mavis Biesanz. *The People of Panama*. New York: Columbia University Press, 1955.
———, and Luke M. Smith. "Adjustment of Interethnic Marriages on the Isthmus of Panama." *American Sociological Review* (December 1951).
———. "Race Relations in Panama and the Canal Zone." *American Journal of Sociology* (July 1951).
Bishop, Farnham. *Panama, Past and Present*, Revised and Enlarged Edition. New York: D. Appleton-Century, 1916.
Bishop, Joseph Bucklin. *Notes and Anecdotes*. New York: Charles Scribner's Sons, 1925.

——. *The Panama Gateway*. New York: Charles Scribner's Sons, 1913.

——, and Farnham Bishop. *Goethals: Genius of the Panama Canal*. New York: Harper & Bros., 1930.

Boorstin, Daniel J. *The Americans: The Democratic Experience*. New York: Random House, 1973.

——. *The Americans: The National Experience*. New York: Random House, 1965.

Bowman, Sylvia E. *The Year 2000: A Critical Biography of Edward Bellamy*. New York: Bookman Associates, 1958.

——, and others. *Edward Bellamy Abroad: An American Prophet's Influence*. New York: Twayne Publishers, 1962.

Bray, Wayne D. *The Common Law Zone in Panama: A Case Study in Reception*. San Juan, P. R.: Inter-American University Press, 1977.

Brosseau, Ray. *Looking Forward: Life in the Twentieth Century as Predicted in the Pages of American Magazines from 1895–1905*. New York: American Heritage Press, 1970.

Bryce, James. *South America*. New York: Macmillan Co., 1913.

Bunau-Varilla, Philippe. *From Panama to Verdun: My Fight for France*. Philadelphia: Dorrance & Co., 1940.

——. *The Great Adventure in Panama*. New York: Doubleday, Page, & Co., 1920.

Burnham, John Chynoweth. "Psychiatry, Psychology, and the Progressive Movement." *American Quarterly* (Winter 1960).

Cameron, Ian [Donald Gordon Payne]. *The Impossible Dream: The Building of the Panama Canal*. London: Hodder & Stoughton, 1971.

Cavallo, Dom. "Social Reform and the Movement to Organize Children's Play During the Progressive Era." *History of Childhood Quarterly: The Journal of Psychohistory* (Spring 1976).

Chamberlin, W. A. "A Table at the Tivoli." *South* (December 1946).

Christian, Shirley. "Foreign Danger." *Atlantic* (October 1983).

Core, Sue. *Maid in Panama*. Dobbs Ferry, N. Y.: Clermont Press, 1938.

Davis, Robert Gorham. "The Professors' Lie." *Columbia Forum* (Fall 1972).

——, and others. "Responses to 'The Professors' Lie.'" *Columbia Forum* (Winter 1973).

Dewey, John. "A Great American Prophet." *Common Sense* (April 1934).

Diamond, Steve. "The Panama Time Bomb." *New Times*, May 14, 1976.

Diggins, John P. *Mussolini and Fascism: The View from America*. Princeton, N. J.: Princeton University Press, 1975.

Dimock, Marshall E. *Government-Operated Enterprises in the Panama Canal Zone*. Chicago: University of Chicago Press, 1934.

Downen, Robert L. "A Sojourner's Refuge in the Senate," *The Free Mason, Official Publication of the Grand Lodge, A.F. and A.M. of Missouri* (Summer 1983).

Dubois, Jules. *Danger Over Panama*. New York: Bobbs-Merrill, 1964.

Dunning, Bill. "Local Boy Blues or Gringo's Lament." *Canal Record* (March 1984).

DuVal, Miles P. *And the Mountains Will Move.* Stanford, Calif.: Stanford University Press, 1947.

————. *Cadiz to Cathay.* Stanford, Calif.: Stanford University Press, 1940.

Ealy, Lawrence O. *The Republic of Panama in World Affairs: 1903–1950.* Philadelphia: University of Pennsylvania Press, 1951.

————. *Yanqui Politics and the Isthmian Canal.* University Park: Pennsylvania State University Press, 1971.

Edwards, Albert [Arthur Bullard]. *Panama: The Canal, the Country, and the People.* New York: Macmillan Co., 1913.

Farson, Negley. *Trangressor in the Tropics.* New York: Harcourt, Brace & Co., 1938.

Fenton, Tom. "Canal Zone Said Much the Same Despite Treaties." A.P., August 23, 1981, reprinted in *Canal Record* (November 1981).

Fitzgerald, Frances. *Fire in the Lake.* Boston: Little, Brown & Co., 1972.

Franck, Harry A. *Zone Policeman 88.* New York: The Century Co., 1913.

Franklin, John Hope. "Edward Bellamy and the Nationalist Movement." *New England Quarterly* (December 1938).

Fraser, John Foster. *Panama and What It Means.* London: Cassell & Co., 1913.

Fussell, Paul. "He Just Keep Rollin' Along." *The Times Literary Supplement,* October 23, 1981.

Gause, Frank A., and Charles Carl Carr. *The Story of Panama: A New Route to the Indies.* New York: Silver, Burdett & Co., 1912.

Gibson, John M. *Physician to the World: The Life of General William C. Gorgas.* Durham, N. C.: Duke University Press, 1950.

Gilbert, James Stanley. *Panama Patchwork.* Colon, Panama: J. V. Beverhoudt, 1920.

Goldstein, Walter. *Shreds from an Old Sun Helmet.* New York: Greenberg, 1947.

Gorgas, Marie, and Burton J. Hendrick. *William Crawford Gorgas: His Life and Work.* Garden City, N. Y.: Doubleday, Page & Co., 1924.

Gorgas, William Crawford. *Sanitation in Panama.* New York: D. Appleton & Co., 1915.

Greene, Eleanor. *Panama Sketches.* Boston: Humphries, ca. 1940.

Greene, Graham. "The Country With Five Frontiers." *New York Review of Books,* February 17, 1977.

————. "The Great Spectacular." *New York Review of Books,* January 26, 1978.

Grier, Thomas Graham. *On the Canal Zone: Panama.* Chicago: Wagner & Hanson, 1908.

Hall, John. *Panama Roughneck Ballads.* Panama City: Albert Lindo, 1912.

Haskin, Frederic J. *The Panama Canal.* New York: Doubleday, Page & Co., 1913.

Haskins, William C., ed. *Canal Zone Pilot.* Panama: Star and Herald Co., 1908.

Heald, Jean. *Picturesque Panama.* Chicago: Curt Teich, 1928.

Hearn, Lafcadio. *Two Years in the French West Indies.* New York: Harper & Bros., 1890.

Heim, Charlie. "Nostalgia." *Canal Record* (March 1981).

Hodges, Donald C. *The Bureaucratization of Socialism.* Amherst, Mass.: University of Massachusetts Press, 1981.

Hollander, Paul. "Intellectuals, Estrangement, and Wish Fulfillment." *Society* (July/August, 1983).

————. *Political Pilgrims: Travels of Western Intellectuals to the Soviet Union, China, and Cuba, 1928–1978.* New York: Oxford University Press, 1981.

Jarrell, Randall. *Kipling, Auden and Co.,* New York: Farrar, Straus & Giroux, 1980.

Jorden, William J. *Panama Odyssey.* Austin: University of Texas Press, 1984.

Kaus, Robert M. "Getting Tough on Trade." *Washington Monthly* (November 1978).

Keegan, John. "The Role of the Officer Class." *New Republic,* June 27, 1981.

Kennan, George F. *The Decision to Intervene.* Soviet-American Relations 1917–1920, vol. 2. Princeton, N. J.: Princeton University Press, 1958.

Kirkpatrick, Jeane, with George Urban. "American Foreign Policy in a Cold Climate." *Encounter* (November 1983).

Kraft, Joseph. "The Imperial Media." *Commentary* (May 1981).

LaFeber, Walter. *The Panama Canal: The Crisis in Historical Perspective.* New York: Oxford University Press, 1978.

Lasch, Christopher. "The Life of Kennedy's Death." *Harper's* (October 1983).

————. Review of *The Shaping of a Behaviorist* by B. F. Skinner. *New Republic,* August 4 and 11, 1979.

Lawrenson, Helen. *Stranger at the Party.* 1972; reprint, New York: Popular Library, 1977.

Lemann, Nicholas. "Success in America." *Washington Monthly* (July/August 1977).

Lessard, Suzannah. "Taste, Class, and Mary Tyler Moore." *Washington Monthly* (February 1977).

Linderman, Gerald F. *The Mirror of War: American Society and the Spanish-American War.* Ann Arbor: University of Michigan Press, 1974.

Lucier, James P. "Another Vietnam." *National Review,* September 12, 1975.

McCormack, Amy. "Panama From Both Sides of the Fence." *U.S. Lady* (April 1964).

McCullough, David. "A Man, A Plan, A Canal, Panama." *American Heritage* (June 1971).

————. *A Path Between the Seas.* New York: Simon & Schuster, 1977.

Mack, Gerstle. *The Land Divided: A History of the Panama Canal and Other Isthmian Canal Projects.* 1944; reprint, New York: Octagon Books, 1974.

McLoughlin, William G. *Revivals, Awakenings, and Reform: An Essay on Religion and Social Change in America, 1607–1977*. Chicago: University of Chicago Press, 1978.

Martin, Harold H. "Why Do They Hate Us?" *Saturday Evening Post*, April 23, 1960.

Meeker, Oden, and Olivia Meeker. *And Points South*. New York: Random House, 1947.

Mellander, G. A. *The United States in Panamanian Politics*. Danville, Ill.: Interstate Printers & Publishers, 1971.

Miller, George A. *Prowling About Panama*. New York: Abingdon Press, 1919.

Miller, Perry. *The Life of the Mind in America: From the Revolution to the Civil War*. New York: Harcourt, Brace & World, 1965.

———. *The New England Mind: The Seventeenth Century*. 1939; reprint, Boston: Beacon Press, 1961.

Minogue, Kenneth. "The Managerial Millennium." *The Times Literary Supplement*, May 29, 1981.

Minter, John Easter. *The Chagres: River of Westward Passage*. New York: Rinehart & Co., 1948.

Morgan, Arthur E. *Edward Bellamy*. New York: Columbia University Press, 1944.

Morgan, Kenneth O. "God's Own Cities." *The Times Literary Supplement*, April 16, 1976.

Morris, Jan. "A Terminal Case of American Perpetuity." *Rolling Stone*, January 1, 1976.

Morris, Stephen J. "Vietnam Under Communism." *Commentary* (September 1982).

Moynihan, Daniel P. "Joining the Jackals: The U.S. at the U.N." *Commentary* (February 1981).

Niemeier, Jean Gilbreath. *The Panama Story*. Portland, Ore.: Metropolitan Press, 1968.

Noble, David W. "The Paradox of Progressive Thought." *American Quarterly* (Fall 1953).

Padelford, Norman J. *The Panama Canal in Peace and War*. New York: Macmillan Co.,1942.

Pastor, Robert. "Ode to Omar." *New Republic*, August 15, 1981.

Paz, Octavio. "Reflections on Mexico and the United States." *New Yorker*, September 17, 1979.

Pennell, Joseph. *Joseph Pennell's Pictures of the Panama Canal*. Philadelphia: J. B. Lippincott Co., 1913.

Pepperman, Walter Leon. *Who Built the Panama Canal?* New York: E. P. Dutton & Co., 1915.

Peters, Joan. "Panama's Genial Despot." *Harper's* (April 1978).

Prewett, Virginia. "The Panama Canal, Past and Present in Perspective." *Seapower* (August 1976).

Pritchett, V. S. *The Living Novel.* New York: Reynal and Hitchcock, 1947.

Quirk, William J. "The Banks Cover Their Assets." *New Republic*, February 17, 1982.

Railey, Hilton Howell. *Touched With Madness.* New York: Carrick & Evans, 1938.

Rasen, Edward. "The Panama Canal Sellout." *Penthouse* (November 1979).

Reid, Alastair. "Ask for Nicolás Catari." *New Yorker*, July 25, 1977.

Revel, Jean-François. "The Trouble With Latin America." *Commentary* (February 1979).

Roosevelt, Theodore. *Letters.* Edited by Elting E. Morison. Cambridge, Mass.: Harvard University Press, 1951.

Rothman, Stanley, and S. Robert Lichter. "Media and Business Elites: Two Classes in Conflict?" *Public Interest* (Fall 1982).

Sadler, Elizabeth. "One Book's Influence, Edward Bellamy's 'Looking Backward.'" *New England Quarterly* (December 1944).

Sands, William Franklin, with Joseph M. Lalley. *Our Jungle Diplomacy.* Chapel Hill: University of North Carolina Press, 1944.

Schiffman, Joseph, ed. *Edward Bellamy. Selected Writings on Religion and Society.* New York: Liberal Arts Press, 1955.

Schorer, Mark. *Sinclair Lewis: An American Life.* New York: McGraw-Hill, 1961.

Scott, William R. *The Americans in Panama.* New York: Statler, 1912.

Seeley, Morris M., R.N. "The Ever Changing Road." *Canal Record* (March 1982).

Shalett, Sidney. "Cities of America: Balboa." *Saturday Evening Post*, December 24, 1949.

Sharpe, Dores Robinson. *Walter Rauschenbusch.* New York: Macmillan Co., 1942.

Showalter, William Joseph. "The Panama Canal." *National Geographic* (February 1912).

Siegelman, Jim. "Playboy Interview: Geraldo Rivera." *Playboy* (November 1978).

Simon, Maron J. *The Panama Affair.* New York: Charles Scribner's Sons, 1971.

Stevens, John F. *An Engineer's Recollections.* New York: McGraw-Hill, 1936.

———. "The Panama Canal." *American Society of Civil Engineers*, Transactions, XCI (December 1927).

Sullivan, Mark. *Our Times, The United States, 1900–1925.* The Turn of the Century, vol. 1. New York: Charles Scribner's Sons, 1926.

Tarbell, Ida. "New Dealers of the Seventies." *The Forum and the Century* (September 1934).

Taylor, John. "A Bad Bargain." *Columbia Forum* (Spring 1975).

Thatcher, Maurice Hudson. *Autobiography in Poetry.* New York: Robert Spiller & Sons, 1974.

Theroux, Paul. *The Old Patagonian Express.* Boston: Houghton Mifflin Co., 1979.
Thomas, John, ed. "Introduction," *Looking Backward, 2000–1887* by Edward Bellamy. Cambridge, Mass.: Belknap Press, 1967.
Tocqueville, Alexis de. *Democracy in America.* Edited by Richard D. Heffner. New York: New American Library, 1956.
Urban, George: "From Containment to . . . Self-Containment, A Conversation with George F. Kennan." *Encounter* (September 1976).
Van Hardeveld, Rose. *Make the Dirt Fly.* Hollywood, Calif.: Pan Press, 1956.
Verrill, A. Hyatt. *Panama of Today.* 1926; reprint, New York: Dodd, Mead & Co., 1927.
Vinton, Kenneth W. *The Jungle Whispers.* New York: Pageant Press, 1956.
Webster, Henry Kitchell. "John F. Stevens." *American Magazine* (October 1905).
Weeks, Edward. *This Trade of Writing.* Boston: Little, Brown & Co., 1936.
West, Richard. *The Gringo in Latin America.* London: Jonathan Cape, 1967.
Westerman, George. *The West Indian Worker on the Canal Zone.* Panama City, Panama: National Civic League, 1951.
Wood, Major R. E. "The Working Force of the Panama Canal," Paper No. 7, Vol. 1, *Transactions of the International Engineering Congress, 1915.* San Francisco: Neal Publishing Co., 1916.

Student Publications

Deviled Ham. (Canal Zone College newspaper).
Gregory, Jackie, ed. *Isthmian Folklore Collected by the Students of Balboa High School,* 1978. Mimeographed.
Saltwater Papaya (Canal Zone College magazine).
Tropical Collegian (Canal Zone College magazine).

Reports, Addresses, Manuscripts, and Privately Printed Sources

Booz, Allen, and Hamilton, Management Consultants. *The Bases for Extra Compensation of Canal Zone Employees,* December, 1953, Vol. 1.
Bowen, Dorothy, with Sharon Holland. *History of the Isthmian College Club, 1925–1975.*
Hibbard, Mary. "Isthmus of Panama: A Sketch, 1904." Typescript.
Investigating Committee Appointed by the International Commission of Jurists, Geneva, Switzerland. *Report on the Events in Panama, January 9–12, 1964.*
Isthmian Historical Society Scrapbooks, 1954–62. 6 vols.
Jackley, John L. *A Study of the Impact of a New Panama Canal Treaty on the Non-DoD, U.S. Citizen Canal Zone Resident, Prepared for the U.S. Embassy, Panama,* June 10, 1976.

Lakas, Demetrio B. "Graduation Address," Panama Canal College Forty-Fifth Commencement Exercises, June 1, 1979.

MacLaren, J. P. *A Brief History of Sanitation in Panama, 1513–1972.*

Manfredo, Fernando. "Speech at Annual YMCA Sports Awards Presentation, Amador Officers' Club, April 15, 1982."

Moody, Dorothy. "Flowering Trees of Panama." Mimeographed. Often reproduced on the Isthmus but in unindexed publications.

[Murphy, Glen]. "Transcription of Governor Fleming's Speech to the Canal Zone Teachers, January 14, 1964."

Panama Canal Society of the United States Souvenir Yearbook, 1947.

Pestillo, Peter J. No title; a report on Panama Canal Zone Government and Panama Canal Company Personnel Policies. July 13, 1974.

Phi Delta Kappa [Lowell C. Wilson, H. Loring White, Michael E. Smith, Charles L. Latimer]. *Schooling in the Panama Canal Zone, 1904–1979.*

Rolofson, Robert H. *Christian Cooperation at the World's Crossroads, Depicting the Amazing Power of Cooperative Christianity as Directed Since 1914 by the General Council and the Seven Parish Units of the Union Church of the Canal Zone.* Panama City, Panama: The Union Church of the Canal Zone, 1950.

Society of the Chagres, *Yearbooks, 1911–17.*

Government Publications

Area Handbook for Panama. Washington, D.C.: U.S. Printing Office, 1972.

Carter, James E. "Address to the Nation, February 1, 1978." Weekly Compilation of Presidential Documents, February 6, 1978.

————. "Question and Answer Session in Denver, October 22, 1977." Department of State Bulletin, November 21,1977.

U.S. Department of Commerce, Bureau of the Census. *General Population Characteristics, Canal Zone, 1970 Census of Population.*

Index